WHEN GOD'S WILL AND MY WILL DISCONNECT

To Bayshore —
"His divine power has given us everything we need" (2 Peter 1:3-4) — Thank you —

TERRY BURLINGAME *Terry*

I often worked on this manuscript during our winter stays (this early printing does have some editorial errors which have been corrected)

CP

www.calvarypress.com

WHEN GOD'S WILL AND MY WILL DISCONNECT
Copyright © 2016 by Terry Burlingame.

All rights reserved. Printed in the United States of America. No part of this book may be used or reproduced in any manner whatsoever without written permission except in the case of brief quotations embodied in critical articles or reviews.

From the ESV® Bible (The Holy Bible, English Standard Version®), copyright 2001 by Crossway, a publishing ministry of Good News Publishers. Used by permission. All rights reserved.

For information contact:
2435 E. North Street, #125
Greenville, SC 29615
www.calvarypress.com

Book Design and Cover Art by Devin Smith (www.artofdevin.com)

ISBN: 978-0-9899796-4-1
First Edition: April 2016

To our Lord and Savior,

who is ever faithful and graciously provides all we need; and to Barbara, my dear wife, who lovingly encourages me and is a wonderful example of making right choices, as she walks in Christ and His love.

"His divine power has granted to us all things that pertain to life and godliness, through the knowledge of him who called us to his own glory and excellence, by which he has granted to us his precious and very great promises, so that through them you may become partakers of the divine nature, having escaped from the corruption that is in the world because of sinful desire."

2 Peter 1:3–4

CONTENTS

INTRODUCTION VIII

SETTING THE STAGE 1

DECISIONS:

ONE—I CHOOSE TO ACCEPT THAT I AM NOT IN CONTROL—GOD IS IN CONTROL 10

TWO—I CHOOSE TO CONFESS SIN 35

THREE—I CHOOSE FAITHFULNESS 57

FOUR—I CHOOSE PURITY 80

FIVE—I CHOOSE TO TRUST GOD TO USE ME 105

SIX—I CHOOSE TO ACCEPT GOD'S TIMEFRAME 126

SEVEN—I CHOOSE GOD'S REALITIES 141

EIGHT—I CHOOSE TO ACCEPT GOD'S BLESSINGS. 159

NINE—I CHOOSE TO REMEMBER GOD'S WORKING. 173

TEN—I CHOOSE TO LIVE ABOVE THE FRAY 193

ELEVEN—I CHOOSE TO FORGIVE OTHERS 208

TWELVE—I CHOOSE TO SERVE OTHERS. 223

THIRTEEN—I CHOOSE TO ACCEPT MY EMOTIONS 236

FOURTEEN—I CHOOSE TO CELEBRATE WITH OTHERS . .251

FIFTEEN—I CHOOSE TO GLORIFY GOD. 266

CONCLUSION. 276

APPENDIX A—SYNOPSIS 282

APPENDIX B—SCRIPTURE USAGE 295

APPENDIX C—THE CERTAINTY OF SALVATION. 305

ABOUT THE AUTHOR 317

WHEN GOD'S WILL AND MY WILL DISCONNECT

Looking at Joseph—making right choices when adversity appears to repeatedly strike

WHEN GOD'S WILL AND MY WILL DISCONNECT

INTRODUCTION

In retrospect we knew there was something "wrong" from day one. My wife had a normal pregnancy; everything went just as planned. The morning of birth went well. There was labor, but not extremely difficult (at least from my perspective). Birth happened naturally. We had a baby boy. He had all five toes on each foot and five fingers on each hand; he looked absolutely perfect. We gave thanks and praise to our Lord. We named him Jonathan—gift of Jehovah.

Little did we know how meaningful his name would be in the coming years. Jonathan didn't crawl until he was 18 months; he didn't walk until he was 2½; and at 41 years, he still does not use expressive language, continues to struggle with toileting issues, and needs near constant supervision. The diagnosis came as "severely impaired with autism." At age 31 he was given an additional diagnosis: epilepsy. This wasn't our plan; it wasn't supposed to be this way.

The events of life do not always, or I should say rarely, happen just the way we plan. This is typical in our lives. We plan and want, we desire and anticipate, and then there's the bump, the pothole, the boulder, the rushing river—something happens and everything

INTRODUCTION

we had expected takes an immediate change, never to return to the anticipated course.

How do we respond to these events of life? What do we do when the circumstances of our days are so contrary to what we expect and life just does not seem to make sense? We think our theology is right and we know of God's omniscience. However, in those difficult days we can wonder if God is even listening, if He cares, and if He is really going to lead us through this valley. The words of Truth bounce around in our minds, but somehow when faced with the reality of a trying moment we are not able to understand how they fit. The road can be a difficult one to walk; we can feel very alone, tired, and fearful.

Believing in Jesus Christ as our Savior, we can know we are Christian. Holding to the truths of Scripture we seek to live a life in harmony with God's design. Yet, it all becomes so confusing. We sit in church and listen to sermons that speak of God's love, the sufficiency of His grace to meet our every need, and His unfailing, unfaltering sovereign plan. But when faced with "our" trouble it is hard to recognize what the truth really means.

We read Scripture, and wonder how our situation fits with God's Truth; we begin to wonder if His Word has any bearing on our particular circumstance. We see God working in the lives of others, His Word being realized and producing fruit, but in us it can just seem empty.

We read:

> *Psalm 118:6; Hebrews 13:6: So we can confidently say, "The Lord is my helper; I will not fear; what can man do to me?"*

…And we wonder where "the help" is. We are filled with fear as

WHEN GOD'S WILL AND MY WILL DISCONNECT

we approach tomorrow.

> *Psalm 92:1-2: It is good to give thanks to the Lord, to sing praises to your name, O Most High; to declare your steadfast love in the morning, and your faithfulness by night*

…And we wonder how to praise the Lord and how to be thankful to Him, as we struggle and as we try to make sense of our seemingly meaningless and hopeless situation, of what has so quickly turned our course from what we had been expecting.

> *Philippians 4:19: And my God will supply every need of yours according to his riches in glory in Christ Jesus.*

…And it seems that we have yet so many needs. We wonder what God is going to do, or if He is going to do anything.

> *Matthew 6:26: Look at the birds of the air: they neither sow nor reap nor gather into barns, and yet your heavenly Father feeds them. Are you not of more value than they?*

…And the birds look like they are better off than we are; they seem to have more for their livelihood; they look happier and more "carefree."

> *Matthew 6:30: But if God so clothes the grass of the field, which today is alive and tomorrow is thrown into the oven, will he not much more clothe you, O you of little faith?*

…And our faith can seem so small. We try to have more faith; we pray for more faith; we try to move the mountains before us. But, it doesn't appear that our faith has any more weight than a feather floating aimlessly through the air.

INTRODUCTION

John 8:32: and you will know the truth, and the truth will set you free."

...And yet we feel like we are in bondage. There seems to be chains around us, and the situation we are in looks hopeless; there appears to be no way out. At times, death looks like a far better option, resulting in the fullness of redemption and true freedom.

Psalm 139:11-12: If I say, "Surely the darkness shall cover me, and the light about me be night," even the darkness is not dark to you; the night is bright as the day, for darkness is as light with you.

...And the darkness looks only darker. There is no light; there is no hope of light. We have a hard time even thinking that there could be light in the midst of our ever daunting and growing darkness.

Psalm 139:15-16: My frame was not hidden from you, when I was being made in secret, intricately woven in the depths of the earth. Your eyes saw my unformed substance; in your book were written, every one of them, the days that were formed for me, when as yet there was none of them.

...And we are saddened, and at times angry to think that God "formed" these days for us. How could He? How could He design such a plan that would hurt so much and seem to do nothing good? And we grow confused with the difference between what God has done and what He has allowed the evil enemy to accomplish.

Psalm 91:1-2: He who dwells in the shelter of the Most High will abide in the shadow of the Almighty. I will say to the Lord, "My refuge and my fortress, my God, in whom I trust."

...And we don't feel like we are in the shelter of the Almighty God, but rather under the dark cloud of His enemy. We don't see a refuge or fortress, only a moat filled with hungry crocodiles waiting to devour us.

> *Job 1:21: And he (Job) said, "Naked I came from my mother's womb, and naked shall I return. The Lord gave, and the Lord has taken away; blessed be the name of the Lord."*

…And we choose to compare ourselves with Job. Maybe Job could praise the Lord after what he went through; but, we are not Job. We don't understand why Job had to suffer, and it makes no sense for us to suffer in this apparent meaningless way, either.

> *Romans 8:28: And we know that for those who love God all things work together for good, for those who are called according to his purpose.*

…And we get tired of hearing this verse. There just doesn't seem to be any possible good that can come out of anything we are experiencing. If what is happening is somehow going to accomplish "good," then we conclude we want no part of good.

> *2 Peter 1:3: His divine power has granted to us all things that pertain to life and godliness, through the knowledge of him who called us to his own glory and excellence.*

…And we look for, we wait for His power. The only thing we seem to have is weakness, and with every passing day it is only our weakness that grows stronger.

> *I John 1:9: If we confess our sins, he is faithful and just to forgive us our sins and to cleanse us from all unrighteousness.*

INTRODUCTION

...And we examine to see if we are harboring sin, if we are blinded to a hidden evil within us. Our guilt only gets worse and heavier. We become convinced we are not doing something right. The sin we do know has been confessed repeatedly, but there is still not relief. Forgiveness should bring peace, and yet our heart is under constant torment.

Then, there is the music of the church which gradually grows elusive. We sing songs, and have sought to sing the words from our heart. We have them memorized as we have repeatedly sung them countless times in the past. However, suddenly the meanings don't seem quite right. We sing, but the depth of our commitment crumbles with the reality of our experience.

> *Take My Life and Let It Be consecrated Lord to Thee.*
> *Take my moments and my days, let them flow in ceaseless praise, let them flow in ceaseless praise.*

Do we really want the Lord to take me, trusting that wherever He does take us is good and that we can fully trust Him in it? Do we trust Him fully with our moments and days; regardless of circumstances, is there "ceaseless praise" coming out of our mouths? Or, are we more inclined to bitterness and complaint, not expecting God to work or to use what is happening?

> *I Surrender All, I surrender all, all to Thee my blessed Savior, I surrender all.*

Do we surrender even what we do not know to the Lord; or are we more inclined to surrender what we know to be safe, when we are confident of the outcome, believing it will be tolerable for us? Somehow, we have the impression that in surrender there is relief. However, we forget that in surrender there is total submission to the will of another and that it can lead to momentary pain. We try to surrender, yet the burden only feels heavier and the wounds deeper.

Have Thine own way, Lord, have Thine own way; Thou art the Potter, I am the clay; mold me and make me after Thy Will, while I am waiting yielded and still.

Do we want the Lord to have His way totally, or are we willing clay just when it meets with our approval, when the vessel being formed is acceptable to us? When what is happening seems disagreeable, we want to be in charge of the wheel as there is a natural inclination to wonder about the potter's skill.

All for Jesus, all for Jesus! All my beings ransomed powers, all my thoughts and words and doings, all my days and all my hours.

Do we stop to consider what "all" means? Or, is there a limitation on "all," changing the definition that "all" doesn't mean "all" except when we want it to mean "all?" At other times, "all" is conditional, as we determine what is best. It is hard to surrender "all" when there is not clarity of purpose and the intensity of struggle only grows greater.

Where He Leads Me I will follow, where He leads me I will follow, where He leads me I will follow, I'll go with Him, with Him all the way.

Do we recognize this repetition indicates our emphasis in commitment? Or, is our following contingent upon knowing where He is leading? Are we able to blindly follow as Abraham did when the Lord led Him out of Ur to a "land I will show you" (Genesis 12:1), or do we want to see the map first, being assured that the destination is good? Following can be frightening; tension can develop; we can be left feeling immobilized.

INTRODUCTION

We sing the words but the meanings bring internal conflict. There are times we do not know how to reconcile God's Truth with our circumstances. The hymns that previously brought encouragement and freedom suddenly result in pain, bringing a dismal outlook and vain purpose.

What has happened? We know truth does not change, that God does not change, and that His Word does not change. He declares Himself to be faithful, and has proven Himself faithful through the years. In these times we recognize we are in spiritual battles. We can give in to the raging doubts, the seeming inconsistencies, the unknown fears, and regress to a point of despair. Or, we can hold firmly to the Truth of God's Word, choosing to believe Him even when it is tough.

This is a choice—a simple choice, a difficult choice. It is simple in that it is a choice to believe and follow, to trust and obey, and to be content not having all the answers or understanding all the incongruences. It is simple in that we are able to trust the faithfulness of God, knowing He will be true to all His promises. Yet, it is a difficult choice as it takes unwavering commitment, sincere devotion, and faithful perseverance; difficult in that it means moving ahead without knowing what will be happening.

The enemy of the Cross of Christ is determined to do all possible to bring about discouragement and render believers ineffective in the service of our Great God. In the moment of our trial, he well knows of our own vulnerabilities and will attack us in our weakest moment and most vulnerable spot. Christians must not let him penetrate the heart, but rather are called to stand firm with the expectation of victory, knowing our Lord and King, our Sovereign Leader, will do what is best for us and for His glory. He has given us His "Armor" and this must not be abandoned, but rather carefully and intentionally worn. Only by the power of God and the work of the grace of God are we able to resist all temptation and escape the resulting failure.

> *Finally, be strong in the Lord and in the strength of his might. Put on the whole armor of God, that you may be able to stand against the schemes of the devil. For we do not wrestle against flesh and blood, but against the rulers, against the authorities, against the cosmic powers over this present darkness, against the spiritual forces of evil in the heavenly places. Therefore take up the whole armor of God, that you may be able to withstand in the evil day, and having done all, to stand firm.*
>
> *Stand therefore, having fastened on the belt of truth, and having put on the breastplate of righteousness, and, as shoes for your feet, having put on the readiness given by the gospel of peace. In all circumstances take up the shield of faith, with which you can extinguish all the flaming darts of the evil one; and take the helmet of salvation, and the sword of the Spirit, which is the word of God, praying at all times in the Spirit, with all prayer and supplication. To that end keep alert with all perseverance, making supplication for all the saints. (Ephesians 6:10-18)*

In seeking to answer the struggles faced during these times of our lives, I began looking more closely at Joseph's life. This is an intriguing story and a fascinating account of God's providential working. Obviously there is much of Joseph's life we do not know, for in 13 chapters of Scripture we are told the story of 93 years of an individual's life. We only have a small sampling of what actually took place. No doubt, many of his days were like ours: the same things happening, much routine, nothing dramatic, and nothing worthy

INTRODUCTION

of the printed page. Some of the things we don't have recorded we would like to know, such as Joseph's emotions, reactions, thoughts, and prayers, but obviously God did not deem those important for us to know. Therefore, I accept what God gave us is what we need to know and what is helpful for us to know in learning about Him and in learning about ourselves. Considering what we do know of Joseph's life, we are able to see God consistently faithful and Joseph repeatedly making right choices when adversity strikes in his life.

Jesus died to forgive us of all sin, cleansing us by His shed blood. He was buried, and so all sin in our lives should also be buried, it should be done away with, put to death, having no hold on us. Jesus rose again, declaring victory over all sin, victory over the enemy, victory over the grave. He did not go through death, burial, and resurrection so that we would be stymied by sin and continue to live under the grasp of the enemy; He did not face death so we would have to face a life of misery. Though we may encounter miserable situations, we do not have to be miserable. His truth makes the difference.

> *So if the Son sets you free, you will be free indeed. (John 8:36)*

In the midst of trouble, we can enjoy a life of joy and peace, knowing our Lord knows, cares, and will meet all our needs.

> *I have said these things to you, that in me you may have peace. In the world you will have tribulation. But take heart; I have overcome the world. (John 16:33)*

> *...I came that they [the sheep, the followers of Jesus Christ] may have life and have it abundantly. (John 10:10)*

Thinking through the events of Joseph's life we can marvel at God's

WHEN GOD'S WILL AND MY WILL DISCONNECT

working and are thrilled with the outcome. The realization of God's perfect design and the wonderful reunion of a family are exciting. However, not all life stories end like Joseph's. When difficulties strike, we can struggle, wondering if God will work in our lives in a similar fashion, accomplishing a perfect purpose. This becomes a matter of faith, of trust, of expectation, of anticipation; of accepting that God will be glorified, and His desire is to use us in bringing glory to His name; of accepting that through the "unknown" or the "unexpected" events of our lives, God will accomplish His purpose.

Believing God is God, and will always be true to Himself and His Word, I come to a foundational conclusion. Recognizing God has a sovereign plan and has given His Word as the final authority for all of life, we are able to submit to the work of the Holy Spirit and claim His enabling in all things. To realize this in our lives, we must make critical choices in following the Lord. We must accept that there will be times when God's will and my will seem disconnected, when they don't mesh, and that there is a real difference in what we are expecting and in what God is doing.

I will initially set the background leading up to Joseph being sold into slavery. In the subsequent chapters I will discuss 15 choices the believer should address when facing the difficult, unexplainable, unwanted situations of life. These are based on specific circumstances in Joseph's life and what would appear to be specific choices he intentionally made. It is my intent to not "read into" Scripture what is not present, but to look at applications in harmony with Scripture from what is present. Though times are different and the situations faced by Joseph will likely not be situations we will experience, these choices are still applicable for the believer today. In making these

INTRODUCTION

choices, I believe we have been given great hope; our Lord will fulfill His promises in our lives and we can look forward with expectation to His gracious working, all for His glory.

These fifteen choices are not intended to be made in a specific order. The order they are placed in the following chapters is largely due to the order they appear in the account of Joseph's life, providing a natural progression of thought. However, in every situation, the first decision addressed is foundational for all others. If we do not have this right, we cannot expect to get any of the others right.

Though primarily focusing on the life of Joseph, I will also reference others in Scripture who have, or have not, made good choices. These individuals will also provide excellent example for us to consider, as we seek to make right choices during the course of events in our lives.

This book is primarily written to those who are believers, to those who have trusted Christ as Savior and know the wonder of His redemptive grace. Additionally, the solid foundation for all that is written is believing and accepting the Scriptures to be absolute truth, to be the inspired, infallible, and inerrant Word of God. If you are uncertain of your salvation, or certain you are not saved, I suggest you begin by reading Appendix C, "The Certainty of Salvation."

SETTING THE STAGE

God is always at work. Something may happen today which will bring about our response, "God's will is not connected with my will—somehow, somewhere there is a disconnect," and we tend to forget about what God has been doing up to now in our lives. Though we may not say it, we deliberately believe that God's will is out of sync, not ours; it is God's will that needs to be changed in order to harmonize with our will. However, the believer must recognize that the events of our lives do not happen in a vacuum, they are not isolated situations which have gone terribly wrong. Rather, they are intentionally designed to accomplish a holy purpose for the glory of God.

Joseph's story does not begin with him being hated by his brothers and about to meet his demise in the bottom of a dried well. Initially we are told of his birth to Jacob and Rachel. From her perspective, she had been cheated from her husband. Though Jacob had worked seven years to gain Rachel as his wife, her father, Laban, deceitfully gave him his older daughter, Leah, in marriage. Jacob is also given Rachel, but the cost is an additional seven years of labor. Once married, Rachel appeared to be nonsensically barren. In order to relieve her shame of being childless, and the envy and disgust she held toward her sister Leah who had born four children, Rachel gave her handmaid to Jacob in hope that she would bear children for her. Eventually after the birth of eleven children, ten sons and one daughter, from three different mothers (Leah, Bilhah, and Zilpah), Rachel gave birth to Joseph (Genesis 30:21-24), meaning "he increases." Jacob and Rachel recognized the act of God in this birth, as she proclaimed, God has taken away my disgrace (Genesis 30:23). After years of waiting, her dreams were fulfilled—she had a son; Jacob's dreams were realized—his beloved wife had born him a son.

The next scene in Joseph's life is at age seventeen.

> *Joseph, being seventeen years old, was pasturing the flock with his brothers. He was a boy with the sons of Bilhah and Zilpah, his father's wives. And Joseph brought a bad report of them to their father. (Genesis 37:2)*

Nothing more is said. There is no indication of what they were doing, what the bad report consisted of, what Joseph's motivation was in telling his dad the details, or what Jacob did about it, if anything. Based on Joseph's character, we can conclude he was giving an honest report, and not fabricating something for his own benefit. Knowing his father's good reputation, he likely thought it necessary to hold his brothers accountable for wrong doing.

Then we see the unwholesome favoritism Jacob shows to Joseph. There is nothing secretive about it; Joseph is his favorite child. If there was a choice between losing his other sons and keeping Joseph, there is no question as to what Jacob[1] would do.

---

1 Though God changed Jacob's name to "Israel" (Genesis 35:10), he is called both Jacob and Israel throughout Scripture.

SETTING THE STAGE

> *Now Israel loved Joseph more than any other of his sons, because he was the son of his old age. And he made him a robe of many colors. (Genesis 37:3)*

Rationale is provided: because of Jacob's age, he justified that this was his special son. It appears that favoritism was not based on anything Joseph had done; it was generated from the heart of his father and his special love for Rachel.

The providential work of God is obvious through the life of Joseph, providing understanding of how Jacob's favoritism was used by God in accomplishing His purpose.[2] This will be seen in later chapters. However, the result of Jacob's favoritism riled his brothers to jealousy and hatred. Possibly because of the deep respect for their father, the brother's anger turned to Joseph. Whether or not Joseph gloated in his preferred position is not known. However, the brother's attitude was obvious.

> *But when his brothers saw that their father loved him more than all his brothers, they hated him and could not speak peacefully to him. (Genesis 37:4)*

Their words became mean and shot out of their mouths like poisonous arrows targeted toward Joseph's heart.

Only to heighten the increased tension, when Joseph had most unusual dreams he told them to his family. One can wonder about the significance of dreams today, and if those nighttime dramas of our mind

---

2 Parents must be very careful not to use Joseph's life as an excuse to show favoritism; parents must be careful not to determine the design of God in regards to their children, anticipating one to be more special to God than another. True, some children may be easier to parent, some may be more in harmony with our likes and dislikes, and some may bring rewarding affirmation. However, there is never an excuse for parents to favor one child over another. When this tendency rises, parents should quickly return to Psalm 139 and recognize the clear design of God in specifically making all individuals, being both planned and purposed by Him. Also note James 2:1-9.

have any meaning or importance regarding our lives.[3] Joseph's dreams were ordained by God, and in years to come would demonstrate His sovereign plan. The first had his brother's sheaves in the field bowing down to the one he had gathered (Genesis 37:5-8). The implication was clear; even though he was the youngest (apart from Benjamin) his brothers would be in submission to him. The second dream carried the imagery one step further, for now the sun, moon, and stars were seen as bowing down to him (Genesis 37:9-10), which included his parents in this acquiescence.

Whether or not Joseph thought the dreams might ever come into reality, he apparently thought it significant to make them public. One can question Joseph's wisdom in this, believing he should well have kept the secret to himself and let matters be. However, he spoke. Was it with arrogance, with intention to put his brothers in their place, or with innocent question as to their meaning, we don't know. But we do know the results of his telling this account.

> *Now Joseph had a dream, and when he told it to his brothers they hated him even more. (Genesis 37:5)*

Their hatred of Joseph in this is of no surprise, and should not have been a surprise to Joseph. The younger brother "predicts" that in days to come his older brothers, those who despise him, will turn in submission to him. It was absurd from their perspective; totally illogical and ridiculous. They would never, in their wildest imaginations, lower themselves to bow to Joseph; they would never place themselves voluntarily under his authority; and they certainly

---

3 Prior to Pentecost, God would speak to people through the use of dreams in order to relay His message, give direction, and convey truth. Today, God has spoken to us through His Word (Hebrews 1.1-2). Though dreams may appear to have significant meaning, we must be careful to consider them for what they are, dreams – our minds working overtime while our body is resting.

could not imagine this younger brother to ever be elevated to a place of rightfully having authority over them.

Or, did they? Knowing Joseph was favored by their father, did they fear that someday he would honor Joseph; that before Jacob's death he would give Joseph the blessing of the eldest son because he was Rachel's first-born. Was some of their hatred for Joseph misdirected, as they were inwardly angered at their father for showing him favor?[4]

With the intensified tension, it appears Joseph both had and didn't have everything going for him. In relationship with his father, he could do no wrong and had a bright future; in relationship with his brothers, he was sickening and could do no right.

Though Jacob initially rebuked Joseph for insinuating his superiority over the family, he didn't hold Joseph's actions against him. Rather, he kept the saying in mind (37:11). Perhaps he recognized there was something unusual about Joseph or something unusual would be happening in and through him. Jacob knew God, and knew God was capable of working in ways beyond his understanding. He wasn't about to forget what Joseph had told him, but rather held on to it for future consideration.

> *Now his brothers went to pasture their father's flock near Shechem. (Genesis 37:12)*

---

4 The motivations and consequences of favoritism are complex. These two principles should be remembered:

(1) When we are the subject of favoritism we should keep careful perspective, realizing that one person's actions do not alter the reality of who we are before God. Our relationship with God is not based on another's decision, but rather on His amazing work of redemptive grace.

(2) When we are part of the consequences of another being favored, having a negative impact on us, again we should remember that this is another person, and he cannot alter the good favor of God, he cannot change God's design. Though we may be neglected by man and disqualified because of their judgments, we can remain confident in the work of God which has made us His child and will keep us for all eternity. Our value and worth are not dependent on another person's acceptance or praise; our ability to be used by God is not dependent on man's evaluations.

WHEN GOD'S WILL AND MY WILL DISCONNECT

We don't know how much time elapsed between verse 11 and verse 12, but likely soon after, Joseph was sent on a mission to check on his brothers, and to once again bring a report back to Jacob.

> *And Israel said to Joseph, "Are not your brothers pasturing the flock at Shechem? Come, I will send you to them." And he said to him, "Here I am." So he said to him, "Go now, see if it is well with your brothers and with the flock, and bring me word." So he sent him from the Valley of Hebron, and he came to Shechem. (Genesis 37:13–14)*

Joseph was trustworthy and willingly obeyed. Jacob waited, knowing a valid report would be brought back to him.

An obvious question arises, "Why didn't Joseph go with them in the first place?" There are three possible answers. One, Jacob knew of his brother's attitude toward Joseph, and didn't want to expose him to their likely cruel treatment. Two, there was a reasonable responsibility Joseph needed to complete prior to leaving home. Or three, because of Jacob's favoritism, he wanted to keep Joseph close to home, which I am inclined to think true. Jacob chose to protect him, to spoil him, to try to insure no harm would come to him.

Upon seeing Joseph, the brother's allowed their jealous and evil minds to plot the most dastardly deed: murder. Before he reached them, they mocked him in his self-proclaimed supremacy: Here comes this dreamer! (37:19). Then they formed their plan:

> *They… conspired against him to kill him. They said to one another, "…Come now, let us kill him and throw him into one of the pits. Then we will say that a fierce animal has devoured him…" (Genesis 37:18–20)*

This would be the last time they would have to deal with Joseph.

SETTING THE STAGE

Once gone, they hoped to finally live in peace, no longer haunted by his preferred status. They even arrogantly stated: and we will see what becomes of his dreams (37:20).

Their design of execution was not in righteous judgment because of Joseph's sin. Rather, it was an evil endeavor born from the root of jealousy and sin in their hearts. The brothers were strongly determined to be rid of him and rid of the affection they perceived he stole from their father.

Reuben, the oldest son, hearing of his brother's plan, sought to thwart it (Genesis 37:21-22). He called on them to not kill Joseph, but rather let him die a slow death in the pit of an empty cistern. His persuasion was not with evil intent, but rather to return after the brothers had left and be Joseph's rescuer. Being the oldest and having a deeper understanding of the family history, perhaps he was able to overlook the dreams and favoritism with his own love for his father. However, in contrast to not wanting to participate in the evil deed, he was not bold enough to stand before his brothers to spare Joseph's life; he wasn't willing to take a stand for what was right.

Reuben's strategy failed. For an unknown reason, he didn't sit with his brothers for supper that night and had ventured off to another place. During this time, a caravan of Ishmaelites traveled by on their way to Egypt. This was a perfect opportunity for the brothers. They could be rid of Joseph, make a little money, and also give respect to their oldest brother's wishes to not murder him. They bargained with the Ishmaelites and agreed upon a "fair" price for this young man who was suddenly translated from being the favored son to an unknown slave.

When Reuben returned, it appears he did not love Joseph enough to run after the Ishmaelite's caravan; he did not care enough to seek Joseph's recovery. He wanted to rescue Joseph when it seemed simple, but now it had become more difficult. He would have to be courageous and stand up to his brothers; he would have to go out of his way. Apparently, the right thing was the right thing in Reuben's eyes as long as it did not require anything extra of him.

There was one more piece of their newly formed puzzle that had to be put into place. What would they tell their father? They knew Jacob would be devastated and likely furious if he knew the truth, and that each of them could likely be disowned. The brothers devised a deceitful plan. Reuben, once the protector of Joseph, now became the protector of his brothers and of his own reputation before his father.

> *Then they took Joseph's robe and slaughtered a goat and dipped the robe in the blood. And they sent the robe of many colors and brought it to their father and said, "This we have found; please identify whether it is your son's robe or not." And he identified it and said, "It is my son's robe. A fierce animal has devoured him. Joseph is without doubt torn to pieces." (Genesis 37:31-33)*

Though their father's heart was broken and his joy was seemingly forever robbed, their deceitfully evil plan had been successful. In their distorted way of thinking, they were free of Joseph, and "not guilty" of any wrong doing. Perhaps they were even favored for returning his special robe to give their father some unresolved comfort.

And Joseph—his life was forever changed. He endured a long ride to Egypt, and then was sold to Potiphar, an officer of Pharaoh, the captain of the guard (Genesis 37:36). Suddenly he is thrust into an entirely new "life" that would take him on a journey he could not have begun to imagine.

SETTING THE STAGE

We will never face the same plight as Joseph, as no two journeys are ever the same. However, the manner of events can be strikingly similar. We may have plans in our lives and a very specific course mapped out for ourselves, or for others (children, friends, others in ministry). We may think we know what is best. Our future may appear to be set on a very clear path.

Our son's story didn't begin at Zeeland Community Hospital in 1975, or even at conception. Rather, his life story began before the foundations of the world in the mind of God (Ephesians 1:4-6). In His sovereign plan He designed a purpose for Jonathan and a purpose for us as his parents. Our responsibility has never been to try to understand all the intricacies of God's design, even though we have spent time walking this path. Rather, our responsibility is to trust our Lord, to walk through life believing Him and choosing to be faithful to what we do know.

Sometimes, because of the decisions we make and sometimes not because of our decisions, circumstances do not go as we anticipate. Many factors can be involved in determining the road we travel. In all this the absolute truth of God's sovereignty must be tightly grasped. Nothing happens out of His control. However, in every decision we make we must not neglect to also recognize we are totally responsible for our every choice before our eternal God. God, in His sovereign design and infinite wisdom is magnificently working together every event and circumstance of our lives, to include those which do not seem to make sense. This foundational truth is critical in looking at the following 15 decisions seen in Joseph's designed and yet unpredictable life.

DECISION ONE

I Choose to Accept that I am Not in Control—God is in Control

I like to be in control. When it was evident that there was something "wrong" with the way our son Jonathan was developing, I wanted to figure it out so that I, or someone, could fix it, so he would be "normal;" so our lives would be normal. We went to various doctors; we looked for explanations and solutions; we had a full examination and evaluation done at Mayo Clinic when he was just three years old. In my thinking, there had to be an understandable reason with an attainable solution. However, the simple solution, or even a complex solution, I had hoped for and prayed for didn't come. In our exit interview with the neurologist, he simply smiled and predicted Jonathan would be a joy to us in our elderly years. That was not what I wanted to hear. But at that point I reluctantly accepted it; there was nothing else I knew to do. Jonathan was our gift from the Lord; we loved him and were thankful for him—regardless of what he

DECISION ONE

could and could not do.

However, acceptance of the situation didn't change my desires. I still like to be in control. I want to be in control. I want to know what is going to happen, how it is going to happen, what the ramifications will be when it does happen, and then what my next step is going to be. I don't like not being in control and not knowing the end results. Only surprises that please me are good; I don't want to face any other surprises.

This is the sentiment of many individuals. Being out of control can produce great fear and anxiety. One's entire world can collapse and he can become immobile in determining the next step to take. For even those few who say they don't "want to be in control," when the unexpected takes place, the resulting fear and anxiety often will be devastating.

Sometimes events will happen in our lives where it first appeared we could have had control. For example: the auto accident. One person had control over what had happened, the other did not. Recently I observed the aftermath of an accident. One car had been sitting at a four-way stop sign. The driver was doing exactly what he was supposed to be doing: waiting his turn to proceed through the intersection. Then the event that considerably changed his plans: a car rear-ended him with force while going about 30 miles per hour. The driver of the moving vehicle obviously was distracted by something, didn't see the stopped vehicle, and didn't see the stop sign. He could have been more alert, made different choices, and prevented the ensuing events. For the first driver, circumstances happened that were totally beyond his control.

What was his response? This is key. In an event such as this, do we respond with rage and anger, do we get upset with ourselves for having been at the intersection instead of taking a different route; do we get upset with the car manufacturer for not building a sturdier car that could have easily withstood such a blow? Or, do we accept the event as being of no surprise to God, knowing that He is in control, and that He will be at work even through the difficult and unexpected?

Another situation could involve a victim of sexual abuse. A young girl being repeatedly molested by a family member, by one who supposedly loves her, is overpowered and convinced that what is happening is good and right. She is told this should be kept a secret and that no one is ever to know; convincing her that others might not understand that the relationship the two of them has is so very special. One person has made choices to sin, has violated God's design and another person. They could have chosen differently, but they did not. The child was wounded; she didn't ask for this to happen, didn't understand what was happening, and didn't know what to do once it did happen. She is left with a dark secret and intense fear and guilt. How does she respond? She may go through life feeling "dirty," may harbor a dark cloud of despair that no one can dispel or understand; may be filled with anger and hurt; or may have any number of other varied responses. Or, in the midst of hurt and pain, she can accept that even in this God is not surprised. Having suffered the consequences of sin and from living in a sinful world and among sinful people, she still has the privilege of knowing the sovereign grace of God which is able to heal her and enable her to live a life which brings glory to His Name.

The types of circumstances that we did not want in our lives or do not like are many. The impact of these circumstances should never be minimized. However, when these circumstances happen, we can choose to respond with one of several options: One, we can cower under the tent of anxiety and choose to become bitter and angry. Two, we can invite others to join us in a pity party, and collapse under the feelings that no one has ever experienced trouble as bad as ours. Three, we can escape into isolation, refusing to participate in our world, fearing that more "bad things" will happen. Four, we can react in rage, blaming others for what has happened to us, seeking revenge. Five, we can turn to worry and fretting, wasting much valuable time in attempting to mentally try and work out a plan to change unchangeable circumstances. Six, we can turn to varying substances, as alcohol or drugs, in seeking to cope with the reality or to neglect its truth; or the turn can be to more "subtle substances" such as television, games, recreation, or work. In each of these the desired result is the same: hoping that somehow our circumstances will be made right, that we will get through them, and that life will eventually and hopefully get better. With each of these there will be a common consequence: emotional and physical weariness in a spiritual desert.

However, there is another option. We can choose to accept that we are not in control, and circumstances will happen that are beyond our control. Recognizing that we do not necessarily have the "right answer" or the "best idea" for what should be taking place, we are then able to submit to the sovereign control of God. This is the first decision and sets the right foundation for all other decisions. In reality, this is the choice of accepting God to be God as He has revealed Himself in the Scriptures; in recognizing His sovereign authority over all things; in knowing He is the source of absolute truth and is always truthful.

Decision One: I choose to accept that I am not in control, that God is in control, and circumstances will happen that are beyond my control.

In the spring of 2001 my wife woke in the middle of the night with an intense case of what was later diagnosed to be vertigo. At the time, we didn't know what was happening. Nearly collapsing to the floor Barbara mentioned to me to tell the children she loved them. She thought she was dying. I quickly called "911" and she was rushed to the hospital. After two months of additional testing, a neurologist, who opened his office to talk with us on Mother's Day, informed us that she had a brain tumor. We were told that it was likely benign, which was later concluded to be true, and that it was imbedded deep within her brain, causing significant balance and hearing issues. If left alone this would only cause further problems as it was also pressing on her brain stem. Seven months later, she went into surgery, and after 15 hours was taken to recovery. Two determined and expert specialists in skull based neurosurgery performed the incredible operation to remove the tumor. Though she lives with enduring consequences, her outcome was as good as could be expected, and for this we are greatly thankful.

This was not our plan. We did not orchestrate that "911" night, we did not plan for her to have a brain tumor, we did not facilitate the surgery, we did not bring about her healing. This was the design of God, and these circumstances were beyond our control. However, knowing our Lord is sovereign, we were able to experience the abundance of peace, and being confident He would accomplish His good purpose

Too often the believer can have a minimized view of God. Though doctrinally correct words may be said, the actuality of what is believed can be very different. We can say we believe God to be good, to be sovereign, to be merciful, and to be actively involved in our lives. However, when circumstances are less than favorable, our actions can demonstrate doubt about all we know, which can result in decisions that are less than honoring to the Lord.

Joseph had a fundamental understanding of God's sovereignty. It wasn't just something he had heard and been taught through the course of his life.[1] In faith, he accepted the truth of God's revelation in the presence of unbelievably difficult circumstances. He didn't just know all the right answers, but saw in his parents and through their heritage an unequivocal belief that God was perfectly orchestrating the events of history for His glory, and all He did was good. He didn't have to know all the answers or foresee the outcome of the situation; he believed God knew.

When the events of life provide either a small interruption to what we expected or a radical disruption to our plans, we must hold to truth. Knowing God as revealed in the Scriptures, we recognize that we cannot change or improve on His design.

The disdain of Joseph by his brothers had been obvious. Yet Reuben came to his rescue:

> *But when Reuben heard it, he rescued him out of their hands, saying, "Let us not take his life." And Reuben said to them, "Shed no blood; throw him into this pit here in the wilderness, but do not lay a hand on him"—that he*

---

1 A sad realization in the church today is the lackadaisical attitude of passing truth to the next generation. Though there can be a proliferation of programs, classes, and studies which children and teens can participate in, the understanding of relationship to the Holy and Sovereign God is missing. Attendance and participation at church are elevated as the practice of Deuteronomy 6 in the family is neglected; having acceptable behavior is emphasized, and the motivation for Christ-likeness is minimized. A fear of man is instilled if "right" is not done, rather than a "fear of God" that will compel righteousness (… and by the fear of the LORD one turns away from evil [Proverbs 16.6]).

might rescue him out of their hand to restore him to his father. (Genesis 37:21-22)

Here Reuben showed a bit of compassion, for Jacob, Joseph, or for both. However, it was not strong enough to stand honestly before his brothers; he didn't have the fortitude to confront them in their evil deeds and argue for what was right. He thought his plan would succeed, but his "secret plan" would soon be thwarted by that of his more cunning brothers.

Judah suddenly had a "better plan." Not only could they be rid of their brother, but they could have personal gain in his demise.

Then Judah said to his brothers, "What profit is it if we kill our brother and conceal his blood? Come, let us sell him to the Ishmaelites, and let not our hand be upon him, for he is our brother, our own flesh." And his brothers listened to him. Then Midianite traders passed by. And they drew Joseph up and lifted him out of the pit, and sold him to the Ishmaelites for twenty shekels of silver. They took Joseph to Egypt. (Genesis 37:26-28)

Reuben's plan was suddenly no longer an option. Joseph had no control over what was happening. He was unheard, overpowered, and sold. Whether he liked it or not, he was on his way to Egypt. He was not responsible to make things different at this point. He could not send word back to his father; he could not bargain with his captors; he could not negotiate with his new owners; he could not escape. He was on a new course in life which he did not choose and would not have chosen had he been given the option. The reality stood.

God has a plan and His design always surpasses mine. If there had been conversation with Joseph regarding what he wanted to do, he likely would not have chosen to be on an Egyptian caravan. He would have chosen to remain with his family, even though he was hated by his brothers. He would have chosen to return to his father, and anticipate his expected inheritance. He would have chosen a life designed for his wealth and pleasure. However, Joseph was not consulted. These circumstances were not about what Joseph wanted, what he thought best, or what he had planned. Rather, it was about God's design.

Often, God's superseding plan can be hard to accept. We may not like what is happening to us. We may grieve a terrible loss. Our hearts may ache because of an awful change of circumstances that appear contrary to God's Word and our expectation of His working. These feelings are part of how God made us. The choice is not to neglect or disregard our feelings, but rather to respond to our feelings in a manner that is in harmony with the character and revelation of God.

God's Character

The Scriptures are clear in the declaration of the character of God and of His sovereign plan. For our purposes here, I will note a few of His characteristics which must be earnestly accepted and vigorously held in order to live through the situations we have and will face.[2] God will always be faithful to Himself and to His working in our lives.

The Lord is Creator

With the words of His mouth, God spoke and brought creation into existence. It didn't just happen through the course of unexplainable events and evolving mutations. It was intentional, planned, and perfectly orchestrated by God to accomplish His purposes. Though man would like to have greater details as to when and how the Creator

---

2 This section is not meant to be a comprehensive study of the character of God, but rather a limited recognition of His character and the believer's response to Him.

worked, it isn't necessary for our faith and our walk in obedience to Him. He has graciously revealed what we need to know, and in this we should be satisfied.

> *In the beginning, God created the heavens and the earth. (Genesis 1:1)*

In creation our Lord specifically made people. We are not here by "chance;" our life is neither an accident nor a mistake; we are not even the decision of earthly parents. Rather, we are here by the grace and design of God. Are our circumstances then a surprise to God? Absolutely not! As we are not a surprise to God, the things that happen in our lives are not surprises to Him. This was true of Joseph, it was true of David, and it is true of us.

> *For you formed my inward parts; you knitted me together in my mother's womb. I praise you, for I am fearfully and wonderfully made. Wonderful are your works; my soul knows it very well. My frame was not hidden from you, when I was being made in secret, intricately woven in the depths of the earth. Your eyes saw my unformed substance; in your book were written, every one of them, the days that were formed for me, when as yet there was none of them. How precious to me are your thoughts, O God! How vast is the sum of them! (Psalm 139:13-17)*

Knowing He is my creator, knowing He is in control of all the days of my life, I am also able to rest in the promise that He is able and will keep me. Everything has been made by Him and everything is kept in order by Him.

> *For by him all things were created, in heaven and on earth, visible and invisible, whether thrones or dominions or rulers or authorities—all things were created through*

him and for him. And he is before all things, and in him all things hold together. (Colossians 1:16–17)

The phrase hold together has the powerful meaning of being "frapped." The concept of "frapping" is a nautical term from the 1540's. The term is used in both ship building and ship preservation. When the slats of wood forming the hull were placed together, pitch would then be placed between the boards. Following this, chains or ropes would be tightly wrapped around the hull to keep it taunt until it dried, preventing it from leaking. This is frapping. Additionally, when a ship was voyaging through rough waters, the crew would frap the hull, securing the hull with heavy ropes to keep it from braking up while weathering the storm. In considering the Lord's working within us, we recognize that He "fraps" us, binding us with His love and holding us together with His power so that we will remain intact through every storm and season of life.

The Lord is Sovereign

God has masterfully designed and implemented the fullness of His desires, all bringing glory to His name. Through His incomparable wisdom and unlimited ability He perfectly completes all that is good. We do not have to understand it; He graciously and sensitively reminds us of our limitations and His limitlessness.

For my thoughts are not your thoughts, neither are your ways my ways, declares the Lord. For as the heavens are higher than the earth, so are my ways higher than your ways and my thoughts than your thoughts. (Isaiah 55:8-9)

When events do not happen for my pleasure, the Lord alone is able to be trusted.

In one of Job's responses to his uncomforting friends, he recognized God as the ultimate controller of all things. The Lord is not surprised, He is not taken off guard, and He is not weakened by the circumstances we face. He unquestionably is God.

> *"But ask the beasts, and they will teach you; the birds of the heavens, and they will tell you; or the bushes of the earth, and they will teach you; and the fish of the sea will declare to you. Who among all these does not know that the hand of the Lord has done this? In his hand is the life of every living thing and the breath of all mankind. (Job 12:7–10)*

Being the author of perfect design, our Lord remains in absolute control even when life seems out of control to us. The prophet Habakkuk understood this as he spoke to the people of Judah who were inflicted with the reign of the evil king Jehoiakim. The hope of the people seemed to be lost, but Habakkuk reminded them that regardless of the circumstances, God doesn't change; He is still sovereign, He is still in control; He is still worthy of praise.

> *Though the fig tree should not blossom, nor fruit be on the vines, the produce of the olive fail and the fields yield no food, the flock be cut off from the fold and there be no herd in the stalls, yet I will rejoice in the Lord; I will take joy in the God of my salvation. God, the Lord, is my strength; he makes my feet like the deer's; he makes me tread on my high places. To the choirmaster: with stringed instruments. (Habakkuk 3:17–19)*

Isaiah understood this as he exhorted Judah to resist all idolatry and recognize God's absolute authority over all creation.

> *To whom then will you liken God, or what likeness compare*

> with him? An idol! A craftsman casts it, and a goldsmith overlays it with gold and casts for it silver chains. He who is too impoverished for an offering chooses wood that will not rot; he seeks out a skillful craftsman to set up an idol that will not move. (Isaiah 40:18–20)

The Lord is Holy

There is nothing of unrighteousness in God; nothing of sin, nothing of error, nothing of chance, nothing of compromise. He is holy through the very fiber of His being, and His holiness encapsulates the fullness of all the attributes of His character.

> For I am the Lord your God. Consecrate yourselves therefore, and be holy, for I am holy… For I am the Lord who brought you up out of the land of Egypt to be your God. You shall therefore be holy, for I am holy." (Leviticus 11:44–45)

> But as he who called you is holy, you also be holy in all your conduct, since it is written, "You shall be holy, for I am holy." (1 Peter 1:15–16)

Believing God to be holy leaves no room for any complaint regarding the events of our lives. If He is holy, then He is all He says He is, and nothing which happens can be anything but part of His most holy plan. Therefore, we can trust Him, we can move forward through the events of our lives with confidence. We don't have to be in control; we can be thankful we are not in control; we can rest in the truth and reality that God is in control.

The Lord is Powerful

God is unequaled in His power; none can surpass Him; none

can even come close to Him. All power which we selfishly claim is in reality only that which has been given by God.

> *Do you not know? Do you not hear? Has it not been told you from the beginning? Have you not understood from the foundations of the earth? It is he who sits above the circle of the earth, and its inhabitants are like grasshoppers; who stretches out the heavens like a curtain, and spreads them like a tent to dwell in; who brings princes to nothing, and makes the rulers of the earth as emptiness. Scarcely are they planted, scarcely sown, scarcely has their stem taken root in the earth, when he blows on them, and they wither, and the tempest carries them off like stubble.*
>
> *To whom then will you compare me, that I should be like him? says the Holy One. Lift up your eyes on high and see: who created these? He who brings out their host by number, calling them all by name, by the greatness of his might, and because he is strong in power not one is missing. Why do you say, O Jacob, and speak, O Israel, "My way is hidden from the Lord, and my right is disregarded by my God"?*
>
> *Have you not known? Have you not heard? The Lord is the everlasting God, the Creator of the ends of the earth. He does not faint or grow weary; his understanding is unsearchable. He gives power to the faint, and to him who has no might he increases strength. Even youths shall faint and be weary, and young men shall fall exhausted; but they who wait for the Lord shall renew their strength; they shall mount up with wings like eagles; they shall run and not be weary; they shall walk and not faint. (Isaiah 40:21–31)*

We can trust the power of God enables Him to do all He has said

He will do; that His power is not weakened in His ability to keep all the promises of His Word. What He says He will do, and in Him we can have complete rest, knowing He will always do what is best on our behalf.

The Lord is Good

We can rest in the truth that a "Good God" is in control. He is not one bent on evil; He is not one only interested in Himself; He is not one that is changeable; He is not one who is untrustworthy. He is good, and His goodness is without flaw; He is good consistently and continually. Everything He is and everything He does is good. In His goodness, He always has our best interest in view, and He will always give us everything we need for our benefit which will result in His glory.

> *Every good gift and every perfect gift is from above, coming down from the Father of lights with whom there is no variation or shadow due to change. (James 1:17)*

We are able to recognize His goodness by being involved in relationship with Him. Knowing Him, walking with Him, observing Him, listening to Him, we can readily conclude that He is good. There is nothing in Him that is anything but good.

> *Oh, taste and see that the Lord is good! Blessed is the man who takes refuge in him! (Psalm 34:8)*

We can begin to experience the Lord's goodness today; we can begin to understand His goodness in our redemption, in rescuing us from the awful judgment and bondage of sin, and adopting us as His own children. But there is yet more to come. We will someday in the glories of heaven and in His eternal presence, see His goodness to yet a fuller and complete extent, unlimited by our frailty.

> *I believe that I shall look upon the goodness of the Lord in the land of the living! (Psalm 27:13)*

The Lord has called us in His goodness, and He will provide for us through His goodness. In Him, we will never have any want of anything at any time. Regardless of what life seems to give us, regardless of circumstances surrounding us, His goodness will never fail.

> *His divine power has granted to us all things that pertain to life and godliness, through the knowledge of him who called us to his own glory and excellence, (2 Peter 1:3)*

His purpose is good, and in His goodness He will accomplish His purpose.

> *For it is God who works in you, both to will and to work for his good pleasure. (Philippians 2:13)*

The Lord is Incomparable

There are no other gods which compare with the Lord God. All others are man-made, derived, designed, formed, and decided upon by man. The Lord alone is dependent only on Himself, as He has always been and always will be—a realization that is beyond our comprehension and must be accepted in faith.

> *Hear, O Israel: The Lord our God, the Lord is one. (Deuteronomy 6:4)*

> *God said to Moses, "I am who I am." And he said, "Say this to the people of Israel, 'I am has sent me to you.'" (Exodus 3:14)*

> *To whom then will you compare me, that I should be like him? says the Holy One. Lift up your eyes on high and see: who created these? He who brings out their host by number, calling them all by name, by the greatness of his might, and because he is strong in power not one is missing. Why do you say, O Jacob, and speak, O Israel, "My way is hidden from the Lord, and my right is disregarded by my God"? Have you not known? Have you not heard? The Lord is the everlasting God, the Creator of the ends of the earth. He does not faint or grow weary; his understanding is unsearchable. (Isaiah 40:25–28)*

The Lord is Redeemer

The Lord is our Redeemer by His Sovereign design. As believers, we should be humbled and stand in awe when realizing the grace of God, the mercy of God, and the love of God, that determined before any of the worlds were ever fashioned, to adopt us as His own children. Our redemption is not a last minute thought nor does it come about by the will of man. Rather, it is totally possible by the will of God.

> *Even as he chose us in him before the foundation of the world, that we should be holy and blameless before him. In love he predestined us for adoption as sons through Jesus Christ, according to the purpose of his will, to the praise of his glorious grace, with which he has blessed us in the Beloved. (Ephesians 1:4–6)*

Our redemption is complete in Christ; it was designed before the foundation of the world. He redeemed us with the price of blood, and that being of His One and Only Son, the Lord Jesus Christ.

> *Knowing that you were ransomed from the futile ways inherited from your forefathers, not with perishable things such as silver or gold, but with the precious blood*

> of Christ, like that of a lamb without blemish or spot. He was foreknown before the foundation of the world but was made manifest in the last times for the sake of you who through him are believers in God, who raised him from the dead and gave him glory, so that your faith and hope are in God. (1 Peter 1:18-21)

Our faith and hope are in Him, and this can be without wavering, knowing His great work to bring us to Himself.

Having redeemed us, we can have absolute confidence that the Lord will do all necessary to keep us throughout our trek on this earth. He came to rescue us from sin, from sin's horrible grasp on us, from bondage to the flesh.

> Who [Jesus Christ] gave himself for our sins to deliver us from the present evil age, according to the will of our God and Father, to whom be the glory forever and ever. Amen. (Galatians 1:4-5)

The Lord is Praise Worthy

The Lord has ordained His people to praise Him, to recognize His marvelous character and work, to choose to not be silent. It is God's intent that He be praised, and He has ordained, ordered, and established this to happen.

> O Lord, our Lord, how majestic is your name in all the earth! You have set your glory above the heavens. Out of the mouth of babies and infants, you have established strength because of your foes, to still the enemy and the avenger. When I look at your heavens, the work of your fingers, the moon and the stars, which you have set in place, (Psalm 8:1-3)

DECISION ONE

If we accept the truth that God is in control, and that all He does is good, then we can and should be filled with praise to Him; there is no cause for silence and there is every reason for demonstrating through our lives His majesty and glory.

> *The heavens declare the glory of God, and the sky above proclaims his handiwork... Let the words of my mouth and the meditation of my heart be acceptable in your sight, O Lord, my rock and my redeemer. (Psalm 19:1, 14)*

The heavens see the work of God and respond with praise; His very creation is a symphony of praise to the wondrous design and work of the Lord. As we have life on this earth, our mouths should also be filled with praise to Him, knowing He alone is worthy and above all existence.

In writing to the Church at Rome, Paul includes a wonderful doxology, a response of praise to the incredible working of God in our redemption.

> *Oh, the depth of the riches and wisdom and knowledge of God! How unsearchable are his judgments and how inscrutable his ways! "For who has known the mind of the Lord, or who has been his counselor?" "Or who has given a gift to him that he might be repaid?" For from him and through him and to him are all things. To him be glory forever. Amen. (Romans 11:33–36)*

How can we not exalt Him in praise? We so selfishly and foolishly think at times that because the order of events in our lives do not meet our standards, that God is intentionally at fault in keeping His blessings from us. We erroneously conclude that we are all wise, or at least have greater wisdom than God, who did not choose to change the flow of our experiences. In this we fail to recognize that His mind is of greater capability than ours, and His discernment of "good" far exceeds our comprehension. Our responsibility is not to understand all things, but rather to trust Him who does, to submit to Him who is holding all things together, and to conclude Him worthy of all praise and adoration; nothing lacks in Him; nothing lacks in His working.

The Lord is Faithful

How can the Lord be faithful if He is not good; how can He be good if He is not faithful? He will be faithful in every way in everything all the time; His faithfulness will never cease.

> *The steadfast love of the Lord never ceases; his mercies never come to an end; they are new every morning; great is your faithfulness. (Lamentations 3:22-23)*

He was faithful in creating perfectly, and He remains faithful to all His creation.

> *Therefore let those who suffer according to God's will entrust their souls to a faithful Creator while doing good. (1 Peter 4:19)*

The Lord is faithful, and it must be proclaimed. If we recognize His faithfulness to us while going through the joys of our lives, should we not recognize His faithfulness when experiencing the dark days of our lives? Ethan, the musician, gladly proclaimed the Lord's faithfulness, and saw no reason for His praise to ever stop.

> *I will sing of the steadfast love of the Lord, forever; with my mouth I will make known your faithfulness to all generations. (Psalm 89:1)*

In response to even a beginning understanding of the character of

God, David's psalm of praise can certainly be repeated by the believer. Knowing our Lord is in control, we can fully rest in His wisdom and strength, knowing He is able to make sense out of everything that doesn't seem to make sense to us.

> *Praise the Lord! I will give thanks to the Lord with my whole heart, in the company of the upright, in the congregation. Great are the works of the Lord, studied by all who delight in them. Full of splendor and majesty is his work, and his righteousness endures forever. He has caused his wondrous works to be remembered; the Lord is gracious and merciful. He provides food for those who fear him; he remembers his covenant forever. He has shown his people the power of his works, in giving them the inheritance of the nations. The works of his hands are faithful and just; all his precepts are trustworthy; they are established forever and ever, to be performed with faithfulness and uprightness. He sent redemption to his people; he has commanded his covenant forever. Holy and awesome is his name! The fear of the Lord is the beginning of wisdom; all those who practice it have a good understanding.*
>
> *His praise endures forever! (Psalm 111:1–10)*

My Responsibility

In our humanistic, science-oriented world we want an answer to everything; we want to understand how everything works, we want to put all the pieces together in the puzzle. At times we can feel that God is playing a childish trick on us and is holding out on the last pieces of the jigsaw puzzle, so we cannot see the finished product. However, a better understanding is to think that we have three pieces of a 10,000 piece jigsaw puzzle and are trying to figure out what the finished picture will look like, while not having a box cover! But we cannot; this is not how life works. Rather, this is called faith—trusting God to be God and believing His plan is perfect. We need to remember that He has directed all the pieces, He made the picture, He formed it perfectly, and He understands the puzzle completely—and it is all good!

I am responsible to believe

Faith is closely related to humility—giving ourselves up and trusting God with the future, with the unknown, with the certainty of His perfect plan. Many have the tendency to foolishly "blame God" for all the "bad" that happens. This is totally contrary to His nature and the truth of His Word. They will say that "if God is sovereign, then why does He not stop the bad, why does He not stop those who are bent on evil" (Proverbs 16:14)? This time will come in future judgment when God fully eliminates all forces of evil from the life of the believer, but that time is not yet (Revelation 20.13-15). Now, God holds man fully responsible for every action. We don't have to understand how God's sovereignty and man's responsibility fit together. We do need to believe it, and then act in harmony with it.[3] We must recognize we live in a sin-oriented, sin-infested world, totally impacted by sin and the fall. God is good, righteous, loving, kind, merciful, perfect, and holy—regardless. His character is not dependent on circumstances or my actions, beliefs, or thoughts; He, and all He does, is totally independent of any other.

---

3 Many have written theology books to further expound on this awesome doctrine, offering their arguments and offering their conclusions. It is my presupposition to accept these seemingly opposing truths to be absolutely true, knowing that in God's mind what appears contrary to me is in perfect harmony with Him. This we can and must accept.

DECISION ONE

Many have experienced circumstances they would not have chosen. Abraham would not have chosen to take Isaac up the mountain to offer him as a sacrifice to God. Jonah would not have chosen to be called by God to go to the Ninevites; he would not have chosen to be swallowed by a great fish; he would not have chosen to proclaim to those of Nineveh the coming judgment of God unless they repented. Jonathan, the son of Saul, would not have chosen to have his best friend be the recipient of his father's wrath. Bartemaeus would not have chosen to be born blind. Yet, in each of these situations, and many more which could be derived from Scripture, we can clearly see how God used and had designed what man would not have chosen.

James states faith can be like a wave of the sea, without certainty and stability, without predictability (James. 1.6-8). Many times I have sat on the shore of Lake Michigan watching the waves, building castles in the sand, digging out moats for the flow of water. Whether the waves are ferociously beating against the shore or gently lapping the sand, several things are certain. The same wave of water never returns; there is no certainty to what the waves will do; the waves have no substance; the waves never stand still; and anything built of sand will disappear. Often those same aspects describe our faith. When we place confidence in ourselves, in what we know and in what we expect, we can anticipate nothing except for discouragement in the demise of our little sand castles.

How different when we place our faith in the certainty of God's Word, in the truth of His promises. His Word doesn't move; His character doesn't change.

> *For God alone my soul waits in silence; from him comes my salvation. He alone is my rock and my salvation, my*

fortress; I shall not be greatly shaken. (Psalm 62:1-2)

Trusting Him makes an absolute difference in how I approach each and every situation of my life. Trusting God to be in control will set the foundation for all other choices I must make when it seems my circumstances are not making sense.

I am responsible to accept God's design

We must remember, our responsibility is not to attempt changing God's design. Rather, we are responsible to believe God—knowing He will always be faithful, will always know what is happening, and will always know what He is doing. The right response is always trusting God with what we do not know and cannot do.

Having been recently diagnosed with cancer, Barbara, my wife, said these words to a group of friends at church: "With new information comes new challenges. The news was not what I was hoping for, but 'it is what it is' and I am thankful it was detected… [while waiting for further tests to reveal treatment] we are in a place of further waiting while hanging on to the things we know. There is comfort in knowing our Lord God knows perfectly."

Regardless of our situations in life, we can rest in His sovereign care, knowing His design is perfect. Peter put it in these words: cast all your anxiety on Him, for He cares for you (1 Peter 5:7). Anxiety in any situation can be abandoned in the gracious arms of the Lord. We don't "have to know" when we know Him who knows all there is to know; we don't have to understand the apparent confusion of our lives life when we know Him who has carefully and perfectly designed our moments for purposes beyond our comprehension.

Choosing to accept that we are not in control and circumstances will happen beyond our control gives us overarching peace, the opportunity to praise God, and the privilege of thanking Him for His wonderful design, thanking Him that He has given us the privilege of being included in His providential plan. We can rest in His truth, knowing He will not fail to accomplish His will for His glory.

This is where we must begin. This is foundational to all other choices we will make. If we have this choice wrong, if we falter here, then we cannot expect any other choice to make sense. We must choose to recognize we are not in control and that God is in control; choose to believe that God is working the intricate details of life in a perfect design that will bring Him glory; choose to accept that situations will happen in our lives over which we are not in control and are contrary to what we would choose to have happen.

There will be times, perhaps numerous and continual, when what we have determined as "our will" and what comes to pass as being "God's will" definitely do not connect. May it be our desire is to surrender our will to take delight in God's will, to accept that we do not have the best idea, and that our Sovereign Lord will never make a mistake. May it be our earnest resolve to know His will, to accept His will, and to walk forward through our days on this earth in the expectation of His working for His glory in and through us in all things and at all times.

Consider:

1. Normally speaking, what is my first response when situations happen in my life that I do not like?
2. In what situation do I most struggle with the truth, "God is in control?"
3. How does understanding specific aspects of God's character

impact the way I look at circumstances?
4. Believing God can never do wrong, what aspects of my character most clash with trusting God?
5. What illustration would best describe my faith?
6. Considering Habakkuk 3.17-19: Am I willing to make a commitment to praise the Lord, regardless?
7. What sin do I need to confess; what thinking needs to be transformed; what practice needs to change?

DECISION TWO

I Choose to Confess Sin

There are times an event happens in our lives life over which we have no control. One has innocently been the target of another's sin and evil actions, and as a bystander their life is dramatically changed. However, there are other times when we have done the wrong thing, made selfish choices and in sin have corrupted the planned path for our life. We can regret it, repent, confess, and seek the Lord's forgiveness, but the circumstance will not change. There are always consequences resulting from our wrong actions. We can be angry, bitter, and enter into rage with ourselves as to how we so stupidly made a particular choice. Or we can seek to inflict those emotional responses on others, trying to justify ourselves and redirect responsibility. But these responses still won't change the scenario; what happened is history.

When it comes right down to it, we do not like to confess sin; we do not like to admit we were wrong; we do not like to accept responsibility for our actions. Our selfish, prideful nature repels being corrected, being confronted, being held accountable. We have a tendency to look for ways to get out of being "caught" in sin as we seek to justify our actions, preventing sin's "conviction." Admitting we were wrong can be embarrassing, it can deflate our overinflated ego, and it can remove another's confidence in us, as well as our own confidence. If we admit we were wrong once, we might have to admit it a second time. We become vulnerable, and we don't like it. Therefore, we will do whatever is possible to get out of it.

Some are inclined to change history and rewrite books, deleting great amounts of known circumstances of the past. The thought process goes something like this: I don't like what happened; it is offensive in today's society and to a number of people; I will ignore its existence; I won't talk of it or let others read of it; I will delete any future reference to it; in time people will forget all about it. At times we would like to do this with the events of our own lives. We would like to rewrite the scenario so the offense is erased and forgotten, so the consequences are not harmful.

However, no matter what we may fantasize in our own minds as to a new reality, what we may delete or how we may rewrite the past, it doesn't change truth. If we are guilty in sin, avoidance isn't going to make it untrue; disregarding it won't bring about a lapse of memory. We must face sin as sin, accept it as sin, and bring it before the Throne of God to confess it as sin. In true heart-rooted repentance the Lord forgives. When forgiveness takes place, the believer can continue down life's path in full confidence that God will waste nothing, and can even use the past situation in a manner to bring glory to His name.

As previously stated, there is much of Joseph's life which is unknown. We do not know what his attitude was like when he told his dreams to his family, when he walked around wearing the special coat given to him by his father, or when he stayed home while his brothers were out in the fields with the sheep. We do not know if Joseph was humble in his favored position or if he walked proudly before others. We do not know the exchange of everyday conversation between him and his brothers, and if his words were kind or filled with conceit. We do not know if he was prideful and enjoyed the thought of ruling over his brothers, over those who relentlessly mocked him, ridiculed him, and didn't like him. Perhaps the thought of his family bowing down to him gave him a false opinion of himself as he thought of being elevated to a rightful recognition. Perhaps he justified inappropriate thoughts in his own mind by recognizing he did not choose to be his father's favorite, he did not choose to be Rachel's son, and he did not choose to be handsome.

We do not have to know of these family interactions or private thoughts. Knowing would add nothing to what God desires to teach us in this passage of Scripture. However, knowing man's sinful nature, it is important to consider the need for examination and repentance when there is a seeming disconnect between God's will and ours.

Decision Two: I choose to confess my own sin, repent, and claim God's forgiveness.

If there was a corner of pride in Joseph's heart, perhaps he was humbled during his trip to Egypt. He would have had time for careful heart examination and recollection of his own actions and thoughts. This could have been a time the Lord brought him under great conviction of sin and to the point of confession and repentance. This may have been a time in life when God was working within Joseph, humbling him, to make him useable for further service in His gracious and providential plan.

When we have a distinct change of circumstances and reflect on the current events in our lives, we can be brought face to face with our wrong choices made. We must then ask the question, "Are the things that are happening in my life now, those things that seem so wrong, and the result of my sinful choices?" This can be a tough question, as it compels us to be honest, to admit sin. However, this cannot be neglected. If we have sinned, we have sinned, and the only good option for the believer is to take responsibility for it. Any other choice will only lead to further frustration and despair, to ongoing guilt and pain. The consequences of sin do not just "go away" on their own.

Consider the man who was dominated by the sinful choice of alcohol use resulting in continued drunkenness which disrupted his entire family. He chose to stop at the store, chose to buy alcohol, chose to not be involved in family events and activities as he chose to sit and drink. He chose to disregard his family; he chose to waste money; he chose self. Feeling defeated, he chose a substance which resulted in feelings of greater defeat. The consequences of sin tore a family apart, losing what could have been so different. Consequences don't just go away.

Or consider the husband who, in a moment of frustration and anger, quits his job. He didn't like what he was doing, what others were doing, how he was being treated, and walked out. The consequences of his sinfully motivated angry responses don't just affect him and his employment. The family is impacted, as now there is the inability to pay bills, purchase food, buy children's clothing, and much more.

Sin never happens in isolation; sin is never without consequences

At times, the Lord permits the difficult and lonely seasons of life to give us a clear vision of our lives and our choices. We can neglect the convicting work of God's Spirit or we can embrace this as God lovingly bringing us back into fellowship with Himself. The Lord's "correcting work" can restore us to be usable in the next phase of life.

A quick review of Jonah can help to illustrate this point. Life did not happen as Jonah planned. God called him to go to Nineveh and preach the message of repentance. Jonah ran. God commanded him out of the great fish, and unmistakably got his attention. Jonah went. The people of Nineveh wholeheartedly repented upon hearing the Word of God. Jonah moped. God provided Jonah relief from the sun's heat through the amazing growth of a plant. Jonah complained. Looking at Jonah, there is a consistent pattern of resisting God and falling into sinful attitudes and practices.

However, the story doesn't stop there. The book of Jonah is written by Jonah. I believe this is evidenced when Jonah was once again confronted by his own sinful actions: he repented and was willing to be used by God. Through the account of Jonah's life, numerous multitudes have been confronted with their own sin of rebellion against God and brought back into usable relationship with Him.

Others may do wrong things that impact our lives. We are not responsible to focus on their sin, blaming others for our difficult plight, and whining in our circumstances. We are each responsible for our own actions.[8] Highlighting another's sin will make no difference in our current situation. But when confronted with our own sin, we

---

8 I am not suggesting that we should not follow the Matthew 18:15-22 principle of confronting those who have offended us to restore them to righteousness and to reconcile any broken relationship. However, for purposes here I am talking about dealing with our sin, with our wrong, with what we have done. When we commit sin, we have full responsibility to seek forgiveness. If another chooses to sin, we cannot stop them or be responsible for them. I will discuss this further in Decision Eleven: "I Choose to Forgive Others." When we commit sin, we have full responsibility to seek forgiveness.

have responsibility to acknowledge it, confess it, repent, and claim the forgiveness of God. Then there can be the expectation of moving forward in honoring the Lord.

Recorded by Luke is the amazing story of what we have come to know as the "Prodigal Son" (Luke 15:11-32). Perhaps this account would be better titled the "Faithful Father" or the "Forgiving Father." This story vividly portrays the sad account of the choice to sin, to follow a sinful pattern of life because it is something "I want to do." The young man had no regard for his father, no regard for the Lord, no regard for his father's hard work that gained him an inheritance, no regard for his example before others. He simply wanted what he wanted, because he wanted it; he thought life had much more to offer if he followed his own design, which had nothing to do with God's design. However, after a period of time (how long, we don't know; it could have been months, or a few long years) this young man realized what he had and what he had lost; what he did not have and what he could have had. His heart was filled with sorrow and shame. Realizing his unworthiness to be called his father's son, he devised a plan to return to his father, begging for mercy and to be treated as one of the hired servants. He returned, repentant of his wayward decisions, with hope for provisions, shelter and security. The father's response: total acceptance and complete forgiveness.

> *'For this my son was dead, and is alive again; he was lost, and is found.' And they began to celebrate. (Luke 15:24)*

This happened as a result of the father's character and the son's willingness to repent and seek forgiveness.

In confronting sin in our lives, we should follow these steps:

First, we must acknowledge our need for a Savior.

The first step is to know that we have become a child of God, to know the loving forgiveness of the Heavenly Father, to know the meaning of reconciliation. However, before we can know this, we must accept the truth that we are sinners, and that we fall far short of being able to please God, fall far short of being able to enter into His holy presence. There is nothing of righteousness in us, nothing of goodness inherent in us.

> *As it is written: "None is righteous, no, not one; no one understands; no one seeks for God. All have turned aside; together they have become worthless; no one does good, not even one." "Their throat is an open grave; they use their tongues to deceive." "The venom of asps is under their lips." "Their mouth is full of curses and bitterness." "Their feet are swift to shed blood; in their paths are ruin and misery, and the way of peace they have not known." "There is no fear of God before their eyes." for all have sinned and fall short of the glory of God. (Romans 3:10-18, 23)*

But this is not the end of the story. God made reconciliation possible through His Son, the Lord Jesus Christ. In Him and in Him alone there is hope, there is forgiveness, and there is justification.

> *And are justified by his grace as a gift, through the redemption that is in Christ Jesus, (Romans 3:24)*

In confession of sin, in repentance, and in faith there is the work of God's grace to draw us to Himself, making us His child.

> *Because, if you confess with your mouth that Jesus is Lord and believe in your heart that God raised him from the dead, you will be saved. For with the heart one believes*

and is justified, and with the mouth one confesses and is saved. (Romans 10:9–10)

Secondly, we must desire to be right in our own relationship with the Lord.

Knowing Christ as Savior does not imply that we are free from sin. Though free from the judgment and penalty of sin, free from eternal condemnation resulting from sin, and having been made a child of the Heavenly Father does not eliminate the potential of sinful behavior continuing in our lives. We must be diligent to carefully examine our hearts through the Truth of Scripture, identifying sin and choosing to eradicate it from our daily living. The true believer wants to be free of sin, doesn't want to be entrapped with the past, wants to repent and be forgiven. Yes, sin can bring shame. But, the far greater shame comes with living in the darkness of guilt, failing to admit sin, and being hindered from doing the will of God. In this, sin is only repeated. First, there is the original offense against God and others, and now there is another offense in refusing to admit sin.

Search me, O God, and know my heart! Try me and know my thoughts! And see if there be any grievous way in me, and lead me in the way everlasting! (Psalm 139:23–24)

Our attention needs to be directed within, not at the sins of another. It is easy to redirect our thoughts, to focus on another's sin, and avoid self-confrontation. We must seek to be right in our relationship with the Lord first, and do what it takes for this to happen.

Why do you see the speck that is in your brother's eye, but do not notice the log that is in your own eye? Or how can you say to your brother, 'Let me take the speck out

> *of your eye,' when there is the log in your own eye? You hypocrite, first take the log out of your own eye, and then you will see clearly to take the speck out of your brother's eye. (Matthew 7:3–5)*

When our focus turns to our actions, repentance, and to God's gracious work in forgiveness, then we are able to see the deeds of others from a completely different perspective. We recognize that sinful behavior can be expected and that we cannot control what others do. However, our own sinful behavior should never be excused or determined acceptable, but rather abhorred and immediately eradicated.

David, in confession of his sin with Bathsheba, called upon the Lord for forgiveness. His first priority was to be right before the eyes of God before he could be usable as the Lord's anointed over Israel.

> *Have mercy on me, O God, according to your steadfast love; according to your abundant mercy blot out my transgressions. Wash me thoroughly from my iniquity, and cleanse me from my sin! For I know my transgressions, and my sin is ever before me. (Psalm 51:1–3)*

He did not seek to justify his actions or turn to blame another ("It was Bathsheba's fault for being on the roof"). After having been confronted by Nathan the prophet, he accepted responsibility and prayed for the cleansing work of the Father to be evidenced in his life. David was termed a man after His [God's] own heart (I Samuel 13:14), yet he sinned. But sin does not end God's work, for God is able to use even the negative events of our lives to accomplish His purpose. In sin, we have the privilege of knowing forgiveness; the joy of being forgiven; the hope of moving forward.

As individual believers, we want to ensure our relationship with the Lord is right and nothing is in the way of His using us for His glory.[9] We must look closely and be willing to ask the right questions. The problems we face, the trial before us, the anxiety of the moment, the difficulty that has become an intense struggle, are these indications of unconfessed sin in our lives?

Though confession is never too difficult, it can seem too difficult. It can seem that we are beyond the point of confession, that repentance won't change anything. The consequences have erupted beyond our control and we feel as if it is impossible to get back on the right track to undo the wrong. But, it is not impossible, for God is able and willing to restore us in relationship with Himself when we willingly admit our sinfulness.

Thirdly, we must repent of sin, having the desire and making the commitment to be free from sin.

We are right in thinking that we cannot undo the sin of the past, that we cannot change what has happened; and that we cannot rewrite history. However, our future does not have to wallow in sin's continuing consequences. Change can happen now, setting a different direction for righteous consequences to our future actions. Decisions can be made today, changing the course for our future days.

We must remember that in Christ, there is freedom: freedom which allows us to resist all sin, and freedom not to be held in bondage because of sin.

We know that our old self was crucified with him in order

---

9 As a church, there may be times when corporate confession of sin is important. Similarly, the leadership must make every effort to lead the congregation in repentance, so that nothing will prevent the further work of the Lord in and through His people.

> *that the body of sin might be brought to nothing, so that we would no longer be enslaved to sin. For one who has died has been set free from sin… So you also must consider yourselves dead to sin and alive to God in Christ Jesus. Let not sin therefore reign in your mortal body, to make you obey its passions…For sin will have no dominion over you, since you are not under law but under grace… But thanks be to God, that you who were once slaves of sin have become obedient from the heart to the standard of teaching to which you were committed, and, having been set free from sin, have become slaves of righteousness. (Romans 6:6–18)*

If there is unconfessed sin, confess it now! Be free from the past. The believer is free to do the will of God. The past cannot be changed, but the future can be impacted by our right choices today. We can claim with full assurance the forgiveness of God and then look forward to what our Lord will do next.

Jonah may have thought, "It's too late." His opportunity to go to Nineveh was over; God had surely sent someone else by the time he recovered from the whole boat and fish scenario. But, that wasn't true, and that wasn't his conclusion. He got up and went. God called him and he followed through, even if it was later than what it could have been.

Forgiveness versus saying "I'm sorry"

Forgiveness is more than words. Though words are important, in requesting and granting forgiveness there is conveyed very important truths.[10] In substituting forgiveness, a conversation may often go like

---

10 In Decision Eleven, I will focus on forgiving others; for our intentions here the focus will remain on seeking forgiveness for our own sin.

this: "I'm sorry" with a quick response, "ok," and then it ends. It is not specific, it takes no responsibility, it demands nothing, and it attempts to cover up the offense as "no big deal."

"I'm sorry" can have a "sense of regret" over something that happened. It can mean: I regret I got caught, I regret I hurt you, I regret this happened, I regret that we are no longer friends. A simple response of "ok" simply pushes the offense aside and lets it lie. No response is demanded; often no response is given. Sorry can have a long line of repetition without any change.

Forgiveness is very different. In seeking forgiveness, we take full responsibility for our sin. It includes the idea of repentance, which is a military term meaning "about face." When we say, "Will you please forgive me," we are saying "I was wrong, I sinned, I did the wrong thing, and I will do my best never to walk down that path again." There is remorse over sin and the consequences that have come with it; there is a grieving in the heart because sin has interrupted relationship with God and with others.

> *As it is, I rejoice, not because you were grieved, but because you were grieved into repenting. For you felt a godly grief, so that you suffered no loss through us. For godly grief produces a repentance that leads to salvation without regret, whereas worldly grief produces death. (2 Corinthians 7:9–10)*

Additionally, there is a commitment to change, to be different, to act differently, having different motives and convictions. Godly sorrow does not want to walk repeatedly in sin.

This follows the pattern set by John when he said:

> *And everyone who thus hopes in him* [the hope of

> redemption and the coming of Christ] *purifies himself as he is pure... You know that he appeared in order to take away sins... No one who abides in him keeps on sinning; no one who keeps on sinning has either seen him or known him.... No one born of God makes a practice of sinning, for God's seed abides in him, and he cannot keep on sinning because he has been born of God.* (1 John 3:3–9)

The Christian will not continue in known sin without having great guilt. Knowing that Christ came to redeem us and to free us from all bondage of sin, the believer will not continue to travel down the path of sin and do nothing about it. When realizing sin, we will repent of it—have the desire to turn from it and never go that direction again. We will follow the command given to Lot upon leaving the city of Sodom, do not look back (Genesis 19:17); leave the sinful patterns behind and never desire to go back and join in them again. Never!

As believers seeking forgiveness, we have this attitude. We want to get out of it, run away from it, and never return to it. We know the awfulness of sin; we see the contrast of sin before the Holy God; we know the cost of being forgiven of sin—the blood of Christ shed on the Cross; and we know victory over sin because of the resurrection of Christ from the dead. We will want nothing to do with sin.

Again, requesting forgiveness is not just a casual admittance of "I'm sorry," but rather a deep conviction of not just having wronged another person, but having sinned against them and having sinned against God.

Fourth, we must humbly ask for forgiveness from God and claim His forgiveness.

We cannot just know what to do and the importance of doing

something—we must act.

This is true in salvation.

> *If you confess with your mouth that Jesus is Lord and believe in your heart that God raised him from the dead, you will be saved. For with the heart one believes and is justified, and with the mouth one confesses and is saved... For "everyone who calls on the name of the Lord will be saved." (Romans 10:9-13)*

This is true in regards to all sin, and in this we have the assurance of His gracious forgiveness.

> *If we say we have no sin, we deceive ourselves, and the truth is not in us. If we confess our sins, he is faithful and just to forgive us our sins and to cleanse us from all unrighteousness. (1 John 1:8-9)*

When sin has been identified, an unrepentant heart is evidence that one is not a child of God. Characteristic of salvation is the desire to seek cleansing, the desire to be free from all sin. When we know the love of God, when we know the atoning work of Christ on the Cross, when we know the powerful working of Jesus in the resurrection, when we know the hope of His return, there will be the desire to be free from sin. How can we linger in sin knowing what Christ accomplished to free us from sin? How can we ignore the awfulness of sin, the misery of sin, the filth of sin when understanding the cost of our redemption? The two don't mix. If we understand what the Lord has done to free us from sin's bondage, we cannot avoid sin in our lives, and we cannot enjoy it. We cannot love two contrary realities at the same time.

> *No one who abides in him keeps on sinning; no one who keeps on sinning has either seen him or known him. Little children, let no one deceive you. Whoever practices righteousness is righteous, as he is righteous. Whoever makes a practice of sinning is of the devil, for the devil has been sinning from the beginning. The reason the Son of God appeared was to destroy the works of the devil. No one born of God makes a practice of sinning, for God's seed abides in him, and he cannot keep on sinning because he has been born of God. By this it is evident who are the children of God, and who are the children of the devil: whoever does not practice righteousness is not of God, nor is the one who does not love his brother. (1 John 3:6–10)*

These are sobering words. Evidence of our salvation is our desire for righteousness. If we have no desire to be free of sin, to walk in the righteousness of Jesus Christ, then we need to go back to step one. We must recognize our sinfulness before the Holy God, earnestly come to Him in repentance and faith, desiring His work of redemption within us, the appropriation of His saving grace in our lives. Once this happens, and we have experienced the new birth (John 3:1-18), we will not live as those who are yet dead; we will live as those who know true life and freedom from sin (Ephesians 2:1-10).

Fifth, we must humbly ask forgiveness from others.

Along with a heart of repentance, confession before the Father, and the determination to be free of all sin, there must also be the commitment to be right in relationship with others. If we have sinned against another, it should not be ignored, it should not be minimized, and it should not be neglected. If we seek to be reconciled to God following sin, there must be the intentional resolve to be reconciled to those we have sinned against. Apart from seeking forgiveness, we cannot expect reconciliation in relationships will happen.

> *Forgive us our debts, as we also have forgiven our debtors. (Matthew 6:12)*

> *Confess your sins to one another... (James 5:16)*

Following the death of their father, Joseph's brothers came to him seeking his forgiveness. They knew they had sinned; they knew their relationship could be in jeopardy; they knew they were guilty. Even though they came deceitfully, they knew they needed to be forgiven.

> *'Say to Joseph, "Please forgive the transgression of your brothers and their sin, because they did evil to you." ' And now, please forgive the transgression of the servants of the God of your father." Joseph wept when they spoke to him. (Genesis 50:17)*

We have no knowledge that Jacob told his sons to go to Joseph to seek his forgiveness; we do not even know if they ever told him the truth of Joseph's disappearance. The brothers likely attributed their request to their father, knowing Joseph would honor him. They feared for their lives, still not certain if Joseph might eventually be vengeful. This was never his intention.

Hearing their confession, their admittance of sin, Joseph wept. These were not tears of sadness, but rather joy in the healing of relationship. He delighted in their repentance, regardless of their initial motivation.

> *Therefore, confess your sins to one another and pray for one another, that you may be healed. The prayer of a righteous person has great power as it is working. (James 5:16)*

The primary instruction of this passage is in reference to illness that has been brought about because of sin or exacerbated because of sin. Open confession of sin enables others to pray and to encourage in righteousness; it also keeps the confessor accountable regarding his intention and practice of being free from sin. At times, through confession and the removal of sin, there can be physical relief.[11]

There is a further application of this passage. This involves the healing of relationships between people. In confession is the admittance of sin, the acknowledgement of guilt. In confession of sin and the request for forgiveness of sin is the firm commitment to change and the humble desire to be restored in relationship. Requesting forgiveness clearly demonstrates a desire to no longer follow in the pattern of past sin, but rather to be transformed through the powerful working of the Spirit of God, and to be in full submission to the will of God.

Paul calls upon believers to not hold grudges, to not develop bitterness, to not embrace sins against another.

> *Let all bitterness and wrath and anger and clamor and slander be put away from you, along with all malice. Be kind to one another, tenderhearted, forgiving one another, as God in Christ forgave you. (Ephesians 4:31-32)*

In seeking forgiveness and granting forgiveness is true reconciliation. Through this commitment, no matter how severely severed the relationship has been because of sin, it can be restored and

---

11 Not all illness is the direct result of sin; the confession of sin does not automatically imply the healing of physical ailments. This must be carefully recognized – there is no "sure cure" from sickness. We live in a sin-infected world, which is cruelly impacted through illness of all kinds. This can be noted, however, that some illness is a direct result of sin, and some illness is worsened because of sinful behavior or attitudes. The removal of these and the effective prayer of others can bring healing, but there is no guarantee.

brought into a stronger bond than previously known. This is possible because in forgiveness is the fullest demonstration of love.

Brian (not his real name) had been involved in pornography and flirtatious relationships with girls and women from his youth. This had become a pattern of his living. Though knowing it was wrong and growing up in the church he believed it to be sin. However, he enjoyed it, didn't want to quit, and actually didn't know if he could quit. Even after being married to Emily (not her real name) his secret was well hid. Finally, his flirting with a particular woman grew into an adulterous relationship. He didn't think anyone would know. However, it was revealed, first becoming known in his work environment. His job was in jeopardy. He had to tell his wife; there was no longer any possibility of hiding what had been hidden for so long. After receiving forgiveness from the Lord and from his wife, their relationship was wonderfully restored and in time continued to grow stronger. However, there was still need to seek forgiveness from family members, as they had been offended by what he had done in violating the marriage covenant with their daughter and sister. In order to carefully express himself, he wrote the following letter to family members.

> As you already know _____ was my final day working at_____. In the interest of full disclosure and seeking forgiveness from my family I want to share with you a few things.
>
> Over the past several years I struggled with involving myself in flirtatious relationships. What made this easy was texting, and having hours and hours of unaccounted for time working nights. Not only did the free time often accompanied by boredom contribute to my struggle, but the seemingly never ending amount of women making known

DECISION TWO

their willingness to engage in relationships added to my struggle. I always thought I would be able to contain this sin struggle to flirtation only, thinking I wasn't really hurting anyone. Little did I know I was spiraling downward into a dark world of lust and selfish gratification. One thing led to another and the next thing I knew I was engaging in an affair. Before I go any further it is important for you to know, that this had nothing to do with Emily or any short comings on her part. She has always been everything I ever wanted in a wife, and more. I took her for granted, and got caught up in an evil struggle, that without God I had no strength to end.

Without going into all the details of how sin compounds and all the details of my situation, I will just say that on_____ God decided for me that He had enough of my sinful behavior. Matthew 5:29 "If your eye causes you to sin pluck it out for it is better to go into heaven with one eye then into hell with both…." My job was my "eye," it was my life. I wasn't going to quit, just as you wouldn't pluck out your own eye. I loved what I did, in fact I loved it too much. Thankfully, God in his infinite wisdom had different plans; he took away my "eye" so that through this situation, my deepest darkest sins would be revealed.

About two months prior to losing my job, I told a close friend that I would never tell Emily of the depths of my struggles. I had plans to overcome my sin on my own. I was even willing to take it to the grave if I had to. I am so thankful that this is not reality anymore. For the first time in our marriage I came completely clean with all my struggles, and secrets.

On_____ I admitted to my employer to having an affair while on duty, even though they were not aware of it.

WHEN GOD'S WILL AND MY WILL DISCONNECT

I had the opportunity to come completely clean and I felt it was the time.

Two days later I told Emily of all the details and asked for her forgiveness. She was gracious to forgive. That night during our devotions I was led to the book of Isaiah 43:1-3 and for the first time in my life I felt complete true forgiveness. I believe in part because I had confessed all my sins to God, and to my wife whom I had been betraying. "Fear not for I have redeemed you, I have called you by your name, and you are Mine. When you pass through the water I will be with you; and through the rivers they shall not overflow you. When you walk through the fire you shall not be burned, nor shall the flame scorch you."

Over the past several years I have questioned my Christianity. Partly because I had everything I ever wanted, including a wonderful wife, two beautiful children, and the job of my dreams, and yet I was living in sin. Was God going to stop me? I questioned often Hebrews 12:6 "For whom the Lord loves He chastens, and scourges every son whom He receives." Where were my trials, I wondered? The Lord must not love me, and I must not be a Christian as I once thought. Praise God for _____ [the date his sin was revealed]. Although I am sure you don't struggle with this sin like I do, I encourage you to confess your sins to your spouse and to God before God stops you in a big way. He will, and it will hurt.

Having said all of this, I want to ask you for your forgiveness. Please forgive me for living a double life, for hurting your sister, for betraying my wife. Emily is the greatest earthly example of love I will ever experience, someone I will never take for granted again.

Pray for us, and pray for me. For the past several years I

was living for myself, I have a lot of making up to do. Please pray for Emily, for strength and confidence. This struggle was not about her, it was about me, but as you can expect she feels like I was searching for something she could not offer. This is not the case. She needs prayer and love.

With Love

Brian[12]

In God's wonderful grace, this family has been restored in relationship. It would not have happened had Brian continued to deny the depth of his sin or been defensive with excuses as to the reason of his choosing sin. He admitted it; confessed it, sought forgiveness, and relationships were restored. Though the temptations continue, Brian now knows victory over sin and freedom from its grave bondage. He is learning the powerful truth of Scripture and their application to his daily living.

Though not every situation is as dramatic as Brian's, every sinful act has the same potential of destroying relationships and negatively altering the course of life. Thankfully, through the grace of God's forgiveness and the desire to be forgiven by others, change can happen.

Consider:

1. Am I a child of God?

   If yes, how do I know this to be true? If no, what keeps me from being a follower of Jesus Christ?

2. Is there unconfessed sin in my life? Have I sought to hide sin, wrongly justifying that it doesn't matter?

   If true, how have I justified my sinful actions?

---

[12] Letter used by permission.

3. Am I aware of and choosing to ignore that my sinful choices have had an impact on others?
   If yes, what have I expected would or would not happen?
4. Am I harboring anger and bitterness toward someone else because of their sin?
   If yes, what do I think my bitterness and anger will accomplish?
5. Have I been stymied under the consequences of sin?
   If yes, how is this realized?
6. Am I characterized more as a "forgiver" or as one who "holds on to sins of others?"
   Is there someone I need to confess sin to and seek forgiveness from, or someone I need to forgive?
   What will I do?
7. What sin do I need to confess; what thinking needs to be transformed; what practice needs to change?

DECISION THREE

I Choose Faithfulness

Faithfulness can be work. We can look at our life circumstances and conclude that in the immediate, laziness looks better. Just "go with the flow;" don't worry about the results, doing anything different right now is just too tiring. We can tend to give up, coming to a point of not caring about what might happen. Thinking the situation is too bad to get out of, we accept the lie that there is no way out, and we just give up. We don't like it, we choose to not like it, and we choose not to do anything that may change our attitude about it.

We can also get into the mindset that "we don't deserve" whatever has happened. Current thought in our society lends itself to this thinking and that we "deserve better." We have come to a place where we think we are worthy of things going well for us; that we deserve to have certain things happen; that we deserve to not be under pressure; that we deserve a certain amount of pleasure; and the list continues ad infinitum. This is a sad commentary in relation to the truth of

Scripture. For in recognizing our sinfulness and inability before the holy and infinite God, there is nothing we can even begin to deserve. Nothing, that is, except judgment. And praise God, that by the gift of His grace, judgment is past and we can be justified through the work of the Lord Jesus Christ.[13]

Individuals will revert to rationalizing sinful actions with the comment, "I don't deserve this; no one, and not even God would possibly expect me to live in this situation. I know that my choice isn't what is right, but I just can't stay here." They give up. Living in a sinful situation, they see their only option is one of sin, a sinful choice to counteract another's sinful choices. Another may say, "I just don't see any way out of this. It has gone on too long, and the pain is too great. I have got to _____, even though I know it isn't the right thing." In desperation, again a choice is made to sin.

A wife says, "I can't do this any longer. You don't know what it is like living with him. I never know who is coming home—whether he will be nice or mean, loving or hateful, calm or angry. God cannot expect me to stay in this situation. I'm fed up! I have got to get away

---

13 Justification is the gracious work of God by which we are declared righteous in Jesus Christ. It is far more than being brought to a condition that is "just as if we had never sinned," because we did sin. We are sinners and that history cannot be changed. In justification we are guilty, condemned sinners who are declared righteous through the work of Jesus Christ.

Romans 3:23-24: For all have sinned and fall short of the glory of God, and are justified by his grace as a gift, through the redemption that is in Christ Jesus.

Romans 5:1: Therefore, since we have been justified by faith, we have peace with God through our Lord Jesus Christ.

Romans 8:1-2: There is therefore now no condemnation for those who are in Christ Jesus. For the law of the Spirit of life has set you free in Christ Jesus from the law of sin and death.

Titus 3:3-7: For we ourselves were once foolish, disobedient, led astray, slaves to various passions and pleasures, passing our days in malice and envy, hated by others and hating one another. But when the goodness and loving kindness of God our Savior appeared, he saved us, not because of works done by us in righteousness, but according to his own mercy, by the washing of regeneration and renewal of the Holy Spirit, whom he poured out on us richly through Jesus Christ our Savior, so that being justified by his grace we might become heirs according to the hope of eternal life.

to where I can have some normalcy in life. I know it is not right, but I don't know what else to do."

Or a young man says, "I know that sex before marriage isn't right, but I just can't seem to help it. We both 'love' each other so much; we are committed to each other; and we plan to marry each other as soon as it is possible. We are taking all the necessary precautions so she doesn't get pregnant, and we do realize our intimacy is an expression of our love for each other. Though it may not be absolutely right, I believe it is right for us and no one can deny what we feel."

The scenarios are innumerable. Seeking to validate sin, we determine we are right. Whether it is those times when we feel out of control, that the things happening around us are very contrary to what we would like, imagine, or even remotely expect. Or, we have chosen to make choices contrary to God's design. Our responsibility is not to sort out all the intricacies of the situation, to try and correctly analyze all our feelings, and to re-determine what is right and wrong, what is good and bad. Rather, our responsibility is to trust God and to do the right thing. We must remember that what may seem totally imperfect to us is totally perfect in God's providential plan. Our guide must be God's Truth, the Holy Scriptures, as our final authority in all things.

Decision Three: I choose to live faithfully before God in imperfect circumstances.

Choosing faithfulness isn't easy when life doesn't make sense and the circumstances are so very contrary to what we hoped for or imagined. It takes faith to trust God, as was outlined in the first decision; it takes faith to live obediently when we "feel" like doing something differently; it takes faith to live faithfully. In looking at

Joseph, we can clearly see he chose faithfulness repeatedly in varying situations. To live faithfully, we must be willing to make the following three choices:

First, I choose to live faithfully before God in circumstances of horror.

It appears Joseph demonstrated his choice to be faithful before the Lord when he didn't understand and didn't know how the future was going to begin to unfold.

> *Now Joseph had been brought down to Egypt, and Potiphar, an officer of Pharaoh, the captain of the guard, an Egyptian, had bought him from the Ishmaelites who had brought him down there. (Genesis 39:1)*

This was likely a moment of horror. Joseph was taken by caravan away from his home and likely treated with little to no respect. The future was totally unknown. He was sold into the Egyptian slave market, placed as a public spectacle for someone unknown to determine his worth and perceived monetary value. What was it like for him to realize that he had suddenly been translated from wealth and prestige to total poverty and dependence, from freedom to slavery, from recognition to abject discrimination? Grief, sorrow, frustration, anger, and fear—all these emotions could have prevailed over Joseph at the same time.

The emotions and attitudes demonstrated by Joseph are not clearly stated in Scripture. However, it appears he chose to respond faithfully in the midst of imperfect, horror filled circumstances. Recognizing his lack of control over circumstances, he chose to remain faithful to the Lord and to live in the manifestation of God's faithfulness to him.

When the unbelievable happens and our lives are suddenly

plunged into an apparent situation of horror, how do we respond? Because of a death, a sudden move, or a broken relationship, our world can abruptly be thrust into turmoil. Nothing seems to be the same as it had been, and there is no longer a "comfort zone" in our lives. At this time will we make the choice to remain faithful, to trust God who is always faithful, or to retreat to a temporarily safe environment or an emotionally spurred activity?

Current thinking about horror is often sadly oblivious to the truth of God's Word. Imaginary horror is marketed as exciting, and some wickedly choose to carry out deeds of horror. However, regardless of the depraved mind's conjecture of fun, living through horror is no fun. Horror is horrible. Horror is filled with fear and danger, with misery, and with an expectation of loneliness, tragedy, and uncertainty. Awful memories can remain for years, if not throughout one's life. Living in the midst horror can be overwhelming, but it does not have to be all encompassing and immobilizing. In recognizing the truth of Scripture and that God will always be faithfully God, we can walk through horror with confidence of not being alone. The believer can be certain of God's gracious working and provision, taking the horrible and translating it into praise for His glory.

> *And if children, then heirs—heirs of God and fellow heirs with Christ, provided we suffer with him in order that we may also be glorified with him. For I consider that the sufferings of this present time are not worth comparing with the glory that is to be revealed to us. (Romans 8:17-18)*

We can experience the "horror situations" because of the acts of others or disastrous situations over which there is no control; in other situations we have made bad choices, and have led ourselves into those tumultuous days. However, walking through the "horror situation" in our lives provides no excuse for unfaithfulness. We can tend to excuse bad behavior because of a seemingly negative situation. We conclude that the expectation to live well when things are bad is an impossible probability. There is a tendency to concede sin as the norm when other areas of life are disrupted. However, before the eyes of God, sin is never excusable. Sin is never permissible. Sin is never necessary.

> *No temptation has overtaken you that is not common to man. God is faithful, and he will not let you be tempted beyond your ability, but with the temptation he will also provide the way of escape, that you may be able to endure it. (1 Corinthians 10:13)*

Some will say the temptation is too difficult to defeat; it is not possible to resist the sinful urge; the lure of the sin is inescapable; we are bound to walk down this sinful path. Others will claim that God is at fault, that He is not fair, that He is not good. No! These statements are not true; they are all in direct contrast to the truth of God's Word. There is absolutely no sin in God, and there is no sin that has unequivocal power over the believer. No sin is so great, no sin is so compelling, no sin is so strong, and no sin is so enticing that through trusting in Christ the believer is not able to resist it. What is the key for overcoming any and all temptations? God is faithful! We can trust His Word, His character, His desire, His power, and His enabling. He is always faithful to all He is, and He is ever faithful to us all the time. We will be tempted to sin—this is a given. The temptations we face can be fierce, attacking us in areas where we are most vulnerable. Sin may even appear to provide the easier and better route for us to travel.

We must hold to the truths of this passage.

I must remember that the temptations we face are not uniquely ours.

Others have faced similar temptation. Though the circumstances will never be exactly the same, the crux of the temptation is similar. We are never able to rightfully say, "No one has ever been through what I am going through."

I must remember God knows what we are facing, when we are facing it, and the depth of our struggle.

Being our loving God and Father, He will always protect us from being overridden by a situation that is too difficult for us; He will always guard us, preventing us from being overtaken.

I must remember our Lord will always provide a way of victory for us while under temptation; He will always make it possible for us to escape the tempter's snare.

We can always say no to doing the wrong thing; we can always resist falling into sin; we can always choose to make right choices. We do not have to succumb to them. Through Christ, through the redeeming power of the Gospel, and by the powerful work of the indwelling Holy Spirit we can resist, we can flee from them, and we can flee to our refuge in Jesus Christ.

> *Be sober-minded; be watchful. Your adversary the devil prowls around like a roaring lion, seeking someone to devour. Resist him, firm in your faith... (1 Peter 5:8–9)*

> *Submit yourselves therefore to God. Resist the devil, and he will flee from you. (James 4:7)*

We must be confident in God's truth and chose to not believe

Satan's tempestuous and evil lies. God will provide a way out, He will give us victory, He will cause us to stand and not fall. God is faithful—we must trust Him, rest in Him, cling to Him, flee to Him, hope in Him, and have confidence in Him, ever praising Him with thanksgiving. How can we be confident of all this? God is faithful. When the believer comes to grips with the truth that God's faithfulness is always trustworthy, then he can respond freely and confidently choosing faithfulness to God in response.

Second, I choose to live in faithfulness before God in circumstances of imperfect success.

Success is imperfect in our minds when it is not the best situation; when we are successful where we don't want to be successful. Joseph's success was imperfect. He took the situation at hand and made the most of it. Being a slave was not his "preferred vocation" in life, not what he had aspired to be. But, if he was going to be a slave, and that was now a given, then it was far better being in charge of his master's household, or being the "slave leader" of other slaves.

> *The Lord was with Joseph, and he became a successful man, and he was in the house of his Egyptian master. His master saw that the Lord was with him and that the Lord caused all that he did to succeed in his hands. So Joseph found favor in his sight and attended him, and he made him overseer of his house and put him in charge of all that he had. From the time that he made him overseer in his house and over all that he had, the Lord blessed the Egyptian's house for Joseph's sake; the blessing of the Lord was on all that he had, in house and field. So he left all that he had in Joseph's charge, and because of him he had no concern about anything but the food he ate. Now Joseph was handsome in form and appearance. (Genesis 39:2–6)*

We can sit, moaning and groaning through our situations, ever frustrated with what has happened. Or, we can choose to respond with integrity, doing our best for God, resulting in glory being given to Him. Instead of focusing on what we don't have, we can accept what God has given us, where He has positioned us, and His desire to use us where we are.

Joseph moved forward. He didn't spend his time complaining and becoming bitter; he didn't connive how he might seek revenge on his brothers; he didn't waste his time wishing he were somewhere else, doing something else, with someone else; he wasn't obsessed with trying to escape; he did not impose on himself "pity parties" hoping that others would see his distress and feel sorry for him, having sympathy for him. No, he accepted his situation and chose to remain faithful to God, doing what he could do. He chose to be faithful to the Lord, knowing the Lord remained faithful to him. Note the key words in this passage:

His master saw that the Lord was with him and that the Lord caused all that he did to succeed in his hands.

There was clear evidence that Joseph had a unique relationship with the Lord, previously unseen by Potiphar, for none of his other "subjects" demonstrated the character qualities found in this slave.

So Joseph found favor in his sight.

God blessed him. Because of his faithfulness in being a man of integrity, God gave him further responsibility.

The LORD blessed the Egyptian's house ... the blessing of the LORD was on all that he had.

Joseph's faithfulness to God resulted in the Lord using him to bless others. We don't always see how this will happen, but we can be assured He will use our faithfulness to encourage and strengthen others, whether it is one or two people or a multitude.

Joseph was handsome in form and appearance.

Joseph did not use his God given characteristics for his benefit and recognition. This was God's work. Our physical characteristics have been designed by God; our responsibility to accept them as from Him, given to us as a tent in which we are able to bring glory to His name.

There was something different about Joseph, and others could see it. Not because of anything that he possessed, but because of his character quality and his commitment to the Lord and the principles he knew as truth. In less than ideal circumstances, Joseph remained faithful before God and others; living in a pagan society, Joseph refused to compromise the truth of God and His Word.

We recognize Joseph wasn't perfect. There may have been areas in his life he compromised, and he may have had the occasional "bad day" when he did or said things which were later regretted. We don't know. But, if those things happened, they are not recorded for us. Therefore, we can conclude that the Lord documented what we need to know, and we are told that Joseph remained faithful in unfavorable circumstances, choosing to do the right thing and not bringing shame on himself, his family, or the Lord.

Joseph's life went from unbelievable turmoil to unbelievable success. The unknown slave was suddenly elevated to a place of prominence and authority. Yet, this change in status didn't change Joseph's attitude; he didn't become proud and arrogant before others. He continued to choose faithfulness before God.

When change happens in our circumstances, either for bad or good, do others see something different about us? Do our actions convey there is a hope and confidence in God? Or, do others excuse our ill behavior with varying comments like: "that is expected after what he has been through," or "I probably would have done the same thing," and "no one can blame him." It is important for the believer to recognize that in these difficult times there is a prime opportunity to stand as a witness of God's love and the power of the Gospel through Jesus Christ. Our responses to life situations should not be fodder for vain excuses, but rather a demonstration of the grace of God actively working in and through our lives.

The Lord never promises the ease of life or the benefit of continual harmony with our plans. However, He does promise His absolute faithfulness to us, and requires our total faithfulness to Him. Anything less doubts the judgment of God, the design of God, and the wisdom of God in completing His redemptive plan in our lives and in these days.

> *I have been young, and now am old, yet I have not seen the righteous forsaken or his children begging for bread. (Psalm 37:25)*

Our Lord will accomplish His good purpose, always and completely.

> *And I am sure of this, that he who began a good work in you will bring it to completion at the day of Jesus Christ. (Philippians 1:6)*

Third, I choose to live in faithfulness before God in reality circumstances.

Joseph has been blessed with an external appearance noted by others. The way it is stated, we can expect that his appearance was the envy of others.

> *Joseph was handsome in form and appearance. (Genesis 39:6)*

We don't know if he had a body builder's body, an athletic physic, or defining physical characteristics that caused others to look his way with great admiration and probable envy. Whatever may have been the specific, he was significantly, positively different from others.

His appearance could have been a snare to him. Knowing he would have been on the cover of the current celebrity magazine as the best looking man in Egypt, the publicity could have filled him with pride. He could have spent time in front of the mirror examining himself and praising his appearance. However, none of this is even suggested.

It is not unusual for us to become overly aware of ourselves, wearing out the mirror of conceit and arrogance. Somehow thinking we are responsible for our appearance or God-given abilities, we become prideful in a false superiority. Taking credit for how we look or what we are able to do is denying the creative work of God; faithfulness to God is suddenly exchanged for faithfulness to self, to "self-idolatry."

Remember the words of the Psalmist earlier quoted:

> *For you formed my inward parts; you knitted me together in my mother's womb... (Psalm 139:13-17)*

Though we may be gifted in various ways, this is not substance for self-praise. God is at work. His creating us as He specifically has is not for our self-sufficiency and self-praise. Rather, in seeing that who we are is a gift of the Lord, our desire should be to use what we have and who we are for His glory (1 Corinthians 10:31).

The prosperity of Joseph's life takes a sudden twist. Though he had chosen right, the resulting consequences were not seemingly to his benefit. Having been placed in charge of Potiphar's household, he had great privilege and responsibility. He recognized this, and so did Potiphar's deceitful and scandalous wife. She sought to entice him into an adulterous relationship. When he resisted, she lied to her husband, resulting in Joseph being thrust into prison. No court, no defense, no jury—just instantaneous judgment. He wasn't guilty, but Potiphar, the prosecutor and judge, wasn't looking for truth.

> *And Joseph's master took him and put him into the prison, the place where the king's prisoners were confined, and he was there in prison. But the Lord was with Joseph and showed him steadfast love and gave him favor in the sight of the keeper of the prison. And the keeper of the prison put Joseph in charge of all the prisoners who were in the prison. Whatever was done there, he was the one who did it. The keeper of the prison paid no attention to anything that was in Joseph's charge, because the Lord was with him. And whatever he did, the Lord made it succeed. (Genesis 39:20–23)*

Again, Joseph chose to live faithfully before God and others, and God's faithfulness prevailed. There is no evidence of Joseph whining, complaining, bickering with others, or trying to justify his actions and prove his innocence. This isn't to say he never did, but that there is no evidence of it. If he did falter in this way, it is insignificant for us, as God did not record it. Again, there are key phrases which are noteworthy regarding God's faithful working:

WHEN GOD'S WILL AND MY WILL DISCONNECT

The LORD was with him.

Joseph knew he was not in prison alone; he had not been deserted by the eternally faithful God. The Lord chose to be with Joseph; He chose to provide Him with confidence of His gracious presence. Similarly, we can be certain that regardless of circumstances, our Lord will also be with us, without fail.

The LORD showed him steadfast love.

Joseph was protected from harshness. Though he had to work hard while enduring the struggles of prison, Joseph remained confident of the Lord's love and kindness to him. The sufficiency of His grace will always take the most difficult situation and use it to demonstrate His sovereign character and His love for His people.

The LORD gave him favor.

God rewarded him and blessed him beyond expectations.

The keeper of the prison put Joseph in charge.

Joseph's actions led to the prison keeper's reward.

Our responsibility is to choose right and to anticipate God working, knowing He will use whatever the circumstance for His glory. He will bring about the accomplishment of His greater purpose, even though we are not able to see it or begin comprehending it. The Lord has never promised us that we will always like everything we do, that we will understand everything that is happening, or that it will always be our first choice. That is insignificant. What is important is knowing we can trust Him to use all for His glory and benefit in His perfect and sovereign plan.

When we first began to realize something was "different" with Jonathan, it was difficult. I had hoped we could somehow "fix"

DECISION THREE

whatever was wrong and he would then have a "normal" life. It didn't work that way. I didn't always like dealing with the uniqueness of Jonathan's characteristics, but it wasn't about what I liked. When we first realized Barbara would have to have brain surgery, we didn't like the idea. The thought of someone cutting through your skull to remove something that doesn't belong there does not necessarily produce excitement. However, it was not about what we wanted. When told I would be spending one year in Turkey on an unaccompanied tour, it was not my first choice; it was difficult to think of being separated from my family, leaving them in a new place in Massachusetts, and being 5,000 miles away. But, it was not about what I wanted. It has always been about God's faithfulness to Himself, to His Word, and to us. Our responsibility is to trust that our Lord will be faithful, and then choose to do what is right according to His Word.

God is faithful, by whom you were called into the fellowship of his Son, Jesus Christ our Lord. (1 Corinthians 1:9)

If we are not willing to accept that God is always faithful all the time, we will have no motivation for faithfulness. However, when we are willing to accept, to believe, to trust in the faithfulness of God, the working of His redemptive plan in our lives, then our only response can be one of faithfulness to Him. Whenever we choose to not be faithful, we are choosing to doubt the faithfulness of God, which in turn doubts God, and is clearly sin.

But this I call to mind, and therefore I have hope: The steadfast love of the Lord never ceases; his mercies never come to an end; they are new every morning; great is your faithfulness. (Lamentations 3:21–23)

WHEN GOD'S WILL AND MY WILL DISCONNECT

Lessons from Paul

Paul is an example in living faithfully. There was nothing "easy" about Paul's life. He could have chosen to live differently; he could have chosen to not confront some people, churches, or issues; he could have chosen not to get into difficult situations, knowing the outcome would be controversial and he would likely result in prison. Yet, he could not make those choices because he had previously made the choice to be faithful to the Lord as a servant, as an apostle, as a representative of Jesus Christ. He could do nothing less than what was right, could do nothing less than stand for Jesus Christ and the Word of God, could do nothing less than be willing to be subject to "whatever" the consequences. And in all this, he remained faithful.

Not in a manner of boasting, but rather in the intention of glorifying God for His faithfulness through the most difficult trials, Paul summarized his life trials.

> *To my shame, I must say, we were too weak for that! But whatever anyone else dares to boast of—I am speaking as a fool—I also dare to boast of that. Are they Hebrews? So am I. Are they Israelites? So am I. Are they offspring of Abraham? So am I. Are they servants of Christ? I am a better one—I am talking like a madman—with far greater labors, far more imprisonments, with countless beatings, and often near death. Five times I received at the hands of the Jews the forty lashes less one. Three times I was beaten with rods. Once I was stoned. Three times I was shipwrecked; a night and a day I was adrift at sea; on frequent journeys, in danger from rivers, danger from robbers, danger from my own people, danger from Gentiles, danger in the city, danger in the wilderness, danger at sea, danger from false brothers; in toil and hardship, through many a sleepless night, in hunger and thirst, often without food, in cold and exposure. And, apart from other things,*

DECISION THREE

> *there is the daily pressure on me of my anxiety for all the churches. Who is weak, and I am not weak? Who is made to fall, and I am not indignant? If I must boast, I will boast of the things that show my weakness. (2 Corinthians 11:21–30)*

Faithfulness without complaint

Paul remained faithful. He did not complain, he did not gripe, he did not argue with God that his plight was too difficult. He moved forward with an expectation God was working in every situation of his life. He was not responsible to understand the details of God's working, to analyze the appropriateness of God's working, or to judge the benefit of God's working. He was to remain faithful to the calling God had given to him.

> *Do all things without grumbling or disputing, that you may be blameless and innocent, children of God without blemish in the midst of a crooked and twisted generation, among whom you shine as lights in the world, holding fast to the word of life… (Philippians 2:13–16)*

Faithfulness in personal struggles

In addition to the trials noted above, he had a defined personal struggle. We do not know what his thorn in the flesh was, but we do know two things. One, it was difficult, and two, God enabled him through it.

> *…A thorn was given me in the flesh, a messenger of Satan to harass me, to keep me from becoming conceited. Three times I pleaded with the Lord about this, that it should leave me. But he said to me, "My grace is sufficient for you, for my power is made perfect in weakness." Therefore I*

> *will boast all the more gladly of my weaknesses, so that the power of Christ may rest upon me. For the sake of Christ, then, I am content with weaknesses, insults, hardships, persecutions, and calamities. For when I am weak, then I am strong. (2 Corinthians 12:7–10)*

Paul did not look at his struggle as an obstacle in doing the Lord's will, but rather as the design of God to bring glory to His name. Accepting his own weakness and limitation, Paul trusted God in His almighty power to give the enablement he needed to walk worthy of his calling (Ephesians 4:1).

Faithfulness in maintaining focus

To maintain a Biblical focus in faithfulness, Paul encourages believers to not be distracted by the thoughts of the world or the feelings we may encompass. Rather, our sights must be kept on the Lord Jesus Christ and His amazing work of grace in our lives.

> *If then you have been raised with Christ, seek the things that are above, where Christ is, seated at the right hand of God. Set your minds on things that are above, not on things that are on earth. For you have died, and your life is hidden with Christ in God. When Christ who is your life appears, then you also will appear with him in glory. (Colossians 3:1–4)*

Paul begins with the basic presupposition for the believer: you have been raised with Christ. Fundamental to our faith is the resurrection of Jesus Christ. Because of His resurrection, the reality of the believer's resurrection is made certain. But note, resurrection only happens after death. The believer dies to sin, and is able to die to sin because of the death of Christ, because of the atoning work of Christ on the cross, because of the efficacy of the shed blood which fully cleanses the believer of all sin. Being cleansed, the believer is made new, he is changed, he is given a new name and the promise of a new inheritance. Life on this earth is known to be temporary, and we wait entrance into the promised land of our full citizenship.

Therefore, knowing our position in Christ, we are exhorted to seek the things that are above, where Christ is, seated at the right hand of God. This seeking is central to our embracing the person and work of Jesus Christ. The believer's desires, motivations, and life are focused on our Savior. This is a response of love. Knowing we are loved by the Gracious Redeemer, by the Almighty Father, we respond in love, desiring to be all encompassed by Him.

When our seeking is focused right, then our minds will follow. Paul says to set our minds on things that are above, not on things that are on the earth. All too often believers embrace the things of the world, thinking it is harmless to enjoy momentary sin. This could be no further from the truth. Sin is never optional; sin is never excusable; sin is never permissible! Sin is nothing less than disgusting filth in the eyes of the all holy God. Our minds are to focus on what has eternal value, on what has eternal purpose, on what has eternal hope. This is not to say we must live in some sort of irrevocable isolation in a godless world. Rather, it is to say that our heart's desire is to focus on His righteousness, on the things of the eternal kingdom, and that of the eternal King.

Faithfulness in praise

> *Rejoice in the Lord always; again I will say, rejoice. (Philippians 4:4)*

WHEN GOD'S WILL AND MY WILL DISCONNECT

Having called the church to rejoice in the Lord, to recognize the grace, mercy, and love demonstrated by God through Jesus Christ, and to see the fulfillment of His sovereign plan working in the believer, Paul said it well to the church at Philippi:

> *Let your reasonableness be known to everyone. The Lord is near. (Philippians 4:5)*

Your manner of life should be consistent with who Christ has made you to be. If you are rejoicing, then rejoice. Don't allow your rejoicing to be contingent upon your circumstances.

> *Do not be anxious about anything, but in everything, by prayer and supplication with thanksgiving let your requests be made known to God. (Philippians 4:6)*

Anxiousness results in the absence of confidence. Confidence in the Lord, in His truth and character, in His design and promise will result in amazing peace.

> *And the peace of God, which surpasses all understanding, will guard your hearts and your minds in Christ Jesus. (Philippians 4:7)*

Knowing the faithfulness of God, the redemptive work of Jesus Christ, the enabling work of the Spirit of God, and the peace of God given to each child of God, and then having absolute confidence in the Lord and His sovereign design, the believer can and should unequivocally rejoice.

In order to remain focused and to have a right perspective on the life Christ intends, Paul reminds believers that their thoughts should be on truth; anything less will lead one down the path of inconsistency instead of faithfulness.

DECISION THREE

> *Finally, brothers, whatever is true, whatever is honorable, whatever is just, whatever is pure, whatever is lovely, whatever is commendable, if there is any excellence , if there is anything worthy of praise, think about these things. What you have learned and received and heard and seen in me—practice these things, and the God of peace will be with you. (Philippians 4:8-9)*

Our thoughts can seem like friends and like enemies; they can bring joy and encouragement, and they can haunt and seem to destroy; at times we seem to have them under control, and at other times they seem to be totally out of control. Paul reminds us of the importance of bringing our thoughts under the control of the Spirit. It takes work; it won't just happen; we must be most diligent to keep them in the right direction. Think about these things... This means that anything contrary or opposing these things must be eradicated; we must refuse to dwell on them; we must reject them. We are exhorted to focus on what will draw us closer to Christ and remove whatever will be a deterrent in our relationship with Christ. Right thinking can be work, and it is worth the work to think like Jesus Christ.

As we consider the things Paul exhorts us to think about, we recognize that all of these—whatever is true, honorable, just, pure, lovely, commendable, of excellence, worthy of praise—are all about Christ. These are Christ characteristics, and our thoughts should be continually about Him. We can also consider other things, people, events that fit into these categories and are in harmony with the Word of God—these should have the focus of our thoughts.[14]

---

14 I have found it helpful to often give the homework of Philippians 4.8-9 to individuals struggling with having right thoughts. After having listed these words used by Paul, I then encourage them to write out those things which fit into each of the categories. They are to answer two questions. First, "What do I know about Christ to be true..." Secondly, "What do I know that is true... which

When our thinking is right, there will be faithful living no matter what the circumstance. Faithfulness is not dependent on our sinful desires being met or on any form of momentary happiness. Rather, faithfulness is rooted in the holiness of God, the character of God, the authority of God, the faithfulness of God. Faithfulness in the life of the believer is demonstrated in response to the perfect faithfulness of the One and Only, the true and complete God.

Choices

Choosing to live faithfully, we should then make these choices:

I will choose to not wallow in unpleasantness.

I will choose to not murmur or complain—about my circumstances or about others.

I will choose to not allow my grief to hinder moving forward.

I will choose to not give up when repeated circumstances are against me.

I will, when all that is familiar is gone, choose to learn my new surroundings and live in them well.

I will choose to place my heart and mind before the Savior that He might renew them in His truth.

I will choose to think on these things… (Philippians 4.8)

I will choose to live faithfully before my faithful Lord and before others, regardless of circumstances.

---

is good for me to think about?" Thinking about our thinking can be most helpful in transforming our minds and thoughts to be pleasing to the Lord. Intentionality in the transformation of our thoughts is critical for change.

DECISION THREE

Consider:

1. Is my faithfulness to God dependent on circumstances pleasing me?
2. Am I confident I have been justified? On what do I base my justification?
3. Have I ever had a "circumstance of horror?"
4. If yes, how did I respond? If I didn't respond rightly, what would have been a better response?
5. Have I been encouraged through the faithful actions of another? How?
6. Can I identify a specific time when the Lord "showed me kindness?"
7. In Colossians 3 Paul commends believers to set their hearts and minds "on things above." What are some practical ways I can do this?
8. What sin do I need to confess; what thinking needs to be transformed; what practice needs to change?

DECISION FOUR

I Choose Purity

As a teenager, Bob (not his real name) was introduced to pornography. His dad had it in the home. His mom expected he would look at it. Pornography was never discouraged. Throughout the teen years, the desire for pornography only increased. The absurd was normal; the perverted was expected. From pornography Bob went into sexual fantasizing. No one knew the depth of his private lust and entrapment. Knowing what he was doing was contrary to God's Word and design of holiness, his guilt was suppressed and sin justified. He delighted in sin, repeatedly giving way to temptation. During college and graduate school, he lived a double life; what people thought of him and what he actually was were diametrically opposed. Even after marriage, Bob was a master at hiding truth from his wife. Life was masterfully hypocritical. Not until numerous years into their marriage was the truth of Bob's activities discovered. This wasn't because of his desire for freedom from bondage, but rather because he was "caught."

DECISION FOUR

His wife providentially learned of his secret life. In the following months Bob began to understand the magnitude of his deception and bondage, confessed and repented of his sin. Life began to change.

Bob was vulnerable and continued to place himself in situations where he knew he would surrender to temptation. There was no joy. There was no victory. There was no hope. His life was characterized by sin, defeat, and deceit. To others in church he was a model Christian. No one knew his secret side as he continued losing battles with temptation and made choices to fall into sin.

Life didn't have to be this way. Though many excuses can be made for Bob's behavior – his father's addiction, his mother's acceptance, and his own vulnerability – there is no clear excuse for choosing sin. Bob could easily excuse his behavior and cast blame on others, but all to no avail. Others can feel badly for Bob, saying it was inevitable he followed a sinful course in his life. However, he chose sin, and he chose to habitually give way to temptation. No one chose this for him; no one else was responsible for his decisions. Knowing right and wrong, knowing the truth of Scripture, Bob continually chose to follow the lust of his sinful nature.

Bob could have lost all he had: his wife, children, job, home, relationships, and future plans. In choosing to give way to temptation he was risking all he had been given. In the moment of temptation, he had repeatedly chosen weakness and lust, justifying his behavior, blinded from truth. The consequences of his choices could have been more devastating than they were. Thankfully, Bob's wife chose to forgive him and work through the agony of his deceptive lifestyle.

Decision Four: I choose purity over temptation, recognizing the cost of consequences is of no benefit.

In considering Joseph, many could have excused him for making sinful choices. After all, he was in a foreign and pagan country, away from family and friends, lonely, under stress in his new surroundings, and unmarried. Additionally, he wasn't the instigator in sinful activity. Another, more powerful and influential than he was the encourager to sin. He lived in a culture that was known for sexual promiscuity; this was an accepted lifestyle, especially among the elite. There was seemingly every reason to choose a sinful path and submit to sexual enticement.

However, Joseph chose a different path. He was willing to stand above the norm and be different, regardless of the cost.

First, I must choose to say "no" to temptation

> *And after a time his master's wife cast her eyes on Joseph and said, "Lie with me." But he refused and said to his master's wife, "Behold, because of me my master has no concern about anything in the house, and he has put everything that he has in my charge. He is not greater in this house than I am, nor has he kept back anything from me except you, because you are his wife. How then can I do this great wickedness and sin against God?" (Genesis 39:7–9)*

Joseph was in a prime position for self-satisfaction. Potiphar's wife came to him; she was a woman of influence; he was expected to satisfy her desires in the house. Would it not have made sense to also satisfy her sexual desires? Could he not have justified in his mind that refusing her, he was in fact refusing his master? There are times in the midst of temptation we can make wrong look right; we can take what is clearly unacceptable before God and determine it is the right thing to do. This was the dilemma facing Joseph.

However, Joseph said no. He made no excuse. He remembered who he was before the eyes of God. He honored God; he honored his master. Having been entrusted with great responsibility, Joseph refused to falter in satisfying another's lusts. It is possible that Joseph was also faced with extreme temptation to lust. Pharaoh's wife may have been very attractive in his eyes. He may well have recognized the temptation facing him, and knew if he even gave thought to it he would be in a very vulnerable position. Regardless of what another desired, regardless of how good the temptation looked, he refused.

Having gained victory over this temptation, life didn't get any easier. Sometimes we wrongly conclude that having resisted temptation once, we will be free of it, and can move forward. The enemy doesn't consider this to be the case; he sees one refusal and is only challenged to continue deceptively confronting us until we break.

Second, I choose to say "no" to repeated temptation

> *And as she spoke to Joseph day after day, he would not listen to her, to lie beside her or to be with her. (Genesis 39:10)*

So Joseph was put to the more difficult test. Having made the right decision once, what would he do when it was repeatedly thrust in front of him? Would he quickly wear down? There comes a time when many will say, "I can't endure it any longer," and presume submission is acceptable. A perverted reconstruction of God's will is manipulated in the mind, and one concludes that the temptation to sin is in actuality God's permission for fulfillment.

This is the design of interrogators with prisoners of war. They do not quit when the prisoner once says "no," and refuses to give any information that may be helpful to his enemy. They continue to press him again, and again, and again. The interrogation can become more brutal; the questioning can become more intense. There is one objective: to see the prisoner crumble before their eyes and speak what he had determined not to speak, to have him divulge the information he had committed to silence.

The enemy knows the tremendous desire of the flesh to submit to sensual temptation, to compromise purity for a moment of intense pleasure. He is also well aware of the deep offense in relationships when one chooses to neglect what he knows to be right to satisfy selfish desires. Paul recognized this unrelenting lure on the Ephesian believers.

> *Now this I say and testify in the Lord, that you must no longer walk as the Gentiles do, in the futility of their minds. They are darkened in their understanding, alienated from the life of God because of the ignorance that is in them, due to their hardness of heart. They have become callous and have given themselves up to sensuality, greedy to practice every kind of impurity. (Ephesians 4:17–19)*

There must be definite and determined change in the believer to be pure. Purity doesn't "just happen" because one has a desire for purity, or because of the embarrassment of impurity. It only comes through a heart-rooted commitment to honor God with our entire life, with our whole body. Paul then exhorts the believers at Ephesus and challenges the church not to give into any form of godless temptation. Knowing the holiness of God and the command for the believer to be holy, there is no room for failure in sensual sin. The cost is too great;

the consequences are too broad; the resulting pain is too deep.

> *But sexual immorality and all impurity or covetousness must not even be named among you, as is proper among saints. (Ephesians 5:3)*

In the face of repeated temptation, sin remains sin. There is no excuse. There is no justification. There is no rationale for choosing to do the wrong thing. Joseph made the right decision. His faith in God and understanding of the holiness of God kept him from falling and enabled him to refuse, regardless of the outcomes. The consequences of making the righteous decision are always superior to the results of choosing evil.

Third, I choose to say "no" when temptation appears to overpower me.

At times there seems no way out – giving into temptation appears to be the only option. The temptation feels so strong and we can feel so weak. However, believing entrapment is disbelieving God's Word.

> *No temptation has overtaken you that is not common to man. God is faithful, and he will not let you be tempted beyond your ability, but with the temptation he will also provide the way of escape, that you may be able to endure it. (1 Corinthians 10:13)*

No matter the power or expectation of the temptation, it is never more powerful than God's ability to give freedom. Even when the temptation appears to have seized the believer, the battle is not over. One must remember the truth: God is faithful. His faithfulness does not falter; it does not change; it does not weaken. He will always provide the ability to resist, to escape, and to run to victory. Temptation never has to overpower the believer; the believer never has to succumb to temptation.

Joseph, when confronted with the inescapable, escaped.

> *But one day, when he went into the house to do his work and none of the men of the house was there in the house, she caught him by his garment, saying, "Lie with me." But he left his garment in her hand and fled and got out of the house. And as soon as she saw that he had left his garment in her hand and had fled out of the house, she called to the men of her household and said to them, "See, he has brought among us a Hebrew to laugh at us. He came in to me to lie with me, and I cried out with a loud voice. And as soon as he heard that I lifted up my voice and cried out, he left his garment beside me and fled and got out of the house." (Genesis 39:11–15)*

Joseph did not stand with his cloak in her hands and try to negotiate with her; he did not look around to see if there was anyone watching as the scenario unfolded; he did not ask her if it was safe and if Potiphar approved; he did not stop and consider the pros and cons of staying and leaving. He ran! There was no option. Joseph knew the weight of the consequence of staying and he chose to run. Had he given any thought to the consequences of running and what Potiphar's wife might do if he didn't please her, it didn't stop him. There was only one right decision. Flee!

Flee from sexual immorality… (1 Corinthians 6.18)

So flee youthful passions and pursue righteousness, faith, love, and peace, along with those who call on the Lord from a pure heart. (2 Timothy 2:22)

It is critical for the believer to determine before ever being tempted how he will respond. If there is a clear heart-commitment of obedience to the Lord, the decision will be clear when confronted with the choice of sin. Problems happen when we begin considering the possibility of choosing sin, of considering the possibility of sin being good, which then opens the door for Satan to masterfully perform his deceptive schemes.

Purity of the heart goes beyond those temptations which may be sensually based.[15] Falling into temptation to sin is to go against the design of God. We can be in a situation that is not as we would have planned and are faced with choices; we may have the best of intentions. But, if those intentions are not based on the truth of God's Word, they will lead to sin; if they are not rooted in a deep love for God, they will mean nothing; if they are not sealed by a firm commitment to righteousness, one will not resist sin. We may seek advice of others and listen to the counsel of those we trust. But if it is unbiblical, our vulnerability to sin only increases.

Giving into temptation may give us momentary pleasure, we may feel good about it, and may even be able to justify it before others. But, the results are the same. We have allowed ourselves to fall, to yield to weakness, and ignore the sovereign design of God to work and bless us.

---

15 The lure of sexual temptation is great; sensual temptations abound throughout societies all around the globe. Men especially are continually being caught in the trap of pornography, and often through the ease of the internet. Through the misuse of technology, sexual sins have become prevalent through the use of the cell phone (texting and sexting), internet chat rooms, and graphic pictures and videos. Men will have internet affairs with numerous women simultaneously; others will have physical affairs with prostitutes, women they don't know, or women they see on a daily basis at work. Sadly, sexual sins have become the norm among many men and women, and acceptable in many circles. Joseph sets a powerful example for all men to flee when faced with sexual temptation. It must be remembered, sexual temptation will happen; sexual temptation is strongly influential; sexual temptation is a part of living in our society; the lure to choose sin will not vanish. However, it must also be remembered that there is no need to fall to sexual temptation; it is never so great that it cannot be defeated. The commitment must be made to the greater loyalty, to the greater love. (Matthew 22:37; 1 John 4:19; 1 Corinthians 10:12-13)

WHEN GOD'S WILL AND MY WILL DISCONNECT

The following principles from Scripture are effective in determining right choices in the face of temptation.

Principle One: All sin is against God

All sin is against God. Sin does not happen in a vacuum; sin is not in isolation of others; sin is never hidden from God. The rebellious teen who disobeys his parents is not just disregarding his parent's authority, he is sinning against God. The young wife who has an affair is not just violating the marriage covenant with her husband, she is sinning against God. The businessman who holds back information in order to look good is not only compromising his integrity, but is sinning against God. The student who cheats on an exam is not just compromising the school standards in order to get a grade, but he is sinning against God. The athlete who ignores team or conference policy in order to be more competitive is not just deceiving the fans, be he is sinning against God. The boy who lies about eating the cookie is not just lying to his mother, but he is sinning against God.

Joseph, enticed by Potiphar's wife, realized that giving in to her advances would be sin. But this would not be just sin against her; it would not be just sin against Potiphar; it would be sin against God.

> *How then could I do this great wickedness and sin against God?" (Genesis 39.9)*

All sin is against God. Following his sinful actions with Bathsheba, David prayed:

> *For I know my transgressions, and my sin is ever before me. Against you, you only, have I sinned and done what is evil in your sigh… (Psalm 51:3-4)*

We must put it in perspective and keep it in perspective. God is holy. All sin is against God. God takes sin seriously. Discipline is serious. Judgment is serious. Consequences are serious. Sin is serious. All sin is against God.

Principle Two: Vulnerability is a reality

> *Therefore let anyone who thinks that he stands take heed lest he fall. (1 Corinthians 10:12)*

As long as we have the breath of life, we are vulnerable to temptation. It is true, that in having repeated victory over a particular area of sin we may have learned how to deal with it successfully so that it is no longer an issue in our everyday Christian living. However, our vulnerability never ceases. If we think we are no longer vulnerable to one specific sin we are faced with in temptation, there will be another. There never will come a time in this life when we will have the ability to declare total victory over all sin. We must expect battles; we must remember victory is always possible.

The battles do not just go away. We do not get old enough to be past them; we do not reach a level of spiritual maturity where we have overcome them; we do not get beyond them at any point in our lives. Paul said it this way:

> *For I do not understand my own actions. For I do not do what I want, but I do the very thing I hate. Now if I do what I do not want, I agree with the law, that it is good. So now it is no longer I who do it, but sin that dwells within me. For I know that nothing good dwells in me, that is, in my flesh. For I have the desire to do what is right, but not the ability to carry it out. For I do not do the good I want, but the evil I do not want is what I keep on doing. Now if*

> *I do what I do not want, it is no longer I who do it, but sin that dwells within me. So I find it to be a law that when I want to do right, evil lies close at hand. For I delight in the law of God, in my inner being, but I see in my members another law waging war against the law of my mind and making me captive to the law of sin that dwells in my members. Wretched man that I am! Who will deliver me from this body of death? (Romans 7:15-24)*

At times it can seem hopeless. We can fight temptation, we can fight sin, we can determine to do differently, and we can even have momentary victory. But, often the next day the temptation stares us in the face and we don't understand it. We may desperately want to be done with that area of sin, but the battle rages. We get tired and worn; we feel like giving up; we think, "What's the use" of struggling.

Thankfully, Paul didn't stop at verse 24. He answered his question and provided the hope that comes through the person of Jesus Christ. Victory can be ours! God is faithful!

> *Thanks be to God through Jesus Christ our Lord! So then, I myself serve the law of God with my mind, but with my flesh I serve the law of sin. (Romans 7:25)*

> *…In all these things we are more than conquerors through Him who loved us. (Romans 8.37)*

Although we may struggle, we are not doomed to failure and defeat. Victory is promised; victory can be realized. We must believe there is hope for victory, and this will only come through a commitment to and belief in the Word of God.

Principle Three: The Armor of God is effective protection

DECISION FOUR

There is no possible way for us to consistently have victory over sin apart from the grace of God and through the work of His Holy Spirit. As Paul stated above, we are vulnerable and weak. In knowing this, God gives His armor to protect us, enabling us to walk into battle unscathed, and come through it victoriously.

Throughout Scripture the Lord reminds us of spiritual warfare and provides us with the ability to succeed, His way. We must not be lackadaisical about warfare; we must not avoid its reality; we must not pretend easy victory.[16] Paul exhorted the believers at Ephesus:[17]

> *Finally, be strong in the Lord and in the strength of his might. Put on the whole armor of God, that you may be able to stand against the schemes of the devil. For we do not wrestle against flesh and blood, but against the rulers, against the authorities, against the cosmic powers over this present darkness, against the spiritual forces of evil in the heavenly places. Therefore take up the whole armor of God, that you may be able to withstand in the evil day, and having done all, to stand firm. (Ephesians 6:10-13)*

The spiritual forces of evil are determined to ruin the believer and make him ineffective in doing the will of God. The enemy is not weak, nor is he easily defeated. We are incapable of gaining victory in our own power and the mere determination of our will. Victory over the enemy only comes through prayerful submission in the holy Throne

---

16 At times, in the light of prevalent conversation about "spiritual warfare," some believers tend to shy away from thinking of its reality. There must be great caution in the danger of overreaction to those who wrongly emphasize activity in the world of evil spirits. We must not neglect the power of the enemy, the reality of spiritual warfare, and the tremendous need to stand firm on the truth of God's Word. In this we must be careful in exposition of the Word of God, to always conclude what Scripture says, and not presuppose what Scripture does not say; it is not about what we "think," but about what God has said.

17 For a powerful and complete exposition of this passage, refer to *The Christian in Complete Armor* by William Gurnall.

Room of God and anticipation of His powerful working within us.

The specific components of the armor are given, each with explicit intention and purpose.

> *Stand therefore, having fastened on the belt of truth, and having put on the breastplate of righteousness, and, as shoes for your feet, having put on the readiness given by the gospel of peace. In all circumstances take up the shield of faith, with which you can extinguish all the flaming darts of the evil one; and take the helmet of salvation, and the sword of the Spirit, which is the word of God, praying at all times in the Spirit, with all prayer and supplication. To that end keep alert with all perseverance, making supplication for all the saints, (Ephesians 6:14–18)*

In choosing purity, each aspect of the armor is most readily required.

First, the belt of truth must be tightly worn. We cannot, we must not, relinquish truth and replace it with any of the worthless lies of the enemy. Joseph knew truth. He knew submitting to the request of Potiphar's wife was sin; he knew God totally disapproved of adultery. This was not optional.

The enemy will twist and contort the Word of God; he will use the tools of trickery and deception. This has been his scheme since the beginning which is seen in his diabolical plot in the Garden. He has not given up and he will not quit. The truth of God's Word must be known and understood; it must be held as our final authority; it must never be relegated to the bottom "dusty shelf of neglect," but must always have the highest position of prominence in our lives.

> *And you will know the truth, and the truth will set you free. (John 8:32)*

DECISION FOUR

So if the Son sets you free, you will be free indeed. (John 8:36)

Truth frees, sin and the lies of the enemy enslave; truth enables, lies debilitate; truth encourages, lies deflate; truth motivates, lies stagnate. In knowing truth, we can move forward in full and complete victory. Apart from truth, the best we can hope for is momentary relief from guilt and pain as we seek change through fleshly wisdom.

Second, the breastplate of righteousness is said to be in place. Having repented of sin, cleansed of all sin by the blood of Jesus Christ, and adopted into the family of God, the believer has the righteousness of Christ imputed to him. Christ's righteousness has taken the place of his unrighteousness; in seeing the believer, the Father sees the perfect righteousness of Christ. Recognizing this, the believer wears the breastplate of Christ's righteousness. Therefore, his every action should harmonize with the righteous actions of Christ; his every thought should be ruled by the righteous thoughts of Christ. If we have been covered by the righteousness of Christ, there is no room for sinful choices.

Third, the feet are to be prepared. Joseph ran. He had no intention of staying to see the next step that Potiphar's wife would take, or to further consider what he should do. They are having put on the readiness given by the gospel of peace; they are ever prepared because of the transforming work of the Gospel in one's life. The Gospel transforms, the Gospel gives hope, the Gospel leads in truth; the Gospel is the herald of peace. When faced with temptation the believer must be ready to respond, knowing that peace with God is priority and nothing should be done that would bring shame on the Gospel; to respond knowing he is at peace with God, and God will do all necessary to give him victory.

Fourth, the believer is to take up the shield of faith with which he is able to extinguish all the flaming darts of the evil one. When faced with temptation, the question is simple: do I believe God and His Word or do I not believe God and His Word. If the shield is not correctly handled, the enemy's flaming arrows can easily circumvent the protection and pierce the believer's side. Doubt begins to grow and the false justification for yielding to temptation begins to make sense. Joseph fundamentally believed God, believed he should do what God says, and believed God would bless obedience. Submitting to sin was not optional. Even before being faced with the lure of Potiphar's wife, Joseph was committed to a life of faith, of believing God's Word, of trusting God when consequences seemed derogatory.

The shield of faith must be held tightly and held circumspectly. It must move to extinguish the enemy's attempts to harm, recognizing the direction and speed of the flying enticements. The shield of faith must be held with the expectation that it will, beyond any fear, be able to successfully thwart the enemy's attacks. How does this work; how does this shield become so powerful? This is possible only through the Truth of God's Word. The believer must be willing to believe God at His Word, fully and completely, and not just when it makes sense to him. In order to have faith in what God will do, the believer must know the command and promises of God. The enabling work of God through His Spirit must be recognized in order to have an enduring hope. This does not happen through osmosis, but rather the careful study and learning of God's Word. Knowing His Truth, before temptation strikes, gives a confident foundation for faith, which is able to rise above any ugly challenge of the enemy.

Fifth, the believer is to wear well the helmet of salvation. This helmet is given him by God and worn to protect the head, the mind, the believer's thinking. One must never forget that he has been redeemed by the blood of the Lord Jesus Christ, cleansed of all sin, justified before the Father, and saved from eternal damnation; freed from the bondage, guilt, and all power of all sin. We must think clearly as we intentionally protect our thinking from ever swaying from the truth of God's Word. When faced with temptation, the helmet protects the mind from ever concluding that sin is good, that evil is right, and right is evil.

Roman helmets were also unit and rank identifiers. For Joseph, he wanted to do nothing that would dishonor the name of the Lord; his commitment to the Lord would be unquestionable. Similarly, for the believer, the helmet of salvation must also be seen as an identifier, by which he is ever declaring his allegiance to the Savior. There should never be doubt as to whom the believer belongs, and he should never forget that he will be fully protected by the King of kings and Lord of lords.

Sixth, the believer is given the privilege of handling the sword of the Spirit, which is the Word of God. Different from the shield which protects and is used defensively, the sword combats and is used offensively. Not only do we know what God has promised and provided, but with the sword of the Spirit we are able to counterattack the enemy with truth. When the enemy says, God has not surely said we are able to clearly state what God has surely said. When the temptation comes to unrighteous living, we can use the sword to declare the righteousness of Christ, the hope of the Cross, the truth of His Word, and His expectations of us as His children.

The sword is not a dormant weapon, kept in its sheath or only drawn for demonstration purposes. It is the powerful Word of God, the eternal Word of God, the absolute true Word of God—the inerrant Word of God. By His Word we know the place, the doom, the ability, the inability, and the schemes of Satan. The Word of God is powerful to stop the enemy from hindering the effectiveness of the Truth of God in our lives.

> *For the weapons of our warfare are not of the flesh but have divine power to destroy strongholds. We destroy arguments and every lofty opinion raised against the knowledge of God, and take every thought captive to obey Christ, (2 Corinthians 10:4–5)*

The Word of God is able to penetrate into the very depths of man and his heart. Through the work of God's Spirit it convicts of sin, demonstrates true life, and reveals the heart condition. It is able to take the hardest and meanest heart and soften it to the Gospel. Through God's Word the unknown can become known, and those in bondage can be set free.

> *For the word of God is living and active, sharper than any two-edged sword, piercing to the division of soul and of spirit, of joints and of marrow, and discerning the thoughts and intentions of the heart. (Hebrews 4:12)*

It is in the Word of God one learns of sin and salvation, knows the horror of being lost and the delight of being found, and knows the depression of enslavement and the joy of freedom. Through God's Word is the pathway for growth and the understanding of God's design.

> *And how from childhood you have been acquainted with*

> *the sacred writings, which are able to make you wise for salvation through faith in Christ Jesus. All Scripture is breathed out by God and profitable for teaching, for reproof, for correction, and for training in righteousness, that the man of God may be complete, equipped for every good work. (2 Timothy 3:15-17)*

Being clothed, the believer is to wear the armor under the canopy of prayer.

> *Praying at all times in the Spirit, with all prayer and supplication. To that end keep alert with all perseverance, making supplication for all the saints, (Ephesians 6:18)*

He comes before the Lord with the desire to be in full submission to Him, enabled by Him, and longing to live in complete harmony with Him. Prayer is not a simple conversation with a good friend in the time of our need, or a routine religious practice to engage in as a receipt of grace. Rather, prayer is communing with the Holy God, in harmony with His Holy Word, concerning a holy subject, and deepening a holy relationship, for a holy purpose. Through prayer one understands the need for full dependence on the Almighty God and he is able to know the perfect enablement for wearing the armor victoriously.[18]

---

18 Prayer too quickly becomes a casual moment in the life of the believer, a quick interruption to a daily life filled with plans and expectations. God calls His people to pray, to enter the Throne Room with delight, with anticipation, with a holy regard for the privilege of communing with the Eternal and Holy God. Prayer is not a two or ten minute exercise – but rather involvement in a relationship with the Almighty God. It brings us to a place of humility before His incomparable Throne, and delights us in the fullness of the relationship between a child and his perfect Father. All too often believers have a coffee house conversation or drive through expectation when coming to prayer. Rather, God's expectation is that it will be one of quietness, one of time, one of commitment; that the believer will come unhurriedly with a prepared heart to the "closet" where he enters into the Throne Room of the Sovereign God.

In private prayer, I have found great help in using the prayer our Lord taught His disciples in Matthew 6.9-13 as a template for praying and to guide my heart and thoughts during the quiet

Principle Four: The consequences of sin are of no benefit to the believer

What do I gain in sin? Momentary pleasure; short lived recognition; fleeting power? What is the long-term benefit? None! The only result is one of disgrace which is brought to Christ, the church of Jesus Christ, the Gospel, and the child of God. Before falling into the pit of temptation, one needs to think: "When is doing the wrong thing ever better than doing what is right?" Never!

A young man wrote the following while battling with sensual sin, after repeatedly realizing there is no lasting satisfaction in doing the wrong thing, in choosing selfishness over righteousness:

> God helps me to push through this hurdle like a train. A failure does not have to mean giving up. His mercies are new every day, so my hope is as well.
>
> *For the weapons of our warfare are not of the flesh but have divine power to destroy strongholds. We destroy arguments and every lofty opinion raised against the knowledge of God, and take every thought captive to obey Christ, (2 Corinthians 10:4–5)*
>
> Don't believe the lie. Demolish it. Smash its face into the ground so it suffocates, never to rise again. Its reign must end

---

"closet" time with the Father.

A. W. Tozer stated: May not the inadequacy of much of our spiritual experience be traced back to our habit of skipping through the corridors of the Kingdom like children in the market place, chattering about everything, but pausing to learn the true value of nothing? (*Intimacy With the Almighty,* Charles Swindoll)

Regarding prayer, Martyn Lloyd-Jones wrote: It is the highest activity of the human soul, and therefore it is at the same time the ultimate test of a man's true spiritual condition. There is nothing that tells the truth about us as Christian people so much as our prayer life. . . . Ultimately, therefore, a man discovers the real condition of his spiritual life when he examines himself in private, when he is alone with God. (*Studies in the Sermon on the Mount*) today. The lie is weak against Truth. It crumbles with every word of it.

So what do I learn? What do I learn that I haven't learned before? The things I've learned from this have been reinforced a hundred times, yet they are still so easily forgotten, so easily thrown away as small rules which only sometimes apply, but not now. It seems my hope is thrown away along with the rules, and it takes so long to get that hope back, so my hope begins to come from my victories. But that's not right. That is what gets me in trouble.

Isaiah 2:22: Stop regarding man in whose nostrils is breath, for of what account is he?

Sometimes I wish I could kill my sense of pride. It doesn't matter if others are proud of me. I don't do anything right without God. I just feel I'm wasting my time when I do things my own way and look back. When trusting in God alone I feel I'm doing what I'm supposed to do. I hope I find these past years were worth the trouble. Worth the time. Jesus never wasted time. What would become of me if I never wasted my time? I see I've learned something.[19]

Many have thought that wrong would be right, that they wouldn't be found out, that their sin would be unnoticed. In speaking to the two and one-half tribes which settled on the east side of the Jordan River, Moses warned them of their loyalty and obligation to the remaining tribes. They were not to forget who they were, where they had come from, or what they were to do in keeping allegiance with the Israelites on the west side of the Jordan. Failure to meet their responsibilities would not go unnoticed.

---

19 Used by permission.

WHEN GOD'S WILL AND MY WILL DISCONNECT

But if you will not do so, behold, you have sinned against the Lord, and be sure your sin will find you out. (Numbers 32:23)

Though it may appear to be hidden for a time, sin never goes unnoticed. Jacob's sons thought their sin would not be noticed, that it would be kept secret. They concluded that once rid of their favored brother, they would be free of the constant reminder of their father's favor toward him. The perfect solution: sell him to the Ishmaelite slave traders. Wrong! They were not free. They lived many years in the guilt of their sin and in the grief of their father. (Genesis 37:17-36)

Following is just a sampling from Scripture of the multiple incidences where the hoped consequences of sin would be kept secret are definitively obvious:

Cain, upset that his offering was not acceptable to the Lord and angered at his brother, chose to follow his emotions and kill his brother thinking none would ever know. Wrong! He was cursed by God and removed from favor. (Genesis 4:1-14)

Hophni and Phineas, sons of Eli, thought they could live above the law and chose to live immorally, thinking that their sensual pleasures would far outweigh any discipline their father might impose. Wrong! They were struck down in battle, never to realize blessings which could have been theirs. (1 Samuel 4:12-22)

Jonah thought that fleeing righteousness and running to self-centeredness would result in peace. Wrong! His response brought the sailors into great danger, which led them to follow what was seen to be their only option – throwing Jonah overboard, expecting his demise as he was swallowed by the great fish. (Jonah 1:1-17)

Achan thought taking a few items of plunder wouldn't hurt anything or anyone. Wrong! People died in battle, and then he and his family were swallowed by the earth. (Joshua 7:1-26)

David thought a moment of sexual promiscuity and satisfaction would go unknown. Wrong! People died, Bathsheba's husband died, his own illegitimate child died, and his escapades were written in the pages of God's eternal Word (2 Samuel 11:1-27).

Ananias and Sapphira thought they could lie regarding their commitment and keep some financial return for their own gain. Wrong! They were struck dead. (Acts 5:1-11)

Judas thought he could gain financially and in notoriety by serving as the Savior's traitor. Wrong! Overcome with guilt and shame, he hung himself. (Matthew 27:1-10)

We must never believe the enemy's lies. Sin always brings consequences; sin's consequences are never good.

Principle Five: *The characteristic behaviors of the unregenerate nature can be eradicated.*

There is no room for sin in the believer's life. In choosing purity, we are choosing to not sin; we are choosing to get rid of all known sin, resulting in freedom from its awful bondage.

> *Put to death therefore what is earthly in you: sexual immorality, impurity, passion, evil desire, and covetousness, which is idolatry. On account of these the wrath of God is coming. In these you too once walked, when you were living in them. But now you must put them all away: anger, wrath, malice, slander, and obscene talk from your mouth. (Colossians 3:5–8)*

> *But sexual immorality and all impurity or covetousness must not even be named among you, as is proper among saints. Let there be no filthiness nor foolish talk nor crude joking, which are out of place, but instead let there be*

thanksgiving. (Ephesians 5:3-4)

At times one will declare that sin is too big to ever know freedom; that the bondage has been too long and is too strong to be released. There is no excuse. We can state again and again our inability, but in doing so we are only affirming our lack of faith and our distrust in the power of God. He who made all creation with the words of His mouth and brought Jesus Christ out of the tomb, is certainly able by the same power to enable us to live above sin.

Believers will not continue in known sin. Though there may be temporary struggles, the pattern of sin will not exist. Knowing the power of salvation, the cost of salvation, the hope of salvation, and the author of salvation, the believer will be compelled to be free of all sin; he will be compelled to live in righteousness.

> *See what kind of love the Father has given to us, that we should be called children of God; and so we are. The reason why the world does not know us is that it did not know him. Beloved, we are God's children now, and what we will be has not yet appeared; but we know that when he appears we shall be like him, because we shall see him as he is. And everyone who thus hopes in him purifies himself as he is pure... No one who abides in him keeps on sinning; no one who keeps on sinning has either seen him or known him. (1 John 3:1-6)*

In making the following six declarations, the believer is able to choose freedom and live in purity.

One, I declare the holiness of God and His abhorrence of all sin.

Two, I declare the desire of God for me to live in complete harmony with Himself.

Three, I declare the power of God, through the Spirit and the resurrection, to free me of all sin.

Four, I declare my own sin, confess and repent all known sin, and determine to live pleasing to God.

Five, I declare the forgiveness of God, accepting the fullness of His mercy and grace.

Six, I declare the joy of God, filling me and allowing me to move forward, free from sin.

In God's redemptive design, I do not have to fall in temptation, but am able to choose purity; I am able to live pleasing to God, being useful to Him for His glory.

> *Therefore be imitators of God, as beloved children. And walk in love, as Christ loved us and gave himself up for us, a fragrant offering and sacrifice to God. (Ephesians 5:1–2)*

Consider:
1. Is there a particular area in my life where I am repeatedly struggling with temptation?
   What is it, and what do I believe is the reason for my continual struggle?
2. Have I fallen into impurity, and tried many times to be free relying on my own strength?
   What have I done?
3. Are there particular lies I am most vulnerable to believe?
   What plan can I implement to recognize the enemy's lies and emphatically deny them?
4. Have I consistently prayed to be clothed with the Armor of God, with an expectation of His victory in my life?
   Can I name the various elements of the Armor in order?

*What do I understand as my need to
be clothed with the Armor?*

5. Am I committed to praying daily, seeking consistency in the place of prayer and in the time for praying?
   *What am I doing; is there something I
   should be doing differently?*
6. Where is my greater love: for God and His righteousness or for selfish impurity?
   What pulls me to God and what pulls me to impurity?
7. What sin do I need to confess; what thinking needs to be transformed; what practice needs to change?

DECISION FIVE

I Choose to Trust God to Use Me

When it seems that my will is disconnected from God's will I can feel battered around, thinking I am on a one way road to nowhere. I don't feel usable, I don't think I am usable, and I am not even certain I want to be usable to God. There are times I just want to be left alone. I don't want to be involved in anyone's life; I don't want to think about anyone else. The situations which have happened in my life are not what they were supposed to be, and I am ready to just quit.

Having completed seminary and anticipating pastoral church ministry, our lives took an unexpected turn. It began with an inquiry into the U. S. Army Chaplaincy, and before long we were heading down a new and adventuresome path. Wearing the uniform, understanding the ways of the Army, and learning military tactics was all completely new to me.

Early in my career, while stationed at Fort Hood, Texas, I was involved in a field training exercise. Feeling somewhat at risk because of my limited knowledge, I sought to do the best I could to fit into the unit, not cause problems, and still minister to soldiers. Early one morning the siren sounded, indicating we had a chemical/biological attack. Still in my sleeping bag and in the dark of night, I did my best to put on my boots, don my gas mask and try to find out what was happening. Being legally blind without my glasses, I had a further hindrance at this point as my glass inserts for my mask had not yet arrived. Therefore, I couldn't see anything. Standing in the middle of a clearing, not knowing where anybody was, feeling vulnerable, and then looking down and realizing I had hastily put my boots on the wrong feet I asked the question, "God, I went through those years of college and seminary education for this? Is this really where you want to use me?" I felt totally out of place and unusable.

This was all part of my training. Looking back on a full career, it is obvious to me this early morning was part of God's design, as are all my days. Though I did not feel usable at that moment in time, I could still trust God to work in me and through me, to use me for His glory. I had to wait, to keep learning, being open and anticipating His working.

Mary (not her real name) had led a difficult life, filled with many wrong choices and unhappiness. Early in life she had great expectations of what might happen. Having attended a Christian college, married a Christian man, and given birth to a son, there was the anticipation of God's working in and through her life and the enjoyment of His blessings. However, this is not what happened. Her marriage was filled with difficulty, with many battles over finances and priorities, and she felt as if her family never fully accepted her. Mary struggled with hopelessness and feelings of uselessness. After growing elderly and widowed, she fought feelings of bitterness, uselessness, and regret. Realizing she had not many years left, she feared having lost the privilege of being usable to God.

Then Mary began to understand the significance of making right choices for God to use her, and not live in the past. Nothing could be changed of the years already spent. However, she could begin to make a difference as she moved forward in the remaining years of her life. Through an understanding of God's grace in forgiveness and His design in giving her life, she began to have a changed attitude. Her desire began to be characterized by what she could do and how she could be used by God; she began to appreciate God's gifting her with purpose; she began to grasp hold of her true identity in Christ as being of far greater worth than what others may have thought of her. In the days Mary has yet to live, she is determined to be the person God has intended, not someone else, and to do what He has designed her to do.

We can feel we missed our opportunity for service; we may think that any moment of usefulness is lost; we can feel weary and tired, old and worn out, past our prime and out of touch; we can feel God is not going to use us, or would not even want to use us at this point in our lives. Perhaps past sins have been so corrupted that the thought of being usable by God is only a vague imagination. We limit what God would want to do, can do, and plans to do. We fail to recognize that though there has been significant change, how God is going to be working in and through our lives could also be changing.

We don't have to understand how God might use us; that's not our responsibility. However, He does call us to be ready to be used, to be faithful, and to be willing to be used for His glory.

WHEN GOD'S WILL AND MY WILL DISCONNECT

Decision Five: I choose to trust God to use me, even though I do not understand how.

Life had not gone as Joseph had hoped. Having been rejected and sold into Egyptian slavery, he sought to do the best he could. However, the unexpected happened, and instead of being rewarded for good work and faithful decisions, he was unjustly committed to prison. How was God going to use him in this environment? We don't know of Joseph's initial attitude, or his struggle with thoughts and actions. We do know he didn't quit. No matter how difficult the days became, how hard the work, how unappreciated he may have been at times, he remained faithful to God.

Regardless of our circumstances, we must accept the truth that God desires to use us. We are His instruments, His ambassadors, His clay pots, and part of the body of Christ. Having made the first choice, "God is in control," we can then move forward in confident trust that our usability to God will not be hindered by our circumstance – it just may not be the way we would like or the way we had thought.

In trusting God to use us, four specific decisions must be made.

First, I choose to be ready for God to use me

Joseph was thrown into prison for a crime he had not committed. He could have become bitter and formed an independent pity party. Rather, it appears he remained consistent, in harmony with his character: walking faithfully before God and doing what was expected of him. I can see his attitude being, "Since I'm here, there is no need to complain as this must be where God wants me. Therefore, I will be ready for whatever He places in front of me."

Being "ready" to be used means I will anticipate God working. Joseph's faithfulness to the Lord demonstrates that he likely anticipated God's working through him in the various situations of his life. In the beginning of his Egyptian journey he obviously did not have a clue as to how God was going to use him, but he remained in an attitude to be used.

Anticipation has the idea of an eager expectation that something is going to happen. As a young man, I anticipated getting married – I looked forward to the day my bride, Barbara, would walk down the church aisle so that we would then walk out of church as husband and wife. Two years later as an expectant father, I anticipated the birth of our first child – anxiously awaiting his arrival and marveling at the incredible working of God. As an U. S. Army Chaplain serving in Turkey unaccompanied for one year, I anticipated coming home; returning to my family whom I loved and hopefully expected once again enjoying life together. These were three different events in my life that I eagerly waited for and looked forward to becoming a reality. I was filled with anticipation.

However, when we think about God working in our lives, do we actually anticipate anything happening? Or, do we simply go through the motions expecting life to continue on a mundane course? I need to remember that God is not in the business of "mundane." Rather, He is in the business of the unusual, of the unexpected, of the phenomenal. Amazing!

Consider Joshua. When God commissioned him to cross the Jordan River and enter the Promised Land, did he actually anticipate God would do anything? Did he go to the water's edge and wonder what he was going to do? Did he begin making plans to build rafts to carry people and supplies across the river? Did he begin sending scouts up and down the river to find a place that would be most accessible?

Did he go back and reconsider if he had heard God correctly? Did he begin a renegotiation with God as to the reality of His plan? Of course not! The reason? He knew God would work. Joshua had absolute confidence in the ability of God to do all He said, and he anticipated God working and accomplishing His purposes.

God does not speak to us audibly as He did to Joshua; I don't hear His voice with my ear. I wonder, even if this were the case, if we would have any stronger anticipation of God's working in our lives. However, He does speak clearly to us in His Word. It is here we must spend time to listen so that we can have honest, realistic, and eager expectations of what our Lord will do.

> *Long ago, at many times and in many ways, God spoke to our fathers by the prophets, but in these last days he has spoken to us by his Son, whom he appointed the heir of all things, through whom also he created the world. (Hebrews 1:1–2)*

We can have absolute confidence that our Lord has provided everything we need in His Word to accomplish His will; everything we need to understand His direction in our lives; everything we need to develop necessary tools to serve Him; everything we need to be successful as His children.[20]

Being "ready" to be used means I will accept my position before God.

---

20 Some speak of the insufficiency of God's Word; how it only is valid for certain areas of life and practice. Some consider His Word to have limitations because it was written by men thousands of years prior to today. Others will seek to prove that God's Word is no longer relevant for the matters and problems in today's world, a world which is far more complex than in the first century. However, God's Word does not change; it is applicable for all of life and practice; and God will accomplish His purpose through His Word (Isaiah 55.11). The authenticity and authority of God's Word is not dependent on man's concurrence; the application of truth is not dependent on man's acceptance of the results. God's Word has, does, and will stand strong; it will not fail; it will not change.

DECISION FIVE

Joseph did not struggle with his identity: he was a child of Jacob, Isaac, and Abraham; His God was the same God as his fathers.[21] Regardless of circumstances, who he was did not change. Even though he had become a slave in the house of Potiphar and then unjustly had become a prisoner, he was still a child of Jacob and a child of God.

Too often individuals in deep difficulties forget who they are in the eyes of God. Because circumstances have changed, they think they have lost their true identity. I understand this. After having served in the military chaplaincy for a career and then pastoring a local church for ten years, I took some time off for refreshment and preparation for the next step in life. However, who was I? Yes, I knew the right Biblical answers, but they were difficult to grasp. My identity was in part tied to what I did, to a position, to a ministry, to relationships with others. Some aspects of my identity did not change: I was still a husband, father, and son; I was still a child of God designed with purpose. But, in my confused thinking, I wanted something more. I was tempted with a lie that my identity was diminished because of what I did, or was not doing.

During this time I came to grips once again that my true identity is in the Lord and this is of the greatest importance; this identity does not change with circumstances. This must be accepted. I cannot anticipate God using me if I do not believe I am usable, if I do not recognize I am a viable part of His divine design. But, I must remember that my usability is not based on who I am and what I can do; rather it is based

---

21 There is a proliferation of materials today regarding the need for individuals to increase their "self-esteem." There is nothing Biblical about this; nowhere in Scripture does it speak of our having to feel good about ourselves, having to "shore up" our identity, having to grow in confidence of our abilities in order to reach our full potential. Rather, the Lord speaks about us having confidence in Him, in His working, in His transforming grace evident in our lives. Our confidence should never be in who we are, but rather in who He is, in who He has made us to be, and in His power to enable us to accomplish His good purpose and will.

solely on who God is and what He is doing in and through me.

In times of difficulty as well as in times of blessing the person we are in Christ does not change. Following are some key words recognizing our identity and God's working. These are listed to generate additional thoughts and realizations of who we are in Christ and how He desires to use us in His ministry. As we think of this, the result should be that of thankfulness and praise for His great work in our lives; there should also be conviction and challenge that we live up to who we are. All of these words identify every believer in Jesus Christ, without exception. This is who we are; this is who He has made us to be.[22]

His child
Redeemed
Justified
Sanctified
Crucified
Risen
Righteous
Brother of Christ
His Ambassador
His clay pot
His instrument
His vessel
Member of His family
Member of His church
Part of His building

---

22 This list is not intended to be exhaustive. It is not placed in a specific order. Some characteristics mentioned are those by which we have been identified in Christ; others are characteristic of what He has called us to do; some encompass both. The intention of this list is to remind us of our tremendous identity in Christ, one which we should never minimize in an obsession of what we can or cannot do; how others evaluate us or seek to have us feel. We must hold on to truth. We have great value, not in ourselves, but in the eyes of the Lord. He providentially saved us, made us, and equipped us with purpose. This usurps all the vain pursuits of the self-esteem crusade which attempts to take us from a negative image to a positive. In Christ, the negative is erased, and we can hold on to what He has positively done in us for His glory.

DECISION FIVE

Co-worker
Branch
Follower
Disciple
Christian
Light of the Gospel
Presenter
Peacemaker
An heir
Minister
Soldier
Warrior
Stranger
Pilgrim
Vulnerable
Dependent
Tempted
Salt
Servant
Slave
Creation of God
New creation
Human
Specifically designed
Forgiven
A forgiver
Sent
Messenger
An epistle
Gifted
A worshipper
One who prays
Loved

WHEN GOD'S WILL AND MY WILL DISCONNECT

Lover
Made new
Anticipator
One who waits
Hopeful
Receiver
Born again
Saved
Alive
Filled
Indwelt by the Holy Spirit
Seeker
Made righteous
Made holy
A treasured possession
A partaker in the divine nature
A recipient of absolute promises
Prisoner
Free
One who sees
A sheep
A celebrator
A praiser
An encourager
A glorifier
A witness
A boaster
A loser
A gainer
A Living sacrifice
A Martyr
A believer
Spiritual

DECISION FIVE

Called
Chosen
Elected
Predestined
Adopted
Accepted
Clothed
Temporary
Eternal
A priest
A walker
A runner
Rich
A sower
A reaper
Recipient of God's grace
Thankful!

The Lord has given believers an incredible identity in Christ. This will never change because of our circumstances. Therefore, we can expect Him to work through us as He has made us, and for His glory.

Second, I choose to do nothing that will detract from my being used by God

Joseph chose to flee sin; he chose to not be compromised in his beliefs. Had he decided differently, his usefulness to God and by God could have been permanently changed. He chose not to be marked by an attitude of complaints and hostility; he chose not to be enticed to fall into sin; he chose not to submit to conceit in his endeavors.

Sin is non-reversible. Many times I have heard someone say, "If only I could turn the hands of time backward and make a different choice." Not possible. In a moment of thoughtless decision, at a time of emotional weakness, by taking a turn and walking down a wicked path, one's life is irreversibly altered. This is not saying God is unable to take our mistakes and still use us. There are many examples of this happening. However, what could be is suddenly erased because of decisions made.

Consider Achan. He did not think anyone would know that he took just a few things from Jericho. Knowing God had said differently, his justifying mind saw the abundance of plunder and determined he could have a little for his own coffers. After all, he had risked his life in participating in Jericho's downfall, and he could use a little extra. However, he clearly disregarded the command of God, placing his desires above those of God.

> *But the people of Israel broke faith in regard to the devoted things, for Achan the son of Carmi, son of Zabdi, son of Zerah, of the tribe of Judah, took some of the devoted things. And the anger of the Lord burned against the people of Israel. Joshua sent men from Jericho to Ai, which is near Beth-aven, east of Bethel, and said to them, "Go up and spy out the land." And the men went up and spied out Ai. And they returned to Joshua and said to him, "Do not have all the people go up, but let about two or three thousand men go up and attack Ai. Do not make the whole people toil up there, for they are few." So about three thousand men went up there from the people. And they fled before the men of Ai, and the men of Ai killed about thirty-six of their men and chased them before the gate as far as Shebarim and struck them at the descent...* (Joshua 7:1–5)

And God judged Achan.

> *And Joshua and all Israel with him took Achan the son of Zerah, and the silver and the cloak and the bar of gold,*

> *and his sons and daughters and his oxen and donkeys and sheep and his tent and all that he had. And they brought them up to the Valley of Achor. And Joshua said, "Why did you bring trouble on us? The Lord brings trouble on you today." And all Israel stoned him with stones. They burned them with fire and stoned them with stones. And they raised over him a great heap of stones that remains to this day. Then the Lord turned from his burning anger. Therefore, to this day the name of that place is called the Valley of Achor. (Joshua 7:24–26)*

His decision to sin cost him his life, the life of his family, and the lives of 36 other men, which in turn affected their families and others. Sin is never in isolation. No matter what we may think, sin will always affect others, and hinder us from fulfilling God's design in our lives.

I remember a pastor saying he made it a practice to tell the young men of the church he served to "never do anything that would disqualify you for serving God in His ministry." Good advice. All too often our decisions made in the passion of a moment will have lifelong consequences, changing the course of our future. What could have been will never be. Our responsibility: always be on guard, always be willing to say no to temptation, always be determined to live so as to not detract from God or His glory.

Third, I choose to have an attitude that is usable and not detrimental to God's purpose

Joseph chose humble submission, accepting his circumstances while moving forward. If given the choice, he would likely have changed his course of events. However, he did not rebel and grumble, he did not fight and seek to justify himself. Nor do we see Joseph choosing an arrogant confidence at any point in his life. We never hear of him saying, "look what I have accomplished;" he did not boast about being favored by his dad, of being a great slave, of having increased responsibilities, of being able to interpret dreams, or of being placed in positions of prominence and power. Rather, we see Joseph being in humble submission to God's design, having an attitude that is compliant to the will of God.

Sometimes our attitudes can become more like Jonah's. His concluding complaint could be summarized as saying, "OK, I'll do it, but I don't like the idea and I don't want to!" Even after having been thrown into the sea and having endured the great fish experience, his attitude was still filled with complaint. His desire was far from pleasing God and quickly reverted to the selfish fulfillment of his own desires. He wanted things to happen his way; he wanted to be in charge. His negative attitude was obvious.

God's desire is for us to have a mind of acceptance.

> *Have this mind among yourselves, which is yours in Christ Jesus, (Philippians 2:5)*

This is the attitude of Christ. Acceptance to God's will, regardless of what it appears to me; a willingness to be usable in my current situation, knowing our Lord can use us and has a definitive plan to use us.

> *Do all things without grumbling or disputing, that you may be blameless and innocent, children of God without blemish in the midst of a crooked and twisted generation, among whom you shine as lights in the world, holding fast to the word of life, so that in the day of Christ I may be proud that I did not run in vain or labor in vain. (Philippians 2:14–16)*

We should choose to have an attitude that will honor the Lord, not be detrimental to His design; one which will reflect His grace and goodness, and not reflect our own self-interested displeasure. If we are to hold fast to the word of life, then we must demonstrate our agreement to the full Word of God, not just our acceptance of that which appears to be for our good. Our attitudes should validate our delight in the full Word of God and the full working of God, as we believe all is happening according to His perfect design.

> *I therefore, a prisoner for the Lord, urge you to walk in a manner worthy of the calling to which you have been called, with all humility and gentleness, with patience, bearing with one another in love, (Ephesians 4:1-2)*

Fourth, I choose to be willing to be used by God

Being ready is being prepared for the day and anticipating God will use me. It is waiting on the porch, fully clothed with all the tools I need, looking for Him to call my name to follow. Not doing anything to hinder my following is choosing to wait, and not walking ahead to the right or to the left in my own judgment. Being willing is following, is seeing every situation as an opportunity for God to work. If I do not follow, I am not willing. Being ready is knowing that whether we are in sleep clothes and the phone rings or whether we are fully prepared, every opportunity has the potential of God using us for His glory.

Joseph was in prison; he was fulfilling his responsibilities; he was making right choices and waiting for the next step in his life. Not knowing where that path would lead, he waited with anticipation and willingness to be used by God. He continued doing what was right. Perhaps we would say he was following the principle of Micah 6.8, years before Micah prophesied.

> *He has told you, O man, what is good; and what does the Lord require of you but to do justice, and to love kindness, and to walk humbly with your God? (Micah 6:8)*

Placed in prison with Joseph were two men of Pharaoh's household: the cupbearer and the baker. The Scriptures don't tell us of their crimes, except that they had offended their master. Obviously it is insignificant for us and we don't need to construe a scenario. Interestingly, by God's sovereign design they were placed in the same area as Joseph. God was at work. How long they were together or what their relationship looked like prior to the eventful occasion is also unknown. Through what may have appeared to be a less than favorable situation for all three of these men, God was about to show His desire and demonstrate His ability. Joseph was ready and willing.

> *They said to him, "We have had dreams, and there is no one to interpret them." And Joseph said to them, "Do not interpretations belong to God? Please tell them to me." (Genesis 40:8)*

Joseph didn't listen to these two men and just shake his head without further considering the possibility. Immediately testifying to the wisdom of God, he demonstrated his willingness to be used by God to convey truth. He chose to accept responsibility as God's instrument, knowing God was able to interpret dreams and that he was in the place ordained by God. Many would have stepped back and said, "I'm not getting involved. Go figure it out on your own." Not Joseph. He was willing to get up and follow the Lord, recognizing he was in a place to be used by God.

We should see our life situations as divine appointments, established by God for a purpose. These appointments are not a meaningless busyness, a standing in line to wait for something insignificant, or an exercise in misery. Rather, they are an opportunity to be used by God in fulfilling His design, knowing He has included me.

God revealed the dream's interpretations to Joseph, and fulfilled His word three days later on Pharaoh's birthday. Disappointment likely soon followed for Joseph, for he had asked to be remembered by the cupbearer when he was restored to Pharaoh's court. This was supposed to be Joseph's ticket out of prison and into a place of more agreeable service. But, he was forgotten.

After two years, Pharaoh had a dream. None of Egypt's wise men could interpret the dream, which caused Pharaoh inner turmoil, grief, and anger. He thought that with the power he wielded in his kingdom, there should have been someone who could perform such a task. Now, in God's sovereign design, the cupbearer suddenly remembered his prior forgetfulness and told Pharaoh what had happened two years earlier. Joseph was still ready and willing to be used. He didn't allow the passing of time to deter his faith and faithfulness; he didn't doubt that God would be still at work; he didn't quit. He desired to be an instrument in God's hands, giving glory to Hm.

> *Then Pharaoh sent and called Joseph, and they quickly brought him out of the pit. And when he had shaved himself and changed his clothes, he came in before Pharaoh. And Pharaoh said to Joseph, "I have had a dream, and there is no one who can interpret it. I have heard it said of you that when you hear a dream you can interpret it." Joseph answered Pharaoh, "It is not in me; God will give Pharaoh a favorable answer."*
>
> *Then Joseph said to Pharaoh, "The dreams of Pharaoh are*

one; God has revealed to Pharaoh what he is about to do. (Genesis 41:14-16, 25)

God used Joseph, and through him blessed the people of Egypt and those in other parts of the world. God also blessed Joseph in taking him from being a prisoner in confinement to being a respected leader, second to none under Pharaoh. After two years Josephs' response was still the same: God is in control; God is able; I will trust God to do what God alone is capable of doing.

God never calls us to understand the fullness of His design for our lives; He never tells us we are to understand all He is doing and will do. What God does do is call us to be faithful. The circumstances of our lives do not have to be perfectly fitting our expectations for us to be used by God; they do not have to be set in an arena that we have deemed appropriate. They will just be. And we are to be faithful: ready, waiting, pure, and willing.

Paul called on the believers in Rome to present themselves before God as a sacrifice. This is complete resignation to God's plan and complete surrender of ours. This is anticipating God is at work and is going to work, for His glory.

> *I appeal to you therefore, brothers, by the mercies of God, to present your bodies as a living sacrifice, holy and acceptable to God, which is your spiritual worship. Do not be conformed to this world, but be transformed by the renewal of your mind, that by testing you may discern what is the will of God, what is good and acceptable and perfect. (Romans 12:1–2)*

It can be so easy to stay in our comfort areas, to be unwilling to do what might lead us to the unknown. However, God wants us to be available to use us, and not have false limitations placed on what He can or will do. He calls us to give up the effort of selfishly holding onto our wants, to quit trying to be in charge, and to fully give ourselves to Him, with no reservations or boundaries. Sacrifice – giving what is valuable to us, what we consider to be of great worth; placing ourselves before Him, relinquishing all authority and control; trusting Him fully to do what is right and best in and through us. Through a willing heart to sacrifice, God works His transforming power in us to make us more like Christ, to use us in His perfect will. In giving ourselves, we learn, we see, we rest in Him; we submit to His control. Our sacrifice should be complete, holding nothing back, anticipating He will use us for His great glory.

When we are willing to be a sacrifice, then we are willing to be used; when we are willing for our lives to not be conformed to the pattern of our thinking, then we are able to experience the working out of God's will in our lives. Why would we not want this to happen, knowing His will is good, pleasing, and perfect? In our minds the answer is obvious. However, in working it out we have to be ready and willing to lose control, which we never actually had, and accept God's wisdom and design.

Paul then reminds us that our pride, our false perception of ourselves, gets in the way of full submission. Though we may not outwardly say it, we have often demonstrated by our actions that we are wiser and clearer in our thinking than God, or that His principles do not apply to our current situation. How wrongly we have concluded!

> *For by the grace given to me I say to everyone among you not to think of himself more highly than he ought to think, but to think with sober judgment, each according to the measure of faith that God has assigned. (Romans 12:3)*

Rather than being caught up with ourselves, the Lord wants us to keep our identity in perspective and His intentional plan in our lives.

For as in one body we have many members, and the members do not all have the same function, so we, though many, are one body in Christ, and individually members one of another. (Romans 12:4–5)

As a member of the body of Christ, He has made us usable; He has made us an integral member that has value in His ministry and service. Our value is not dependent on circumstances, but rather on the grace of God and His working in and through our lives.

During the times of trial, spiritual battles can rage within us. The enemy wants to destroy us, rendering us ineffective as servants of the Most High God. He will do all possible to bring about doubt and discouragement, seeking to convince us of our lack of worth as a believer and inability to be used by God for anything; he will attack us, wanting us to retreat from faith. Therefore, it is critically important to be clothed with the Armor of God (Ephesians 6:10-20). As we raise the shield of faith and tightly hold it in front of us, we will be able to extinguish all the flaming darts of the evil one. (Ephesians 6:16).

We make a choice based on truth, trusting God to use us, even when we don't understand how or think it possible. May we wake each day with the expectation of knowing and seeing God's working in and through our lives for His glory.

Consider:
1. Has there been a circumstance or circumstances in my life that I believe has rendered me unusable to God? What happened?

2. Am I willing and desiring to be in submission for God to use me, even though it might be very different from what I had imagined?
   How do I demonstrate this?
3. How have I seen God using me in past situations?
4. What difference does my understanding of my identity in Christ, as compared to the world's view, make in my life?
5. What are the major distractors in my life hindering me from being used by God?
   What will I do about removing those hindrances?
6. What is my attitude in serving: is it one of humble submission, arrogant confidence, complaining compliance, or something else?
7. What sin do I need to confess; what thinking needs to be transformed; what practice needs to change?

DECISION SIX

I Choose to Accept God's Timeframe

In some situations our response is "please wait, life is going too fast, I just need some time to slow down." And, at other times we plead, "Hurry up, how come I have to wait so long, it seems like these things take forever, I just want to get going." Speed up, slow down; slow down, speed up. At times we never seem to be fully content with the ways things are happening; we want it to happen differently, in our timeframe.

Many times during my military days did the "timeframe" seem to be out of whack. I could be busily involved in a project, meeting what I thought to be a deadline, when suddenly the deadline became now. How come? Someone, on a different level of authority than me, made the decision. For some unknown reason the requirement was suddenly urgent. Or, there was the opposite: the command to hurry up and get somewhere, only to wait. How come? I could have used my time more productively had I continued doing what I was doing.

DECISION SIX

Just waiting can seem so meaningless. Yet, from another's perspective (yes, one of greater authority than mine) there was a reason. My responsibility wasn't to understand; rather, I was simply to obey.

Our interrupted timeframes can include every day experiences such as waiting in a line at the store when the customer ahead of us seems to question the price on an item; it can be the proverbial red light when we are in a hurry to meet an appointment, or the train that just decides to stop in front of us when we are the next in line to cross the tracks. There is the hospital "emergency room," where our emergency is not seen as an emergency at all; triage has deemed others needs or crises to be more serious than ours, yet from our perspective we should be the next to see the doctor. Then there is the long awaited vacation to someplace warm during the midst of a cold northern winter, only to arrive and find they are experiencing record breaking cold temperatures. Times of waiting can be tests as we look forward to the promotion, the raise, the new home, the new car, the finalization of an adoption, school grades, graduation, the birth of a child, special events – the list can be significantly long. Our timeframe design isn't happening; reality doesn't ask for our input.

Disappointments can abound! How do we respond? Frustration? Anger? Despair? Depression? Anxiety? We can move forward with many varied emotions and reactions. At these times we need to step back to consider the bigger picture of our lives, and ask the question, "What is God doing?"

Decision Six: *I choose to accept God's timeframe, knowing His timing is always perfect*

Joseph likely thought he knew what was about to happen. Having rightly interpreted the dreams of both the cupbearer and baker, he couldn't imagine not being remembered. He was on his way out of prison. "Where was he to go;" and, "what would be his next position?" These were the unknowns. But, he knew he would be getting out. After all, the cupbearer was in a place of influence; he had Pharaoh's ear. Then, reality hit.

> *Only remember me, when it is well with you, and please do me the kindness to mention me to Pharaoh, and so get me out of this house… Yet the chief cupbearer did not remember Joseph, but forgot him. (Genesis 40:14, 23)*

The cupbearer forgot! We think, "How could he be so thoughtless after Joseph had correctly interpreted his dream?" This wasn't supposed to happen this way; the chief cupbearer was to be Joseph's passage out of prison. Joseph may have been counting the hours, the days, which then led into weeks and months; he could have been waiting, thinking, anticipating with every footstep coming down the hall that he was about to be released. However, it did not happen. The grateful cupbearer demonstrated an ungrateful heart and forgot. He became so involved in his own work and interests, his own delight with a new found freedom, that remembering Joseph was not a priority. He was just happy to resume doing what he did, sleeping in a real bed, eating regular food, and enjoying the prestige of his position.

God was not surprised. In His design, the time wasn't right for Joseph to be out of prison. Joseph may have thought himself ready, but God said "not yet." How could this be possible? What could be the rationale for Joseph staying in prison another day? There was much more he could do in other places, he had too much talent to be in the pit of the dungeon. But, that is where he remained for two more full years (Genesis 41.1). Maybe a few weeks could be understood and accepted, or even a few months. But two years? This could well have been seen as the never ending plight for the rest of his life.

God's plan was not altered, nor did He suddenly have a lapse of memory. It is a conscious decision for us to remember that God's timeframe is perfect. Life is not all about what we can see or try to comprehend. We must not forget that if we could see the "big picture" we would not want to alter what He is doing. The key is remembering truth, knowing His perception of what is happening is far greater than ours, and that He will never make a mistake in the events of our lives.

> *For my thoughts are not your thoughts, neither are your ways my ways, declares the Lord. For as the heavens are higher than the earth, so are my ways higher than your ways and my thoughts than your thoughts. (Isaiah 55:8–9)*

God who formed all of creation, who set the stars and planets in perfect motion, and who keeps all things in perfect order at all times, thinks on a different level than we do. This tremendous truth is easy to disregard. We somehow imperfectly think that God is on a similar level to us, and that He should be consulting us regarding what happens and when things happen. Not true. His ways and His thoughts are not in the same category as ours, and when we consider the truth, it is far easier to trust Him, to believe Him, and to accept His timeframe as superior to anything we might try to invoke.

The following five reminders can help us learn and accept God's timeframe as always best.

One, I will have disappointments.

This is a given. As long as we have a timeframe in mind for things to happen, as long as we set expectations, there will be disappointments.

WHEN GOD'S WILL AND MY WILL DISCONNECT

Our timeframe is different than Gods. Sometimes they connect; often they don't.

Jacob longed to see his son Joseph. It appeared this would never happen again, as he concluded Joseph had been killed by an animal and the body never recovered. He wanted Joseph to come back with his brothers, or before them, after he had been sent out on the scouting mission. It didn't happen. Years passed before he finally was able to see Joseph face to face, and then the setting was far different than he ever could have imagined.

The unexpected timeframes are evident throughout Scripture. Abraham was disappointed when Sarah didn't have children. God had promised he would have a son, that he would become the father of a great nation. Yet, it didn't happen, and he sought to fulfill God's Word his own way. It didn't work. It wasn't time yet. Sarah did have a son; she just had to wait until she was 90 years old and Abraham was 100.

Moses thought it was time for him to rescue his people. With the knowledge and authority he possessed in Pharaoh's kingdom, he thought the Israelites would surely welcome him and recognize he was their "gift." They didn't. He was rejected and fled. God's timeframe was fulfilled forty years later when Moses led the people out of Egypt to new found freedom. However, their timeframe for entering the Promised Land didn't materialize. Instead there was forty years of wandering through the desert wilderness. Many thought they would never see the Promised Land; many didn't. Eventually, the Israelites did, but it was when God determined the time was right.

David is an example of one who was not disappointed with timeframe. He was anointed king by Samuel; he knew the authority over all Israel was soon to be his. However, he didn't covet it, he didn't rush to make it happen, he didn't devise mutiny; he didn't raise his hand against the Lord's anointed (1 Samuel 24.6). He waited. In God's timeframe he took the throne. However, there were many times David prayed, "How long, O Lord." He longed to have God do something, now. David became weary in waiting for deliverance, for relief from despair. Some days seemed so long and nights never ending. Yet, in all these things he knew and trusted God.

> *Why are you cast down, O my soul, and why are you in turmoil within me? Hope in God; for I shall again praise him, my salvation. (Psalm 42:5, 11; 43:5)*

Then we see people flocking around Jesus. He was their hope; they thought Him to be the answer to their Roman bondage. They thought He would establish His kingdom on earth and lead in a previously unknown righteousness. It didn't happen. Instead, He was sought like an animal, hunted down by authorities who wanted to see Him killed, to put an end to the disruption He was causing the established religion. He was unjustly arrested, unjustly tried, and cruelly executed on the Cross of Calvary. For the people, their timeframe came to a smashing halt. What they had expected was suddenly impossible. However, God's timeframe is different. The earthly Kingdom of Christ will come, though the time is not yet. However, His kingdom has already been established in the heavenly realms as well as in the hearts of those who believe in Him, who trust Him, who know Him as Lord and Savior, as King of kings.

Disappointments happen because our agenda isn't satisfied. The pattern is nothing new. However, when things seem to be repeatedly going contrary to what we expect, as believers we need to stop. It is time for evaluation. Are we working only on our timeframe, or are we willing to trust that God's timeframe is different from ours, and His plan may not be what we are expecting.

How do we redirect our disappointments? Consider these truths from God's Word.

Practice truth

> ...Trust in the Lord, and do good; dwell in the land and befriend faithfulness. Delight yourself in the Lord, and he will give you the desires of your heart. Commit your way to the Lord; trust in him, and he will act. He will bring forth your righteousness as the light, and your justice as the noonday. Be still before the Lord and wait patiently for him; fret not yourself over the one who prospers in his way, over the man who carries out evil devices! Refrain from anger, and forsake wrath! Fret not yourself; it tends only to evil. (Psalm 37:2-8)

We are called to do the right thing. Our delight is to be in the Lord, be fully committed to Him and His ways, trusting Him, listening to Him (through His Word), to make choices in harmony with Scripture. Trust will lead to patience as we wait for His working, knowing what He is doing is best. Trust also leads to confidence and contentment when things don't happen according our plan. Trusting our Lord, who is in control, prevents anger and frustration, resentment and bitterness, as we willingly accept we are not in control.

Practice patience

> I waited patiently for the Lord; he inclined to me and heard my cry. He drew me up from the pit of destruction, out of the miry bog, and set my feet upon a rock, making my steps secure. He put a new song in my mouth, a song of praise to our God. Many will see and fear, and put their

trust in the Lord. (Psalm 40:1–3)

In His timing, God will work; His purposes will be accomplished. The work of the Spirit of God in the believer's life will produce patience. It is part of His given fruit:

But the fruit of the Spirit is love, joy, peace, patience, kindness, goodness, faithfulness, gentleness, self-control; against such things there is no law. (Galatians 5:22–23)

If we are indwelt by the Spirit of God, and every believer is, then we should be controlled by the Spirit of God. As believers led by the Spirit, the fruit of the Spirit is the natural response in our lives.

Practice faith

Now faith is the assurance of things hoped for, the conviction of things not seen. (Hebrews 11:1)

How do we do this? Simply do it. There doesn't need to be a complex formula or a list of ways to make it happen. Believe and do. We are to trust, without having to understand; trust, without having to know; trust, without having to put all the pieces together in a nice little box. We choose to believe; we choose to be certain of what we believe; we choose to be absolutely convinced that what we believe is true.

And without faith it is impossible to please him, for whoever would draw near to God must believe that he exists and that he rewards those who seek him. (Hebrews 11:6)

If we want to please God, and every believer should, then we must practice faith; we must learn to trust our Lord even in the most difficult situations and complex experiences.

> *Looking to Jesus, the founder and perfecter of our faith, who for the joy that was set before him endured the cross, despising the shame, and is seated at the right hand of the throne of God. (Hebrews 12:2)*

We consider Jesus. He is truth and always true. He alone is able to perfect our faith, to bring it to maturity. The more we look to Jesus, the more we consider who He is and what He has said, the more we choose to believe Him, the more our faith will increase and impact the daily events of our living.

> *I have fought the good fight, I have finished the race, I have kept the faith. (2 Timothy 4:7)*

Here is the believer's desire: to keep the faith until the very end of our days. Not allowing doubt to filter in and rob us of what God desires to do; not giving way to our disappointments, because things don't go as we want. Rather, trusting our Lord in all things at all times, knowing His working in His timeframe is absolutely best.

Two, God is never surprised.

We can be readily surprised and quickly caught off guard. Not long ago I drove over the crest of a highway hill only to realize my little truck was not going to stop as quickly as the vehicle in front of me. Afterwards, I attempted to play "Monday morning quarterback" and try and figure out what actually happened. Was it a quick glance at another car or a billboard that diverted my attention for that critical moment; though not speeding, could I have been going too fast for the amount of traffic and road conditions; perhaps it was totally unavoidable. Regardless, my morning was changed and my plans had to be rearranged. After having left the scene (with ticket in hand) I was now in a different traffic pattern moving at a different time. What had happened affected my actions, reactions, and interactions. Through all of this, God wasn't surprised. He had a different timeframe for my day.

If we have honestly adhered to the first choice mentioned, "Choosing to accept that we are not in control" and accepting that "God is in control," this is easy. No, not necessarily. We are still in the flesh, and these choices all work together. If we say God is in control, then we must agree that He will not be surprised by any of the events of our lives, and when the things we expect happen or don't happen.

God was not surprised by the fall of man in the Garden of Eden. He was not surprised by the rebellion of Israel. He was not surprised by the crucifixion of His Son, the Lord Jesus. He was not surprised by His resurrection on the third day. And, He is not surprised by anything that has happened or will happen in our lives.

David wrote:

> *O Lord, you have searched me and known me! You know when I sit down and when I rise up; you discern my thoughts from afar. You search out my path and my lying down and are acquainted with all my ways. Even before a word is on my tongue, behold, O Lord, you know it altogether. You hem me in, behind and before, and lay your hand upon me. Such knowledge is too wonderful for me; it is high; I cannot attain it. Where shall I go from your Spirit? Or where shall I flee from your presence? If I ascend to heaven, you are there! If I make my bed in Sheol, you are there! If I take the wings of the morning and dwell in the uttermost parts of the sea, even there your hand shall lead me, and your right hand shall hold me. If I say,*

> *"Surely the darkness shall cover me, and the light about me be night," even the darkness is not dark to you; the night is bright as the day, for darkness is as light with you. (Psalm 139:1-12)*

Here is great encouragement. There is no place that we can go, there is nothing we can do, there is no time in our lives that the Lord is not fully aware of us. We are never out of His sight. In all things, He is never surprised. Remember: ... In your book were written every one of them, the days that were formed for me, when as yet there was none of them (Psalm 139.16). There are no surprises.

Three, I live in a perfect timeframe.

We can trust the perfection of God's timeframe to be absolutely true. And in this timeframe, He will give us everything we need – even the faith to trust Him in it.

His divine power has granted to us all things that pertain to life and godliness, through the knowledge of him who called us to his own glory and excellence. (2 Peter 1:3)

When doubting the perfection of God's timeframe, the following questions help us to relinquish doubt and life in faith.

When has God's timeframe not been perfect?

When has God failed in the past?

When has God not provided everything I have needed?[23]

---

23 We can question the provision of "all our needs." We read Paul's writing, And my God will supply every need of yours according to His riches in glory in Christ Jesus (Philippians 4:19), and wonder how it will happen. We know that Christians throughout the world suffer extreme devastations and persecutions, and it doesn't seem as if their needs are being met. However, we must carefully understand that God's perception of needs can vary dramatically from our expectation. He didn't promise us freedom from trouble, but rather said we would have trouble (John 16:33). He didn't promise us deliverance from all enemies, but He does promise full and complete salvation, and eternal deliverance. We live in a sin-sickened world, and every part of life suffers under the curse of the fall. However, our greatest need – salvation and deliverance from

When has God forgotten me?

When has God said who I am and where I am is unimportant?

When has God not been good?

The obvious answer to these questions is: Never! Therefore, whatever our circumstance, we can trust He will perfectly complete His will, and give us everything necessary to trust Him and walk with Him in doing His will.

Four, I recognize that time doesn't stop with the disruption of my timeframe.

Immobilization does not happen. When our timeframe isn't met, we must recognize that time keeps going. For Joseph, his dad and brothers still had a life. They were still involved in work, in family, in the regular activities of their every day. Potiphar and his household continued to function. Potiphar's wife was still his wife, to our knowledge, and was never discovered of her deceptive deed. The cupbearer and Pharaoh completed their daily tasks. When Joseph was freed from prison, the prison guard still had work to do.

At times, it can seem that time stops for us. A loved one suddenly dies, shattering our hopes and dreams. We fear what may happen next and don't know how to continue, or if we even want to move to the next step. Time seemingly stops. A long awaited promotion doesn't happen; conception doesn't happen; application into a college or graduate program is rejected. Time seemingly stops. In this we must remember truth. God hasn't stopped; He is still working. All we know about our gracious Lord isn't suddenly rendered false. Rather, it is our understanding of His reality that must be deepened, perhaps adjusting

---

eternal damnation and the influence of the evil one – will always be met through the riches of Jesus Christ, His amazing grace.

our own awareness of His unchanging character.

As time doesn't stop, so we must be careful to not stop and claim abandonment because we don't know what to do next, as what we had planned is not going to happen. Our responsibility is to claim and use the time we have to the best of our ability, and in a way to honor and please the Lord.

Consider Paul. Having been placed in a Roman prison, separated from those he hoped to minister to, he didn't stop. He still found ways to proclaim Christ to the prison guards. He still connected with churches, assuring them of His concern for them, teaching them how to practice truth.[24]

Five, I am to practice contentment.

Many will say they can accept that they will be disappointed when things don't happen in their timeframe, that God is never surprised by anything that does happen, and that His timing is always perfect. But, to be content in it, that's another matter. The same person will respond with, "I can accept it, but I am not content in it; I don't have to like it, and I don't want things to be the way they are."

If this is true, then we must ask the following questions:

Am I willing to go against God?

Do I realize my decision to be discontented with the way things are doubts God's design?

Do I remember that to doubt God is to sin against God?

---

[24] The "Prison Epistles" (Ephesians, Philippians, Colossians, and Philemon) are powerful letters of instruction to the churches, inspired by God. Being confined to the Roman prison and unable to visit the churches, Paul scribed, under the inspiration of the Holy Spirit, clear and specific instruction for the believer to live pleasing to God. Apart from his imprisonment we could wonder if these letters would have been written; God used our difficulties in accomplishing His perfect purpose.

Then others may ask, "Ok, I will be content with the now, but how long until I 'get my way?' When will things get better for me, and I end up with what I want? How long do I have to accept what I consider as 'less than desirable' to be the way things are?"

In these questions, there is no contentment; there is not true believing that God is doing good and right. Then, in the responses there is only a "masked contentment." It is only a presumptuous façade on a spiritual stage to fool ones' self and others. Contentment is acceptance which brings satisfaction; it brings restful peace knowing our Lord is in control and is completing His purpose.[25] True contentment accepts God's working, and His timeframe in His working.

Paul, imprisoned and facing death, related a powerful example for believers to follow.

> *Not that I am speaking of being in need, for I have learned in whatever situation I am to be content. (Philippians 4:11)*

Hoping, expecting, desiring, and even at times demanding my timeframe to be the reality must be recognized as sin and replaced. Trusting the Lord's design, knowing His timeframe is perfect, and then using the time we have to please and honor Him demonstrates true contentment; this makes all the difference in our daily living.

Consider:

1. In considering the "big" disappointments in my life, do I continue to grieve their loss?

---

25   One should also recognize there is a righteous discontentment. This is never being content in my own faith and the ongoing work of sanctification in my life. Where the "contentment" mentioned above is in relation to God and His working, I must never be resigned to a lackadaisical contentment in my growth process as a child of God. We should always be learning, seeking to grow in the grace and knowledge of our Lord and Savior Jesus Christ (2 Peter 3.18), becoming more like Him, as we are transformed by the renewal of your mind (Romans 12.2).

What do I want to have happen at this time?
2. When have people disappointed me that changed the way things happened, or didn't happen, in my life?
   What did I do?
3. Are some "truths" more difficult for me to practice than others; are some commands more difficult for me to obey than others?
   If so, what are they and what makes them difficult?
4. What can I plan to do differently to change wrong thinking or wrong behavior?
5. Do I struggle with the reality of believing God is not surprised?
   Do I question God's goodness in letting my "surprise" happen?
6. Has time ever "stopped" for me, or have I wanted it to stop?
   What did I do? What could I have done differently?
7. What sin do I need to confess; what thinking needs to be transformed; what practice needs to change?

DECISION SEVEN

I Choose God's Realities

I was a young seminary student and recently married. After celebrating our second anniversary we were expecting our first child. Since this was before the days of "routine ultrasounds" we didn't know if this child would be a boy or a girl. Having carefully selected names for both, we thought we were ready. On February 26, 1975 my wife woke in the night and informed me it was time to go to the hospital. We called the doctor, and before long we were on our way. At 7:25 in the morning our son was born. We named him Jonathan Haddon: Jonathan, meaning "gift of Jehovah" and Haddon after Charles Haddon Spurgeon, the influential English Pastor of the 1800's.

Did I have expectations of this son of ours? Absolutely! Trying not to predetermine his life vocation, I had hoped he would choose to be in vocational ministry. Since I was preparing for pastoral ministry, in my mind I determined this would also be a good direction for him, and the name "Haddon" would serve him well.

Then, reality hit. As those early years began to unfold, it became apparent that Jonathan wouldn't be used by God as I had anticipated. The Lord had a very different design for him. My dreams were not being fulfilled, and short of an unusual miracle of the Lord, they would not be. Reality hits again. Life isn't about what I dream, want, think best, or predetermine should happen. Rather, it is about being faithful to what God desires and designs, doing my part in obeying Him. In his thirty-nine years, the Lord has used Jonathan in ways we would not have determined, in our lives and the lives of countless others. This was His design, and it became my reality.

There are many situations I could innumerate in my own life which have reinforced the need to give up my dreams. Everyone has them. Sometimes they creep up on us and the dream slowly fades into oblivion, and at other times they smack us hard, like the unforeseen automobile accident leaving the car irreparably totaled. These unforeseen experiences can hurt, leaving a heart-rooted pain that is unexplainable. Life changes, and will never be reversed to what it used to be. The new path being traveled is not one that would ever have been imagined. Lives are affected and the far-reaching impact can be baffling. Pain, tears, a dreadful silence can infect our every moment. The memories of what isn't and never will be can be torturous, as we long for something different to place on the landscape of our lives.

What will we do; how will we face the unknown of our new life direction when it is different from what we wanted and dreamed?

Decision Seven: I choose to give-up my dreams and replace them with God's realities.

Joseph was known as the "dreamer," as he had shared the dreams of his brothers and parents bowing down to him, giving him homage, being under his authority. However, I doubt these are the dreams he thought would come into reality during those days of slavery and imprisonment or during the time of power and influence over Egypt. He may have remembered them, and thought they seemed like an impossibility. Only near the end of his story did the realization of God's plan and timing strike him as he saw his brothers come in search of grain.

Likely there were other dreams he didn't understand, that had similar characteristics to the disappointments we often face. Though not the dreams where God miraculously worked in delivering His message, these were likely dreams of the heart. There could have been the "dream" of growing up in Canaan and having a family. Perhaps there was the "dream" of inheritance and improved relationship with his brothers as they grew older together, and with what had been their father's flocks. Later in Egypt, he likely dreamed of being released from prison and being restored to a position of prominence, or perhaps even satisfied in a position of servitude. We do not know, but I can imagine that as a man these thoughts and dreams were on his mind at various points in his life.

If these were Joseph's unfulfilled dreams, how did he respond to them? Every indication is that he moved forward, not sulking over what was not, but rather living in what was the reality. Though it would have been easy to fall into the pitiful slump of unfounded regret, he remembered the first choice – "I am not in control, God is." When placed in perspective, had these potential dreams of his been fulfilled, the course of history would have been changed. Had he never traveled to Egypt, the Israelites likely would not have been in bondage under Pharaoh. Had he lived in serenity in Canaan, he would never have been used in the court of Pharaoh and in the salvation of his own family. In short, had his dreams been fulfilled, what we know of God's providential working in revealing His redemptive plan would never have been written. God's reality was far better than anything Joseph could possibly have thought.

There comes a time when we recognize our need to completely resign ourselves to the full design of God. In recognizing our dreams are not going to come to fruition; that which we wanted, expected, and hoped for is not going to happen, we need to readjust. We need to re-examine and evaluate the basis for our dreams and look at them through the reality of God's Word. We need to look at our situation and accept that God is on His Throne, and even when we feel like we are forgotten in the dungeon, God's realities will always prove to be best.[26]

Rather than remain in the painful hopelessness of shattered dreams, the believer should choose to anticipate the joy of God's realities. These six areas of examination will help us make good future choices in determining the next step, the acceptance of a new and unplanned, to us, direction designed by God.

I need to reassess God's call.

I had planned for pastoral ministry. In preparing to leave seminary, my name was submitted to a number of churches, but nothing developed; the connection didn't happen between this young aspiring pastor and a local church. Then I was introduced to the possibility of

---

26 I am not suggesting God speaks to His people today through the means of "dreams." Scripture clearly states this is not God's way of communicating with people (Hebrews 1:1-2; 2 Timothy 3:16-17). Unless specifically referring to Joseph's dreams which were ordained by God with the purpose of showing and affirming His sovereign design, I am referring to "dreams" as our own plans, desires, and goals; those ambitions we have and long to see come to fruition.

the Army Chaplaincy. I had not thought about this; I had no military background; I knew no one in my family that had ever served in the military. This was a totally foreign arena to me. I had not spent a lot of time in "outdoor activities." I did not hunt, fish, backpack, or go camping. These were not a part of my background, and they were not part of my present.

What was the full extent of what I knew about military structure, ranking, promotions, positions, missions? Almost nothing. But the possibility came and we reassessed God's call. Could this be an area of ministry He would have us enter; is this where we were to serve? We asked questions, we talked to people who understood the military, we inquired about the possibility of our being accepted. A year and a half later I was wearing a uniform. This was not what we had imagined, and it certainly was not what my wife had thought when she agreed to marry this young seminary student. But, God had a plan, and He was redirecting our steps.

On the road to Egypt or the path to prison, Joseph needed to reconsider God's call; he needed to rethink what God was going to be doing in his life. The future was not going to be what he had anticipated. Rather than focus on what was not going to be, he chose to look ahead to what was the reality God had intended for his life.

Later in Israel's history, Moses also had to reassess God's call. He thought he would be the one to help the Israelites out of bondage and to a better way of life. That did not happen. Instead, he ended up in Midian and became comfortable in his new surroundings. He married, had a family, and was stable in his position. There was no need for him to do anything different.

Then, in the most unusual setting, God spoke to him from an

unconsumed burning bush. He revealed Himself to Moses, got his attention, and conveyed the mission he was to fulfill.

> *And the angel of the Lord appeared to him in a flame of fire out of the midst of a bush... God called to him out of the bush, "Moses, Moses!" And he said, "Here I am."... Then the Lord said, "I have surely seen the affliction of my people who are in Egypt and have heard their cry because of their taskmasters. I know their sufferings, and I have come down to deliver them out of the hand of the Egyptians and to bring them up out of that land to a good and broad land, a land flowing with milk and honey, to the place of the Canaanites, the Hittites, the Amorites, the Perizzites, the Hivites, and the Jebusites. And now, behold, the cry of the people of Israel has come to me, and I have also seen the oppression with which the Egyptians oppress them. Come, I will send you to Pharaoh that you may bring my people, the children of Israel, out of Egypt."... (Exodus 3:2-11)*

Moses' response? Not me! Even in knowing God was audibly speaking with him, and in seeing the miraculous burning bush, Moses still sought to reject God's call. This was not what Moses had planned. He began a series of arguments with God, giving varied excuses as to the reasons God had made a mistake in calling him (Exodus 3.11-4.17). He did not want to accept the fact that God had other plans for him. Though his current dreams were being fulfilled and he was just fine with the way things were, God had other plans.

When our dreams seem to have faded away, or are quickly shattered with the unthinkable, it is important to reassess what we thought God was doing and to accept what God is doing. We must be careful not to reject God's call, but rather to accept His design as perfect.

DECISION SEVEN

I need to review my actions.

Perhaps on the caravan to Egypt, Joseph reviewed his previous actions and interactions with his brothers. There was time to think, to rehearse multiple times what had taken place, the reasons he was so desperately hated, the root of his being rejected by those older than him, by those who would normally be protective of a younger sibling. If he had done some things wrong, now was the time to reconsider and determine to live differently in the days ahead with whatever was in store for him.

Joshua is another example. He had been given the reigns of leadership to lead the people across the Jordan River and into the Promised Land. God assured him of his provision and protection, of His enabling him to be victorious.

> *Be strong and courageous, for you shall cause this people to inherit the land that I swore to their fathers to give them. Only be strong and very courageous, being careful to do according to all the law that Moses my servant commanded you. Do not turn from it to the right hand or to the left, that you may have good success wherever you go. This Book of the Law shall not depart from your mouth, but you shall meditate on it day and night, so that you may be careful to do according to all that is written in it. For then you will make your way prosperous, and then you will have good success. Have I not commanded you? Be strong and courageous. Do not be frightened, and do not be dismayed, for the Lord your God is with you wherever you go." (Joshua 1:6-9)*

There was hope. The dream and realization of finally arriving "home" was within reach. The promise of victory was clear. God's presence with them through every movement was assured. They were ready to move forward, in confidence and courage, having the full hope of success. They knew the Word of the Lord, and as both leader and people they made a commitment to follow Him completely.

The river crossing was successful. Conquering Jericho was unusual and complete. But then, they were defeated at Ai. Suddenly the dreams of continued victory and success were shattered. What happened? Had God failed them? Did they miss His instructions in some way? The reality – they had failed.

It was time to review their actions. Achan sinned and failed to obey the Lord. He plundered Jericho in defiance of God's Word. His sin had sweeping effects over the entire people. Instead of victory, there was stunning defeat (Joshua 7:3-5). God rebuked Joshua and the people.[27] In time, Achan confessed his sin; judgment was final (Joshua 7:24-26), and the people were regrouped to once again face Ai. This time there was victory (Joshua 8:1-29).

When dreams are broken, we need to review our lives. Is there sin? Have we ignored or avoided God's Word and chosen disobedience, believing the lie that it won't make any difference. At times, our dreams are good, and in complete harmony with God's design, but our own sin becomes a hindrance. Only in confession and repentance of sin can the believer anticipate moving forward in God's blessing.

> *If we confess our sins, he is faithful and just to forgive us our sins and to cleanse us from all unrighteousness. (1 John 1:9)*

I need to rejoice in God's mercy.

Do we rejoice when God is merciful? I am not talking about when

---

27 Sin is never isolated. Though we may think it is done in seclusion, it will have an effect on countless others. Its impact may come in small ripples over time, or it may be like a sweeping tsunami, causing unforeseen devastation.

He is merciful to those we like, but when He is merciful to those we do not like. Is God's mercy for others part of our heart's desire, or do our dreams hold only consternation and the hope of judgment? Are there times when our dreams include the infliction of misery on someone else? Have we taken the role of judge and determined there is only one course of action in regards to another?

> *Beloved, never avenge yourselves, but leave it to the wrath of God, for it is written, "Vengeance is mine, I will repay, says the Lord." (Romans 12:19)*

We must carefully recognize that our responsibility is not to "get even" or to delight in evil coming upon another person. Rather, our Lord gives us a new paradigm to follow, a different course of action to demonstrate to others the mercy of God that we enjoy as believers.

> *To the contrary, "if your enemy is hungry, feed him; if he is thirsty, give him something to drink; for by so doing you will heap burning coals on his head." Do not be overcome by evil, but overcome evil with good. (Romans 12:20-21)*

There is no indication Joseph held bitterness towards Potiphar's wife, and once out of prison and in a place of prominence that he desired to "make her pay" for his jail time. We do not read that Joseph ever sought retaliation with Pharaoh's cupbearer. Even though his forgetfulness brought two more years of imprisonment, Joseph accepted his reality. When seeing his brothers, years after being sold into slavery, he didn't look at them grudgingly. Though their words of hatred toward him likely rang loudly in his ears from the time they threw him into the cistern and then sold him to the Ishmaelite slave traders, he did not retaliate. He accepted God was sovereignly at work and his reality was part of God's eternal plan.

Again, Jonah serves as a good illustration in the neglect of reality. In his thinking, there was only one reasonable outcome for the city of Nineveh. Judgment! They were a pagan, wicked, Godless, miserable, people with no redeeming value. His dream was to see their demise.

When God called, he fleetingly resisted. He ran the opposite direction, went to the port city of Joppa, and quickly boarded a ship headed to Tarshish. Determined to be "out of sight and out of mind" he went to the lower deck and fell asleep, no doubt weary from his quick and guilty escape. God didn't let him rest. The entire scenario was horrific: the entire ship endured a terrible storm, Jonah was thrown overboard to save the sailors, and he lived in the great fish's belly for three days, and ended his excursion by being vomited onto the shore. When Jonah woke up – God had captured his attention. It was time to quit resisting God's mercy. Jonah went to Nineveh, and the city became the scene of a unique revival.

Have our broken dreams been wrong dreams, seeking judgment for another hoping for their pain, wanting them to suffer? Rather than resisting God's mercy, may our dreams be redirected to rejoice in God's mercy, as we pray to be clear proclaimers and obedient servants of God's mercy.

I need to reformat my future.

When my dreams involve my vocation and those dreams dissolve, how do I determine the next step? What takes the place of what I thought, of what I anticipated doing? Individuals can feel they have no identity, no training for anything else, and no heart for another work or ministry, no motivation to learn something new. Perhaps the dream quickly ends with being laid-off from work, an unexpected inability to continue doing what had been done for years, or being dismissed from a position, either with or without cause. What's next? Depression can set in and hopelessness can prevail.

On the road to Egypt in an Ishmaelite caravan, Joseph likely did some reformatting of thoughts regarding his future. He did not know what was ahead for him, but he did know life would never be the same. Rather than fight reality, he needed to accept change, knowing God was not surprised and had an unknowable, yet perfect design.

We need to stop, think, and honestly consider "what does God have for me next?" He never leaves us in a place of despair, counting us worthless to His Kingdom and ministry.

Consider Paul. He could have quit. He could have determined that he had done all he could do. Three missionary journeys later, having started or helped to start numerous churches, impacting countless lives for Christ and eternity, he could have put his imprisoned feet up and said, "I'm done."

But, he did not quit. He wrote, he encouraged, he taught, he witnessed. He was willing to relook and reformat his future. He never gave up. In writing to the Philippian believers he said:

> *Not that I have already obtained this or am already perfect, but I press on to make it my own, because Christ Jesus has made me his own. Brothers, I do not consider that I have made it my own. But one thing I do: forgetting what lies behind and straining forward to what lies ahead, I press on toward the goal for the prize of the upward call of God in Christ Jesus. (Philippians 3:12-14)*

He looked at his life, and said, "I'm not done yet. I haven't gained perfection. There is more yet to do." He chose to press on, to consider what was yet ahead and willingly do all he could for the cause of Christ. Rather than sulk in his unfortunate state, he sought to be used of God in his current circumstances.

When our dreams are gone, it is time for "new dreams;" dreams that are in harmony with the Word of God, dreams that look ahead to what God desires to do in and through us. It isn't a time to quit and resign to obscurity, but instead it is a time to reformat and push forward.

I need to readjust my attitude.

Through the entire account of Joseph's life, it appears his attitude remained consistently positive. True, we don't have the insight of all his days; there may have been the times of grumpiness, irritability, and despair. However, it appears these did not characterize his life; he was distinguished by steadfastly anticipating God's working.

Our attitude can take a nosedive when dreams dissolve. Negative responses can quickly spew out of our hearts and mouths. Paul writes that these things have no part in the believer's life:

> *Put to death therefore what is earthly in you: sexual immorality, impurity, passion, evil desire, and covetousness, which is idolatry. On account of these the wrath of God is coming. In these you too once walked, when you were living in them. But now you must put them all away: anger, wrath, malice, slander, and obscene talk from your mouth. (Colossians 3:5–8)*

When these things are given license, the downward spiral can lead to great disappointment, despair, and total frustration.

What does God call us to do? His command is simple; His command is clear.

> *Give thanks in all circumstances; for this is the will of God in Christ Jesus for you. (1 Thessalonians 5:18)*

DECISION SEVEN

Reminder: God is not surprised; His design is perfect. Regardless of our life situations, there is never an excuse to fall into sinful patterns. He always desires for us to be in complete harmony with His Word. Paul said to the believers in Ephesus:

> *I therefore, a prisoner for the Lord, urge you to walk in a manner worthy of the calling to which you have been called, (Ephesians 4:1)*

Walking worthy involves thankfulness; it is an acceptance of what is God's design, of knowing our current situation will be used by God for our good and in harmony with His purpose.

> *And we know that for those who love God all things work together for good, for those who are called according to his purpose. (Romans 8:28)*

Consider Jesus. Though His dreams were not shattered as He did exactly what He came to do, in perfect timing for a perfect purpose in harmony with the will of the Father, He maintained an attitude that did not revolve around Himself, around what would be best for Him, or what would be least painful. His attitude focused on others, on us, as He willingly gave Himself in sacrifice for our redemption.

> *Have this mind among yourselves, which is yours in Christ Jesus, who, though he was in the form of God, did not count equality with God a thing to be grasped, but emptied himself, by taking the form of a servant, being born in the likeness of men. And being found in human form, he humbled himself by becoming obedient to the point of death, even death on a cross. (Philippians 2:5–8)*

Do we have this attitude: a willingness to be humbled, to put our interests to the side, and consider how the Lord might use us in His

WHEN GOD'S WILL AND MY WILL DISCONNECT

Kingdom work?

In the absence of prior dreams, what is our attitude in moving forward? He calls us to be thankful.

> *It is good to give thanks to the Lord, to sing praises to your name, O Most High; to declare your steadfast love in the morning, and your faithfulness by night, (Psalm 92:1-2)*

In recognizing we are the children of God, redeemed by the blood of Christ, secured for eternity in His presence, sustained by His loving grace, how can we be anything but thankful? Our attitude should never be based on what we are getting out of life, or what we are doing, or what others may be doing for us. Rather, our attitude should always be focused on the person of Christ and the assurance of His unconditional grace, sufficient for us in every moment of life.

I need to realize God's answers.

We can pray and anticipate the coming answers of God, and then totally miss them. Why? They weren't what we were expecting, or our faith was minimized in our current circumstances. We may desperately want something to happen, to change what may appear to be the present course of life. But, when it does, do we recognize it? Are we so caught up with what we had anticipated in our "dream world" that we don't see God working.

Peter was imprisoned.[28] He had boldly stood for the Gospel. King Herod, in attempting to gain favor with the Jews had executed James, the brother of John, and then jailed Peter. The intention was to bring

---

28 Often God's people, both in Scripture and throughout history, have faced imprisonment. Sometimes, even though we are not physically imprisoned, we can feel like we are bound in chains. In these times and as we look at the examples of Scripture, we can see God works in ways that we would not have imagined, as He works in and through His people to accomplish His purposes.

him to public trial following the observance of Passover, with the expectation he would be judged, condemned, and then serve as an example before others. For believers, this was not supposed to happen. Peter was a leader among them, a teacher, an encourager, and an example to follow. Thinking he was to be tried and probably executed dashed their dreams of seeing the church growing and flourishing.

> *So Peter was kept in prison, but earnest prayer for him was made to God by the church. Now when Herod was about to bring him out, on that very night, Peter was sleeping between two soldiers, bound with two chains, and sentries before the door were guarding the prison. (Acts 12:5-6)*

The church prayed – earnestly. They were intent on "storming" the Throne of God with the request for Peter's freedom and for the furtherance of the Gospel. Then the unexpected happened. Peter, asleep in prison, was wakened by an angel of the Lord, freed, and led out of prison unharmed and unnoticed. Once out of the prison gates and confident the Lord had released him, he went directly to the home where he knew believers were praying. Peter knocked. The servant girl, Rhoda, answered the door. Recognizing Peter, she neglected to open the door and quickly ran to tell the believers.

> *Recognizing Peter's voice, in her joy she did not open the gate but ran in and reported that Peter was standing at the gate. They said to her, "You are out of your mind." But she kept insisting that it was so, and they kept saying, "It is his angel!" But Peter continued knocking, and when they opened, they saw him and were amazed. (Acts 12:14-16)*

They had nearly missed God's answer. They didn't believe He would hear their prayer and respond with Peter's freedom. Their dream had been realized. God answered. They doubted.

We also often doubt.

When we are left without the direction we once had, we pray. This is good and right, as it always is to submit before God's Throne when seeking His direction. However, there is a key that must not be missed: being open and sensitive to His response. He may well be opening a path for us to follow that perfectly coincides with what we had at one time hoped.

I need to remember God's truth.

God does not stop halfway through His plan. Everything He has always done and everything He will do in the future will be perfectly and completely brought to conclusion. We need to focus on this truth. When our dreams are suddenly altered, we must remember that His plans have not changed.

> *And I am sure of this, that he who began a good work in you will bring it to completion at the day of Jesus Christ. (Philippians 1:6)*

This good work of our Lord did not begin at our salvation, it didn't begin at our birth or conception, it did not begin at creation. His good work in our lives began before the creation of the world. This was not a last minute thought or that which was connived to correct a bad situation. God had a plan; He has always had a plan.

> *Blessed be the God and Father of our Lord Jesus Christ, who has blessed us in Christ with every spiritual blessing in the heavenly places, even as he chose us in him before the foundation of the world, that we should be holy and blameless before him. In love he predestined us for adoption as sons through Jesus Christ, according to the purpose of his will, to the praise of his glorious grace, with*

which he has blessed us in the Beloved. (Ephesians 1:3–6)

In His sovereign design, our Lord worked through our ancestors for us to be just as we are. He chose us to be His own, redeemed us through the blood of Christ, indwelt us by His Holy Spirit and sealed us for the Day of Redemption, and additionally gave us His fully inspired Word. Having accomplished all this, we can now rest in absolute assurance He will bring us to completion.

We do not know the process, but we do know the outcome; we do not know all the events, trials, circumstances along the way, but we do know the Master Designer. In remembering God's Truth we can accept God's realities with confident expectation of the fulfillment of His divine purpose.

Faith in our Lord frees us to release our dreams and replace them with grateful acceptance of His realities.

Consider:
1. Has there been a time when my "dreams" were suddenly shattered? What happened?
   How did I respond?
2. What has made accepting God's realities most difficult for me?
   How do I respond to Romans 8:28, Ephesians 4:1,
   Philippians 1:6, and 1 Thessalonians 5:18
3. In recognizing God's reality is very different than our expectations, we need to consider what we have done and are doing, and our motivation for our actions.
   Am I willing to consider, admit, and confess that
   I may have done wrong, which has negatively

impacted what I had hoped would happen?
4. When plans abruptly change, do I tend to blame others? In doing this, what am I hoping to accomplish?
5. How do others describe my attitude when my plans change? Would their description of me be one that pleases God?
6. When my "dreams" are shattered, how do I pray? Are my prayers focused on changing my situation, changing me, or bringing glory to God?
7. What sin do I need to confess; what thinking needs to be transformed; what practice needs to change?

DECISION EIGHT

I Choose to Accept God's Blessings

The first time Barbara and I were in the hospital delivery room the Doctor told us, "You have a son." We named him Jonathan Haddon, and knew we had been richly blessed by our Lord. Almost three years later we were once again in the delivery room and the Doctor said, "You have a daughter." We named her Anna Kristin (Gracious Christian) and knew we were again richly blessed by our Lord. The third time, we were in an adoption courtroom and the judge said, "You can have a son." We left his given name as Barry (Spear, indicating one who is a warrior), as this was a perfect blend of Barbara and Terry. For his middle name we gave him mine, Daniel (God is my Judge), and once again, we were richly blessed by our Lord.

The Lord has given us three children; each very different from the others; each a gift from our Lord; and each a great blessing to us. Anna and Barry are now grown, married, and have been blessed with children; and we have been blessed with eight grandchildren.

These are easy blessings to accept and appreciate. We are constantly reminded of them, whether we are physically together or together through their pictures, enjoying memories, and seeing how the hand of our Lord has worked.

Other blessings are not so easy to recognize or accept. When they don't fit our plan or are not the blessings we were hoping for or anticipating, we can sometimes step back and wonder what God is doing. And often the richness of those blessings comes alongside the difficulty of trial.

That eventful night in March 2001 was the beginning of a series of events which changed our lives. At that time we understood little of how our Lord would work and bless us through an unwanted brain tumor. Options were discussed regarding forms of treatment, and after several more months of testing and observation, the decision was made to have the tumor removed.

Going into surgery, the Lord gave both of us an overwhelming peace. We knew what could happen. Barbara would definitely lose all potential of hearing on her left side. There could be severe facial nerve damage or brain damage. From the time she left for the surgical room to the time she was wheeled into recovery, 15 hours had elapsed. The surgery was successful. The entire tumor had been removed; there was no damage to the facial nerve which meant no paralysis of the facial muscles. Though recovery time was long and effects of the surgery remain today, we could not have anticipated better results.

The blessings we experienced were numerous; all these would have been unknown had we not gone through this time in our lives!

- ➢ The Lord gave us a remarkable peace. We knew He was in control, and that He could bring about exceptionally good

results. But even if the "worst thing" happened, we knew He would provide everything we needed. His goodness is unwavering regardless of surgery results.
- Providentially, a doctor had recently arrived in town that specialized in the resection of acoustic neuroma tumors. He, along with an excellent neurosurgeon, worked carefully and tediously as a team to microscopically remove the tumor with no unforeseen negative results.
- Our church family was overwhelmingly supportive. They spent time around the clock praying. They visited, sent cards, called, and provided encouragement in ways that could not have been imagined.
- We gained a renewed appreciation for the gracious gift of life, as we were confronted with our fragility in daily living.
- He gave us a unique sensitivity to others experiencing surgery and having to endure resulting side effects.
- After the initial diagnosis we stopped by the local Christian bookstore and purchased a picture, using a gift card that had been given to us. This Scripture at the bottom of the picture states: Be joyful and glad of heart for the good that the LORD has done (2 Chronicles 7:10). Many times since this purchase our Lord has blessed us with these words and His promise, as we are confident of His continued goodness working in our lives.
- Barbara and I have enjoyed special times together – both before and after surgery. The difficulties were used by our Lord to unite our hearts in a freshness of love and appreciation.

There are ongoing challenges due to the resulting side effects of this surgery. Disrupted nerves are still active and being one-sided hearing now changes the way Barbara hears the world. Some days end with a painful head or weariness from noise stimulation. However, even in the ongoing challenges, we have much to be thankful for as we consider the incomparable blessings of God.

Blessings can come out of trial. We need to look for them; to stop and think about them; to recognize that God is uniquely working His will and purpose. Seeing His blessings is a choice. The opposing choice which can be made is focusing only on the trial, the difficulty, the unwanted circumstance. In doing this, we forego what God wants us to experience. We choose misery rather than knowing His blessing; basking in difficulty rather than seeing His joy.

Decision Eight: I choose to accept and appreciate God's unusual blessings as His perfect design.

Joseph was repeatedly a recipient of God's unusual blessings. Though sold into Egypt and considered to be a common slave, he quickly rose to a place of prominence in Potiphar's household. He didn't remain focused on what he didn't have and where he wasn't, but rather accepted what God was doing in his life. Out of his trial, God brought him blessings he never would have or could have experienced elsewhere.

> *The Lord was with Joseph, and he became a successful man, and he was in the house of his Egyptian master. His master saw that the Lord was with him and that the Lord caused all that he did to succeed in his hands. So Joseph found favor in his sight and attended him, and he made him overseer of his house and put him in charge of all that he had. (Genesis 39:2-4)*

When in difficult situations we need to continue doing what we should be doing.

Joseph did what was expected of him; he followed through on his responsibilities. Notice what the Scriptures state: the LORD caused all that he did to succeed. His blessing in coming to prominence wasn't just because of what he did. Rather, it was the Lord's goodness that brought him success. Because Joseph was not prone to sulking in his supposedly less than favorable circumstances and because he did what he could do in being trusted in his responsibilities, he was able to know God's blessings.

When in the midst of trial, we need to carefully consider and ask the question, "Am I doing what I should be doing, right now?" Too often individuals take "a break" from work, excuse themselves from fulfilling their responsibilities, and then justify irresponsibility. Out of their own misery they begin to complain, things continue to go badly for them, and they know nothing of God's blessings. Regardless of how we feel about circumstances encompassing us, or the dreaded outcomes that may be looming over us, we have no excuse for being unreliable. In determining to be faithful before God and others, we can expect the Lord's blessings. However, we must be careful not to determine what these blessings will look like; rather, we need to be open and accepting of how God chooses to bless.

When in difficult situations we need to remember God is working far beyond our purview.

We also are told that Joseph's blessings reached far beyond him. When God works in one person's life, we can well anticipate that others are going to be positively affected because of it.

From the time that he made him overseer in his house and over all that he had, the Lord blessed the Egyptian's house for Joseph's sake; the blessing of the Lord was on all that he had, in house and field. (Genesis 39:5)

Potiphar was blessed; his household was blessed; all that he owned enjoyed blessings from the Lord.

Joseph was blessed as a slave; he was also greatly blessed as a leader. After interpreting Pharaoh's dreams, Joseph was elevated out of prison to a place of prominence in the kingdom, second only to Pharaoh. All of Egypt was subservient to him.

> *Then Pharaoh said to Joseph, "Since God has shown you all this, there is none so discerning and wise as you are. You shall be over my house, and all my people shall order themselves as you command. Only as regards the throne will I be greater than you." And Pharaoh said to Joseph, "See, I have set you over all the land of Egypt." Then Pharaoh took his signet ring from his hand and put it on Joseph's hand, and clothed him in garments of fine linen and put a gold chain about his neck. And he made him ride in his second chariot. And they called out before him, "Bow the knee!" Thus he set him over all the land of Egypt. (Genesis 41:39–43)*

Joseph's life radically changed. He went from being a rejected Hebrew to a common slave to a forgotten prisoner to ruler over all of Egypt. He was changed from being excluded by family and losing all expectation of ever returning to the life he once had or hoped for, from great trial and sorrow, to being placed in the most responsible position in a foreign kingdom. This is God at work; this is God blessing in unusual ways when we do not expect it. Joseph remained faithful, and God, in His sovereign design, used him as a blessing to others.

DECISION EIGHT

> *When all the land of Egypt was famished, the people cried to Pharaoh for bread. Pharaoh said to all the Egyptians, "Go to Joseph. What he says to you, do." So when the famine had spread over all the land, Joseph opened all the storehouses and sold to the Egyptians, for the famine was severe in the land of Egypt. Moreover, all the earth came to Egypt to Joseph to buy grain, because the famine was severe over all the earth. (Genesis 41:55–57)*

Joseph, being responsible in all the Lord gave him to do, was given greater responsibility, and in turn greater blessing and the privilege of being used to bless others. All of Egypt, as well as those from many surrounding nations, were sustained in life while Joseph held the storehouse keys.

When in difficult situations we need to remember God does not quit working.

In the midst of our trials, God does not quit working. He uses the most trying situations of our lives at times to pour upon us the fullest of His blessings. It is important for the believer to see the "unexpected" as the "expected" in God's book.

We never want to minimize the difficulty and pain one may be experiencing. The turmoil of divorce, the inner pain of a rebellious child or the loss of a child who was not born alive, the grief over the death of a loved one, the heartache of a broken relationship are all severely traumatic in their own way. There are many other times in our lives which seem to overwhelm and appear to have no solution. These are tough situations, tiring, and life-changing.

However, as the chapters of our lives are written, we are able to see that God is unusually putting the words together to make our story. What He does and how He writes may not be anything like we expect, but we can trust Him to be accomplishing His purposes. In this we are blessed in knowing we are part of His spectacular design and the recipients of His most gracious blessings. We may not realize them at this time, or even in this life. We don't need to. Still, we can have confidence that God is doing what is best, and that which is best for His children.

In addition to the blessings coming to the believer as a result of the circumstances when it seems that our will and God's will are disconnected, we can hold on to the truth of an abundance of further blessings He has given, is giving, and promises to give in the future. Looking at Paul's letter to the church at Ephesus, some of these blessings are highlighted below. When fighting despair in the midst of difficulties and feeling alone or forgotten, a great exercise for the believer is to carefully consider the magnitude of the blessings of God. Walk through the Scriptures seeing how God works, and enjoy knowing He is the same God today as He has been and always will be.

Jesus Christ is the same yesterday and today and forever. (Hebrews 13.8)

The believer is blessed:
- We are blessed with every spiritual blessing in Christ (Ephesians 1:3). Now! Though we don't know what these necessarily involve, we can know that God has so looked upon us in His favor, that currently in the heavenly realms there are innumerable blessings for us, and they are present in His presence now.
- We are blessed in having been chosen in Christ before the foundation of the world (Ephesians 1:4). To know that as believers we were in the design of God before He ever spoke in

DECISION EIGHT

Genesis 1:1. In His love and grace, beyond any of our possible comprehension, He chose to make us His children. Knowing we would be lost, sinful, rebellious created beings, He desired to bring us into the fullness of His blessings.

- We are blessed in being chosen by God to be holy and blameless before him (Ephesians 1:4). We have been blessed with the promise of being remade into perfection by the design of God.
- We are blessed in that He predestined us for adoption as sons through Jesus Christ (Ephesians 1:5). He has made us His very children and taken full responsibility for us. The believer is not made to be an angel, or some other heavenly being, but rather made an heir of the eternal kingdom and a joint-heir with Jesus Christ (Romans 8:17), His one and only Son (John 3:16), enjoying all the rights and privileges of a natural born son.
- We are blessed as we have been made part of His holy family in according to the purpose of his will (Ephesians 1:5). It pleased the Father to make us His own; it was His sovereign design that we should be called His child, by His Name.
- We are blessed to be able to be to the praise of His glorious grace (Ephesians 1:6). Praising God is not a burden; it is not an unwanted task. Rather, to give Him praise because of His gracious transforming work is a blessing; to be a testimony of what He has done, reserved only for those who can call Him Father, is a blessing; and to praise Him for His work of redemption is a privilege and blessing.
- We are blessed to be the recipients of His blessing us in the Beloved (Ephesians 1:6). The believer is in the Beloved – a

recipient of His grace, placing us in Christ and filing us with His glory; His grace is not based on anything of our worth, but is rather the very opposite of what we so rightly deserve.[29]

- We are blessed in that we have redemption through His blood (Ephesians 1:7). Redemption – having been purchased by God to be His child. He desired us, He chose us, and He purchased us to be His own. His purchase was not with anything of monetary value. Rather, He purchased us with the very sacrificial blood of His one and only Son, the Lord Jesus Christ. It was the blood of Christ shed on the Cross of Calvary, the blood of Christ spilt on the heavenly altar, the blood of Christ that alone is able to cleanse us of all sin, the blood of Christ that is all sufficient for a once and for all cleansing (Hebrews 10:10); it is through the blood of Christ we have obtained redemption.
- We are blessed in that we have the forgiveness of our trespasses, according to the riches of his grace (Ephesians 1:7). Sin forgiven, (1 John 1:9), sin remembered no more (Jeremiah 31:34), sin cast into the depths of the sea (Micah 7:19), sin removed as far as the east is from the west (Psalm 103:12). This is the work of God's rich grace; this is the work of a sovereign, loving, merciful God; this is the work of the Eternal Father who has desired to bless His children beyond anything we could ever possibly deserve.
- We are blessed with that his grace has been lavished on us in all wisdom and understanding (Ephesians 1:8). In Christ we

---

29 To have a fuller understanding of the blessings given to the believer by God, it is important to periodically consider the depth of despair which was our plight before His redemptive rescue.

are able to know Him, to know His work of grace, to know the wonder of His love and mercy. He not only accomplished this great work on our behalf, but He has also given to us the wisdom and understanding to know His love and mercy that we might be filled with the fullness of praise.

- We are blessed in that He has made known to us the mystery of His will, according to his purpose, which He set forth in Christ (Ephesians 1:9). He has blessed us with an understanding of His incomparable and incomprehensible redemptive plan. This is His desire for us to know Him, to know His working, and to understand that our redemption has been His plan before time.

- We are blessed to know the end of the story, that the Lord has a plan for the fullness of time, to unite all things in him, things in heaven and things on earth (Ephesians 1:10). There is more to come. Yes, there may be trials today, problems may abound, difficulties may be beyond our comprehension, but we can know that God is at work. And, in the end, He will show Himself to be victorious, as all things are brought into subjection before Him.

> *At the name of Jesus every knee should bow, in heaven and on earth and under the earth, and every tongue confess that Jesus Christ is Lord, to the glory of God the Father. (Philippians 2:10-11)*

- We are blessed in knowing that He is working all things according to the counsel of his will (Ephesians 1:11). Nothing goes to waste; God uses everything. We may not understand the "how" and we don't have to know. However, we can have absolute assurance that every situation in our life, whether we look at it as one of great delight or of great trial, is being used by God and is in total harmony with His will.

- We are blessed in knowing that we have been sealed with the promised Holy Spirit (Ephesians 1:13). Being made His child and being purchased by Him, we are secured in Him through the work of the Holy Spirit of God. He has sealed us, and nothing can break that seal; there is nothing that can remove us from His family; there is nothing that can ever separate us from the love of God in Christ Jesus our Lord (Romans 8:39).
- We are blessed in knowing that we are secure until Jesus comes, until we acquire possession of our inheritance (Ephesians 1:14).

And this is just the beginning of the blessings He has revealed to us in just 12 verses of one chapter of the entire Scriptures. His blessings abound abundantly filling us with the completeness of His bounty above our ability to fully perceive.[30]

Praising God for His blessings and then turning to complaints do not agree, they cannot come from the same person. We are to be those who praise, or we will be those who complain. After meditating on these blessings from Ephesians 1, the succeeding exercise is to consider our own lives. How has God been at work in blessing us? Take time to think, to carefully review, to consider the events of life. Be careful not to look for just the "big event blessings," but for those

---

30 In reading Scripture there should be the expectation that God is at work, that God wants to convey something to us, that God wants to communicate to us His truth. This list of blessings is from one portion of one chapter in Scripture, but can be multiplied innumerable times throughout His Word. Our responsibility is to read seeking His blessing, seeking to understand further, seeking to grow in the richness of what God has done, to be filled with the knowledge of His will in all spiritual wisdom and understanding (Colossians 1.9).

daily blessings we so quickly tend to forget, those "small" moments that may seem insignificant and are often overlooked. However, when seen from a broader vision, when seen from a heavenly perspective, we know they have powerfully changed the direction of our lives.[31]

This is what we are to bask in, this should be our meditation, and this is our hope and joy: the fullness of the riches of His blessings. There is no need for the believer to be overwhelmed by the circumstances of life, of those seemingly negative things which happen. The entire scope of our countenance, within and without, is changed when our focus is turned to our Lord – who He is, what He has done, what He is doing, and what He has promised to do in the future.[32]

Consider :

1. It is easy for me to accept the obvious blessings from God, those which are enjoyable and are pleasing to me. However, the "blessings in disguise" are far more difficult to appreciate. How have I seen the reality of God's blessings come out of the initially undesirable circumstance?
2. What do I hope to gain by resisting God's working when it is unpleasant?
3. How do I define success?
How does the Lord define success?

---

31 We have a tendency to give praise for the "big blessings," for those things considered to be answers to prayer, for those things that are life changing in a positive form in our view, or preventative of negatively changing the course of our lives. However, it is equally important to consider the "moment blessings" – those things that happen as a matter of routine, those things we piously take for granted, the people that God is using to shape and develop us, the positive influences in our lives as well as the difficult people we must learn to work and live with on a daily basis.

32 We will never appreciate the blessings of our Lord apart from "thankfulness." "Thanklessness" scorns God's blessings. When we learn the principle of giving thanks in all circumstances, we are being obedient to the Lord and are present in doing His will (1 Thessalonians 5:18). The thankful heart enjoys the blessings of God and appreciates every good gift and every perfect gift, coming down from the Father of lights (James 1:17).

4. Do I tend to "take a break" from my responsibilities when facing difficult situations?
   Am I willing to ask the question, "Am I doing what I should be doing, right now" and then respond appropriately?
5. Focus on the blessings of Ephesians 1:3-14 and Romans 8:1-39. Are there certain of these blessings I have difficulty accepting? If so, what can I do to better grasp their reality in my life?
6. What additional blessings can I identify in my life as having come from the Lord?
7. What sin do I need to confess; what thinking needs to be transformed; what practice needs to change?

DECISION NINE

I Choose to Remember God's Working

Why is it we often tend to forget the things we want to remember, and remember the things we would like to forget? This happens to me invariably, and even more so as I get older. I use sticky notes, pieces of scrap paper, and 3 x 5 cards. When preaching or teaching, my notes have become more specific. When in a phone conversation or a counseling session, I make careful summaries. These things are important, and I don't want to forget what I should be remembering.

However, there are other things; those things that I'd just as soon forget, those things that don't seem to get out of my mind. When I least expect it, the memory can quickly pop back into my head, and I respond with "Where did that come from?" I had not planned on thinking about it, I did not want to think about it, and I do not even see any point in ever thinking about it again. Whether it was a previous casual conversation or a sinful act, a plaguing thought or a fleeting idea, these reminders can hound us.

As believers, Peter exhorts us to be constantly on guard of such things, recognizing the enemy is intent on hurting us, destroying us, disenabling us as God's representatives.

> *Be sober-minded; be watchful. Your adversary the devil prowls around like a roaring lion, seeking someone to devour. Resist him, firm in your faith, knowing that the same kinds of suffering are being experienced by your brotherhood throughout the world. (1 Peter 5:8-9)*

In telling us to be sober-minded we recognize we don't have to fall under the enemy's tactics. Just because his desire is to inflict spiritual harm on us, does not mean we have to submit. What is the key? Being firm in your faith. Knowing, growing, and practicing this faith given by our Lord, keeps us from submitting to sin.

Paul encourages us as believers to be pro-active in our thinking, placing ourselves on the altar of sacrifice for the Lord's use.

> *I appeal to you therefore, brothers, by the mercies of God, to present your bodies as a living sacrifice, holy and acceptable to God, which is your spiritual worship. Do not be conformed to this world, but be transformed by the renewal of your mind, that by testing you may discern what is the will of God, what is good and acceptable and perfect. (Romans 12:1-2)*

He calls us to be transformed by the renewal of our mind. In full submission to the Lord, giving ourselves to Him as a living sacrifice, He is commanding us to have our minds transformed, to reconsider and redo the way we think.

Though we may struggle with remembering certain things and always need those proverbial sticky notes, we can accept the fact that they are helpful in reminding us of the things we want to know. And those other thoughts, those things we want to forget, we do not have to ruminate on them, we do not have to meditate on them and give them unwanted and unnecessary "air time." That is the result of being transformed; learning to quickly move on and refocus on the thoughts God would have for us.

Paul spoke of his personal struggle in the battle with right and wrong, with pleasing God and falling into sin.

> *For I do not understand my own actions. For I do not do what I want, but I do the very thing I hate... So now it is no longer I who do it, but sin that dwells within me. For I know that nothing good dwells in me, that is, in my flesh. For I have the desire to do what is right, but not the ability to carry it out. For I do not do the good I want, but the evil I do not want is what I keep on doing. Now if I do what I do not want, it is no longer I who do it, but sin that dwells within me. So I find it to be a law that when I want to do right, evil lies close at hand. For I delight in the law of God, in my inner being, but I see in my members another law waging war against the law of my mind and making me captive to the law of sin that dwells in my members. Wretched man that I am! Who will deliver me from this body of death? (Romans 7:15–24)*

We must not give up; we must not resign ourselves to sin. In regards to our thoughts, we must continue to strive to take every thought captive to obey Christ (2 Corinthians 10:5). We must seek to remember that our only hope in remembering what is good and right is through the power of Christ.

God knows our struggle. When those difficult times hit us and our world may seem to shatter, He well knows of the wrestling matches we have with thoughts. Quickly our mind reverts to all the things we should forget, we focus on those things that will only hinder us from believing God and knowing He is at work. We need to determine to not forget what we know about God and His Word; we must strive to trust Him, to believe Him, to anticipate the realization of His sovereign design.

Decision Nine: I choose to remember God's working in the past, knowing He will work in the future.

This is a decision to remember; a decision to not forget.

It is also a decision to not consider and ponder on those things which should be put behind us, which should not be remembered.

Jacob, his sons, and their families were beginning to struggle in Canaan. The famine that plagued Egypt was widespread, affecting other nations. Jacob's family was not immune. Having heard there was grain in Egypt, he directed his sons to take the journey and purchase what was needed. It is either go and live or stay and die; he saw no option. Ten brothers went; Benjamin stayed behind. Having lost Joseph, Jacob wasn't about to lose Rachel's other son, as he had likely taken Joseph's place as "the most favored."

In Egypt, perhaps it was a typical day for Joseph. Listening to people and their needs, making decisions regarding the distribution of grain, seeking to help needy people in the best way he could. Typical, that is, until he was told there were visitors from Canaan.

> *Now Joseph was governor over the land. He was the one who sold to all the people of the land. And Joseph's brothers came and bowed themselves before him with their faces to the ground. Joseph saw his brothers and recognized them, but he treated them like strangers and spoke roughly to them. "Where do you come from?" he said. They said, "From the land of Canaan, to buy food." And Joseph recognized his brothers, but they did not recognize him. (Genesis 42:6–8)*

DECISION NINE

The brothers paid homage to this "unknown" leader; the one who had the power to sell them grain or withhold from them blessing, the one who would determine their future. Joseph chose not to reveal himself to them at this time. Perhaps he wanted to hear more from them; perhaps he wanted to judge their sincerity. We don't know; we don't need to know.

We do know that Joseph's memory became clear.

> *And Joseph remembered the dreams that he had dreamed of them. And he said to them, "You are spies; you have come to see the nakedness of the land." (Genesis 42:9)*

Joseph remembered. Whether or not he often thought about these dreams is unknown. But now he did. And possibly, at this time he was reminded of the powerful working of God. What had at one point been predicted through a dream had now become a reality years later.

Not having revealed himself to his brothers, Joseph initially confined them for three days. He wanted them to bring Benjamin to Egypt; he wanted to see his youngest brother, the brother of his mother Rachel. He put a plan in motion. Nine of the brothers would remain confined to prison; one could go to bring Benjamin. Joseph told them his motivation, "Do this and you will live, for I fear God" (Genesis 42:18).

During his years in Egypt, he had not forgotten the Lord God. He knew Him and he feared Him. He had determined not to do anything that would be contrary to His Word.

Having changed his strategy, the brothers were told that one must stay until their youngest brother is brought to Egypt. In their guilt they remembered their action toward Joseph. The horror of what they had done, the grief brought to their father, and likely the death or miserable life they had brought upon Joseph began to freshly haunt them. Additionally, there would now be the added stress of their future, and that of Simeon having been left behind.

> *Then they said to one another, "In truth we are guilty concerning our brother, in that we saw the distress of his soul, when he begged us and we did not listen. That is why this distress has come upon us." And Reuben answered them, "Did I not tell you not to sin against the boy? But you did not listen. So now there comes a reckoning for his blood." They did not know that Joseph understood them, for there was an interpreter between them. Then he turned away from them and wept. And he returned to them and spoke to them. And he took Simeon from them and bound him before their eyes. (Genesis 42:21-24)*

Reuben wanted to be remembered as "the righteous one" with his "didn't I tell you not to do this" comment. "I told you this wasn't a good idea; I told you not to sin." However, Reuben had forgotten what he didn't do and how he didn't stand up for him when they threw Joseph into the cistern, how he didn't flee after the caravan; he didn't tell his father the truth.

Often we remember what makes us look good, and choose to forget our own faults.[33] To the brother's credit, when confronted, their

---

33 Regarding past sins, these three things should be noted:

1. When sin has been confessed, repentance made, and forgiveness granted there is no need to continue down the path of constant guilt. Sin happened, the event is past, and consequences are now to be dealt with appropriately. The past cannot be changed; we need to move forward.

2. When sin has not been confessed, confession and repentance are the first step. It is then possible to move forward in God's favor when no longer harboring known sin.

3. To not be hounded by the guilt of past sin, we should be intentional to learn from the past, never forgetting the lessons learned, being committed to never repeat past sins, and standing guard against all temptation.

memory resurfaced. They knew they had done wrong and recognized they were faced with the consequences of their prior wicked choices.

The brothers remembered their past sins, but made no confession. Returning to Canaan, they told their father about their unusual experience. However, there is no indication they told him of their assumption that their current plight was a result of the evil they had done years earlier. They saw no value in speaking the truth. They were sworn to secrecy.

Joseph remembered and wept. He knew his brothers; he heard them talk and understood their language. Nothing had been forgotten. He may have been surprised to see them, but in remembering his dreams, the surprise quickly fled. I think he would have had a new sense of awe at the wonder and working of God. All he had been through had a purpose. God was using all he had experienced for the protection of his own family. Some of Joseph's tears were likely in realization of God's gracious design. The rejection, the slavery, the imprisonment, Pharaoh's dreams, his rise to power, were now clearly seen as all having been providentially designed by God. And now, he stood before his brothers seeing the unexplainable dreams of his youth coming to fruition.

When sold to slavery and then imprisoned, Joseph never forgot the Lord. Upon seeing his brothers, there was a commanding reinforcement of God's working.[34]

---

34 A great exercise in helping individuals refocus is what I have termed "Picking up Stones," coming from Joshua 3-4. I ask individuals to begin writing short statements on a pad of paper what they know about the Lord and His working in the lives of His people from the Scriptures, how they see Him blessing people, and how they have seen Him working in their own lives. Each time they write something down, they are to pick up a small stone and place it in a bowl or basket, positioned in a visible place in their home or at work. Whenever they see the stones, they can visually and quickly remember the power of the Lord and all the good things He has done for His people, and be reminded that He is the same God today, still doing good things among His people.

In those darkest days of our lives when the will of God does not seem to even come close to what we thought was His will, we must remember that God has not changed. As He had worked in the past, so He is at work and will work in the future.

Sometimes we need reminders; there is nothing wrong with prompts. The Lord provides a powerful illustration with rocks which can help us remember. At the crossing of the Jordan River, Joshua was given an unusual command to follow before the river flowed back over dry ground.

> *When all the nation had finished passing over the Jordan, the Lord said to Joshua, "Take twelve men from the people, from each tribe a man, and command them, saying, 'Take twelve stones from here out of the midst of the Jordan, from the very place where the priests' feet stood firmly, and bring them over with you and lay them down in the place where you lodge tonight.'" (Joshua 4:1-3)*

Though the request may have seemed strange initially, the Lord had a very clear purpose.

> *Then Joshua called the twelve men from the people of Israel, whom he had appointed, a man from each tribe. And Joshua said to them, "Pass on before the ark of the Lord your God into the midst of the Jordan, and take up each of you a stone upon his shoulder, according to the number of the tribes of the people of Israel, that this may be a sign among you. When your children ask in time to come, 'What do those stones mean to you?' then you shall tell them that the waters of the Jordan were cut off before the ark of the covenant of the Lord. When it passed over the Jordan, the waters of the Jordan were cut off. So these stones shall be to the people of Israel a memorial forever." (Joshua 4:4-7)*

The advice to the Israelites was clear and simple. Pick up rocks. Put them in a place where you can see them. When people ask you about them, tell them about God's working. When struggling, choose to remember. When struggling to remember, choose to pray for the transforming work of God to change your thoughts. When your thoughts go in the wrong direction, choose to resist them, and refocus on the great things that God has done. He hasn't changed; He is still at work.

Principles for remembering

The following six principles are those which many believers have been taught from their youth. However, being taught them and choosing to practice them can be very different. We must be careful not to overlook truth because of its simplicity, but determine more aggressively to adhere to its challenge. The following Scriptures, mostly taken from the Psalms, attest to the truths presented. The Scriptures given are only a sampling; many additional passages could also be looked at and discussed to further emphasize the importance of God's Word and remembering its truth. Practicing these principles will lead us in making the right choice: to remember God's working in the past, knowing He will work in the future.

Principle #1: Interact with the Word of God.

We have to read it. Believers should develop a definite discipline of spending time in God's Word. We cannot expect to understand the character of God, to understand His desire for us, or grow in our appreciation for His working apart from reading His Word. We must interact with God through His Word to know Him.[35] Interacting requires thinking; thinking leads to interaction. If we are honestly reading the Scriptures with the desire to learn and grow, we cannot be passive; we must be actively involved with what God says.

Recently I heard Woodward Kroll,[36] a noted author, speak. He commented that he always enjoys hearing that people have read one of his books. He then reminded us that God only wrote one book, and it is His book that we should become vitally familiar with; it is His book that should have priority over all other books in our libraries. We should know His book, knowing more than having scanned it from cover to cover.

> *Open my eyes that I may behold wondrous things out of your law. (Psalm 119:18)*
>
> *When I told of my ways, you answered me; teach me your statutes. (Psalm 119:26)*
>
> *Teach me, O Lord, the way of your statutes; and I will keep it to the end. (Psalm 119:33)*
>
> *The earth, O LORD, is full of your steadfast love; teach me your statutes! (Psalm 119:64)*
>
> *Teach me good judgment and knowledge, for I believe in your commandments. (Psalm 119:66)*

---

35 I always encourage reading Scripture with a pen in hand. Underlining phrases, verses, or sentences, circling words, noting lessons, writing in margins will all help us to think, to interact, to remember, and to review. The reading of Scripture should not just be an exercise in reading, but rather a time of interacting with the God of all creation who has given us the Scriptures with definite purpose.

36 Woodward Kroll is the President and Senior Bible Teacher at "Back to the Bible" Ministry.

You are good and do good; teach me your statutes. (Psalm 119:68)

It is good for me that I was afflicted, so that I might learn your statutes. (Psalm 119:71)

In your steadfast love give me life, that I may keep the testimonies of your mouth. (Psalm 119:88)

Principle #2: Meditate on the Word of God.

Think about what God says; contemplate truth; consider the wonder of God's unchanging, eternal character; ponder deeply the implications of God's redemptive plan. This is not a casual reading of the Word, but making the interaction meaningful. Early in the military a friend commented to me that we had lost one of the great arts. Perplexed by his comment, I could not think of any "art" that had disappeared from our society. He then told me, "Terry, we have lost the fine art of thinking." We have become so busy in our daily routines, in seeking to meet our expectations of ourselves and those others place upon us, that we have become simply a "doing people," and not a "thinking people." This comment, true 30 years ago, is certainly magnified in today's fast-paced, activity filled, entertainment consumed society.

We need to intentionally develop the discipline of thinking, of meditating, of ruminating on the Word of God. Carefully considering what it says, what it means, and how it applies to us, we then are called to make decisions as to what we are going to do with what we know.

This Book of the Law shall not depart from your mouth, but you shall meditate on it day and night, so that you may be careful to do according to all that is written in it. For then you will make your way prosperous, and then you will have good success. (Joshua 1:8)

Blessed is the man who walks not in the counsel of the wicked, nor stands in the way of sinners, nor sits in the seat of scoffers; but his delight is in the law of the Lord, and on his law he meditates day and night. He is like a tree planted by streams of water that yields its fruit in its season, and its leaf does not wither. In all that he does, he prospers. (Psalm 1:1-3)

I will meditate on your precepts and fix my eyes on your ways. (Psalm 119:15)

Make me understand the way of your precepts, and I will meditate on your wondrous works. (Psalm 119:27)

Principle #3: Memorize the Word of God

Often people will tell me they are unable to memorize Scripture. However, when I ask them of certain things they know, they may quickly be able to recount sport's statistics, specific details relating to their job, song lyrics, phone numbers, dates of their children's activities, and numerous other details that have become a part of their daily routine. These things they know, and know well. What is the difference? They have learned the particular aspects of their lives, those things they are continually involved with, because they are important to them; they have repeated them in their minds until they are fully secure. Should this not be even more vitally true in regards to the Word which God has given to us?

Memorizing His Word is a discipline. Memorization accomplished in our younger years is especially important. First, because the Word will lead us as we begin to make life decisions. Second, because the youthful mind more quickly retains information. Three, those things memorized in our youth will be kept more secure as we grow older.

There is not a simple, "one size fits all" way of memorizing Scripture. We just have to do it. We have to work at it. We have to be disciplined not to stop, committed to persist. In so doing, we will reap great benefit of having the Word of God planted within our hearts, which God will use to accomplish His purpose.

> *The law of his God is in his heart; his steps do not slip. (Psalm 37:31)*

> *How can a young man keep his way pure? By guarding it according to your word. With my whole heart I seek you; let me not wander from your commandments. I have hidden your word in my heart that I might not sin against you. (Psalm 119:9-11)*

> *And take not the word of truth utterly out of my mouth, for my hope is in your rules. (Psalm 119:43)*

> *For I have become like a wineskin in the smoke, yet I have not forgotten your statutes. (Psalm 119:83)*

> *So shall my word be that goes out from my mouth; it shall not return to me empty, but it shall accomplish that which I purpose, and shall succeed in the thing for which I sent it. (Isaiah 55:11)*

Principle #4: Trust the Word of God

It is one thing to say I trust God's Word, it is another to "trust Him," to actually believe what He says to be absolutely true. His Word is the guide for our life. We can know it; but if we don't trust Him in it, His Word means nothing to us. Trusting the Word of God will produce change; it will have impact. Trusting is a choice, a decision to unequivocally and unquestionably believe God's Word is true and will always prove to be fully true.

> *Trust in the Lord with all your heart, and do not lean on your own understanding. In all your ways acknowledge Him, and He will make straight your paths. (Proverbs 3:5-6)*

> *I have chosen the way of faithfulness; I set your rules before me. (Psalm 119:30)*

> *The insolent utterly deride me, but I do not turn away from your law. (Psalm 119:51)*

> *Those who fear you shall see me and rejoice, because I have hoped in your word. (Psalm 119:74)*

> *All your commandments are sure... (Psalm 119:86)*

> *Your word is a lamp to my feet and a light to my path. I have sworn an oath and confirmed it, to keep your righteous rules. (Psalm 119:105-106)*

Principle #5: Walk in the Word of God

Live it. Let it be that which has our full attention every day, which runs through our veins, which is part of the very fiber of our being.

DECISION NINE

The Word of God is not for special occasions, not for particular events, not for specific times during the week. It is not given to us to "pick and choose" what we like, what makes sense to us, or what produces the results we desire. Rather, believers are to choose to live in harmony with the full Word of God, to choose obedience, knowing our Lord knows best.

> *Now this is the commandment—the statutes and the rules—that the Lord your God commanded me to teach you… that you may fear the Lord your God, you and your son and your son's son, by keeping all his statutes and his commandments… Hear therefore, O Israel, and be careful to do them, that it may go well with you… Hear, O Israel: The Lord our God, the Lord is one. You shall love the Lord your God with all your heart and with all your soul and with all your might. And these words that I command you today shall be on your heart. You shall teach them diligently to your children, and shall talk of them when you sit in your house, and when you walk by the way, and when you lie down, and when you rise. You shall bind them as a sign on your hand, and they shall be as frontlets between your eyes. You shall write them on the doorposts of your house and on your gates. (Deuteronomy 6:1–9)*

> *Blessed are those whose way is blameless, who walk in the law of the Lord! Blessed are those who keep his testimonies, who seek him with their whole heart, (Psalm 119:1–2)*

> *I will keep your law continually, forever and ever, and I shall walk in a wide place, for I have sought your precepts. (Psalm 119:44–45)*

> *I remember your name in the night, O Lord, and keep your law. This blessing has fallen to me, that I have kept*

your precepts. (Psalm 119:55-56)

In your steadfast love give me life, that I may keep the testimonies of your mouth. (Psalm 119:88)

Principle #6: Love the Word of God

I love my wife. I love my family. I love certain other people. At times, I might even say that I love a particular food or being in a particular place. Each of these expressions of love will look differently, will have varying depth, and will bring about diverse responses. It all depends on who, or what, is the object of my love.

But, do we love God's Word? Loving God's Word will lead us to loving God, for we cannot love God without loving His Word; and if we learn to love God's Word we will learn to more deeply love God.

During our military days, I was stationed in Sinop, Turkey for one year while my family remained in Massachusetts. This was before the days of cell phones, email, or Skype; we had a scheduled 15 minute phone call weekly and "snail mail." Barbara and I were committed to daily keeping connected by writing to each other. Every day I would make the trek to the postal area to see if a letter had arrived. Because of the mail process, often the box was empty; on other days, there may have been three or four letters which arrived at once. I devoured these letters. Barbara would write of her activities and the events of the days, would keep me informed as to the joys and difficulties of our children, and share with me her heart, her struggles, and her love. I would often reread these treasures, as from a distance I grew in my love for my wife and our children.[37]

---

37   Having made the commitment to write daily, we also kept every one of our letters. They are

Reading God's Word with a similar anticipation will lead us to growing in love for God's Word. Further, loving God's Word will continually take us to His Word, will compel us to spend time in His Word, and will lead us to great delight in His Word. Learning to love God's Word, we will be eager to read God's Word, to interact with God's Word, and to meditate on God's Word. Loving His Word will change our motivations, our intentions, our goals, our desires, and our delights. Loving begins with a choice, and leads to a passion; loving is a discipline that develops into a deep desire.

> *The law of the Lord is perfect, reviving the soul; the testimony of the Lord is sure, making wise the simple; the precepts of the Lord are right, rejoicing the heart; the commandment of the Lord is pure, enlightening the eyes; the fear of the Lord is clean, enduring forever; the rules of the Lord are true, and righteous altogether. More to be desired are they than gold, even much fine gold; sweeter also than honey and drippings of the honeycomb. (Psalm 19:7–10)*

> *I will delight in your statutes; I will not forget your word. (Psalm 119:16)*

> *Your testimonies are my delight; they are my counselors. (Psalm 119:24)*

> *Lead me in the path of your commandments, for I delight in it. (Psalm 119:35)*

---

in large yellow binders, reminding us of those days of separation, the hard times faced, the things learned, and of our commitment to each other.

Based on our own experience, I always encourage those who are facing separations to commit to daily contact. Though it is easy to be caught in the daily busyness of life, taking the time to "talk" through some format keeps the relationship connected and enhances the bond of love.

WHEN GOD'S WILL AND MY WILL DISCONNECT

For I find my delight in your commandments, which I love. (Psalm 119:47)

Their heart is unfeeling like fat, but I delight in your law. (Psalm 119:70)

The law of your mouth is better to me than thousands of gold and silver pieces. (Psalm 119:72)

Let your mercy come to me, that I may live; for your law is my delight. (Psalm 119:77)

As believers in Jesus Christ we make a choice to believe our Lord is at work within us; as He has been working in the past so He will faithfully work in the future. We know our lives have been changed, our hearts have been changed, and our desires have been changed. We cannot and will not be the same person we were before knowing Christ as Savior; our attitude towards and commitment to the Word of God will not be the same as it was before our salvation.

So put away all malice and all deceit and hypocrisy and envy and all slander. Like newborn infants, long for the pure spiritual milk, that by it you may grow up into salvation— if indeed you have tasted that the Lord is good. (1 Peter 2:1–3)

We must be intentional in removing those characteristics of our lives which dishonor Christ. These vices mentioned by Peter must be completely eradicated, allowing none of them to remain in any degree. They each have to do with our relationship with others, each securing our attention, each monopolizing our emotions.

Rather than focusing on the ill of others, Peter calls us to "crave pure spiritual milk." Our cravings cannot pursue two conflicting directions simultaneously. If we selfishly desire good for ourselves by seeking the ill of others, we will not desire God's Word; contrarily, if we are craving Scripture we will not be focusing on ourselves or others. He encourages our cravings to be intense, like a young baby calling out for milk, only to be satisfied when milk is received. When hungry, no amount of walking, rocking, singing, or holding will be sufficient; only milk will satisfy. May we so crave and only be satisfied in the Word of God. We must not cling to reading books, listening to sermons, singing hymns and songs of faith, or fellowshipping with the saints. Though each of these is good in the believer's life and in worshipping God, they must never be substituted for time in the Word of God. Our diligence, our craving must be for God and His Word, for it is here we learn of His grace and goodness, here we learn of His redemptive plan, here we see His mercy and faithfulness, here we learn of true worship, and here we learn to love Him. May we have a never-satisfied and always-growing craving for our Lord and His Holy Word.

Choosing to remember is a discipline. I remember because I want to remember, because I choose to remember.

Consider:
1. What do I tend to most easily forget?
2. What have I done to help myself remember important truths of God's Word?
3. What does it mean to present my body as a living sacrifice to God?
   How do I do this?
4. Based on Joshua 3–4, "stone collecting" is a good way to

remember God's working in our lives.
What are the initial "stones" I can collect, ensuring certain truths and experiences will not be forgotten?

5. Memorization of God's Word is a discipline of the Christian life.
What passages of Scripture will I commit to begin memorizing right now?

6. What particular areas of Scripture are most difficult for me to trust?
What can I do to grow in faith and practice trusting the truth of Scripture?

7. What sin do I need to confess; what thinking needs to be transformed; what practice needs to change?

DECISION TEN

I Choose to Live Above the Fray

Revenge. It can come so naturally. Someone does something that affects us negatively and we seek for ways to "get back" at them. Revenge is mean spirited, plays by the rules of "getting even," and conveys the message that no one is going to do something to us and get away with it. Some will take great strides in revenge becoming a reality; there will be plans and schemes carefully laid to ensure the victory messages are loudly heard. Revenge can eat away like a killing cancer until the plot is implemented and the opponent is successfully attacked. For many it is the only normal response; the conniving thoughts often come easily; and rest is disturbed until vengeance is applied.

The desire for revenge can result from a failure to accept responsibility for our failed actions and sinful responses. Cain, having perceived that his brother Abel had wittingly offered a sacrifice as acceptable, became angry that his was rejected.

> *But for Cain and his offering he [the Lord] had no regard. So Cain was very angry, and his face fell. (Genesis 4:5)*

Rather than coming before the Lord in repentance and admitting his failure to do the right thing, he looked for a way to have Abel "put in his place." The thought process could have gone something like this: "the Lord likes Abel better than me; there is no reason why my sacrifice shouldn't be accepted, since I brought those things I had grown and they were some of the best; I'll show Abel that he is no better than me; once he is dead, then I will be the favored one." Cain vigorously sought to be the one in the right, and to "get even" with Abel for having an acceptable offering. It wasn't Abel's wrongdoing; Cain failed to obey the Lord. However, rather than accept responsibility for his own actions, he took out his frustration and anger on his brother.

Revenge can also swell within us when we have honestly been wronged, or someone we love has been clearly offended by another. An evil passion had grown within Amnon, the Son of David, for his half-sister, Tamar. In his sexual promiscuity and lustful heart, he physically desired Tamar:

> *And Amnon was so tormented that he made himself ill because of his sister Tamar, for she was a virgin, and it seemed impossible to Amnon to do anything to her. (2 Samuel 13:2)*

Having been ill advised by his wicked friend, he devised a plan to have his way. He succeeded in his sexual action, but with miserable consequences, resulting in turmoil and hatred.

> *Then Amnon hated her with very great hatred, so that the hatred with which he hated her was greater than the love with which he had loved her. And Amnon said to her, "Get*

DECISION TEN

up! Go!" (2 Samuel 13:15)

Tamar's brother Absalom, upon hearing of Amnon's violation, quietly hated his brother. For two years, he said nothing and did nothing, but during that time his hatred only grew. Rather than confront Amnon regarding his sin, rather than talk to David about it, who could have rightly disciplined his son Amnon, Absalom took matters into his own hands. He was focused on "getting even"; doing what needed to be done, in his mind, to judge the evil action of Amnon.

> *...Amnon alone is dead. For by the command of Absalom this has been determined from the day he violated his sister Tamar. (2 Samuel 13:32)*

Absalom sought revenge; he harbored hatred; he carried out his evil deed in response to Amnon's evil deed. Sin gave birth to further sin.

How different is David's response to Saul. Having been hunted by Saul, wrongly accused by Saul, having stood under Saul's failed attempts to kill him, David still refused to take matters into his own hands and seek revenge. At least twice David had clear opportunity to end Saul's life, in what some might say would have been justified revenge. But, he didn't do it. He chose to leave the matter of judgment to God.

> *And the men of David said to him, "Here is the day of which the Lord said to you, 'Behold, I will give your enemy into your hand, and you shall do to him as it shall seem good to you.' " Then David arose and stealthily cut off a corner of Saul's robe. And afterward David's heart struck him, because he had cut off a corner of Saul's robe. He said to his men, "The Lord forbid that I should do this thing to my lord, the Lord's anointed, to put out my hand*

against him, seeing he is the Lord's anointed." So David persuaded his men with these words and did not permit them to attack Saul. And Saul rose up and left the cave and went on his way. (1 Samuel 24:4–7)

But David said to Abishai, "Do not destroy him, for who can put out his hand against the Lord's anointed and be guiltless?" And David said, "As the Lord lives, the Lord will strike him, or his day will come to die, or he will go down into battle and perish. The Lord forbid that I should put out my hand against the Lord's anointed. But take now the spear that is at his head and the jar of water, and let us go." (1 Samuel 26:9–11)

God is not surprised by the actions of others towards us; He well knows those who have wickedly offended us, have in meanness caused us harm; have brought trouble on us in seeking to advantage themselves. God is righteous, and He will bring all acts to judgment. This is His responsibility, not ours. He calls us to be faithful, to make righteous choices, regardless of what others have done. Our choice to sin against another in retaliation to their sin against us is never condoned by God.

Beloved, never avenge yourselves, but leave it to the wrath of God, for it is written, "Vengeance is mine, I will repay, says the Lord." (Romans 12:19)

Do not say, "I will repay evil"; wait for the Lord, and he will deliver you. (Proverbs 20:22)

Decision Ten: I choose to live above the fray and not seek revenge.

DECISION TEN

It is easy for us to look at Joseph and put him in the category of one who "had every right" to seek revenge. Who would have blamed Joseph for immediately identifying himself to his brothers and sending them to prison? If we were watching Joseph's story unfold on the "big screen" would we not be cheering for him, laughing as he reminded them of his dreams, and then standing behind him as they were placed in the deepest, moldiest, dankest dungeon?

But that is not what Joseph did. He had no need to stoop to their level and respond to them, as they may have responded to him. He had no need to correct them when they identified themselves as honest men (Genesis 42:11). He chose to live above the fray, to live above the mean competitions of his brothers and the internal quarrels that would accomplish nothing. He chose not to seek revenge.

Instead of revenge, Joseph blessed them.

> *As they emptied their sacks, behold, every man's bundle of money was in his sack. And when they and their father saw their bundles of money, they were afraid. (Genesis 42:35)*

Even before he had revealed himself to them, he demonstrated that he had no evil intention toward them. Though he had accused them of being spies, had left them in prison for three days, and held back Simeon until they returned with Benjamin, this had nothing of the flavor of revenge. He had not seen his brother's in years; he didn't know their hearts and if they were truly looking out for their families, or had another hidden agenda; he probably assumed they were not spying for another ill motive, but made this accusation to hear their responses. His brother's actions and words demonstrated their honesty. Joseph chose to bless them.

WHEN GOD'S WILL AND MY WILL DISCONNECT

At the brother's second visit, instead of revenge, Joseph is delighted to see them, and blesses them with assurance of kindness.

> *And Joseph said to his brothers, "I am Joseph! Is my father still alive?" But his brothers could not answer him, for they were dismayed at his presence. (Genesis 45:3)*

Joseph reveals himself to his brothers with delight! Though alone in the room with his brothers, those without knew his emotion of joy, as he wept aloud, so that the Egyptians heard it (Genesis 45.2). This wasn't a sad time; this wasn't a time to blame; this wasn't a time to "get even." This was a time of rejoicing as a family had been reunited, and God's providential plan was being revealed.

> *Then he fell upon his brother Benjamin's neck and wept, and Benjamin wept upon his neck. And he kissed all his brothers and wept upon them. After that his brothers talked with him. (Genesis 45:14–15)*

In talking with his brothers he confidently assured them of his absolute acceptance of the events of the past. He declared it all as the wonderful work of a sovereign God. Yes, they had plotted evil. Yes, they rejoiced in his absence. Yes, they shed no tears as the caravan took him away, and in their minds he was as good as dead. But, that was in the past. Now, they could look and see that God had been at work in ways they could not have begun to imagine. Even their emotions of despising Joseph and their hatred toward him were all used by God to bring him to this place of influence.

> *And now do not be distressed or angry with yourselves because you sold me here, for God sent me before you to preserve life. For the famine has been in the land these two years, and there are yet five years in which there will be*

> *neither plowing nor harvest. And God sent me before you to preserve for you a remnant on earth, and to keep alive for you many survivors. So it was not you who sent me here, but God. He has made me a father to Pharaoh, and lord of all his house and ruler over all the land of Egypt. (Genesis 45:5-8)*

Interestingly, Joseph doesn't give them credit for their actions. Rather, he said to them, God sent me before you and it was not you who sent me here, but God. Joseph made the first choice – he was not in control, his brothers were not in control; God was in control. When we start here, the rest of the events of our lives begin to make sense. Sometimes, years go by before we begin to realize what God was doing; in some things we may never know how our experiences all work together. But, knowing they do, we can trust our Lord. And then, when those repeated circumstances happen that seem so out of place with our desires, when others work against us seemingly without cause, we can have confidence that our God is at work.

Again, Joseph takes the next step. He doesn't just not seek revenge, or just provide what we might term as a "small blessing" (their money returned to them), he went further in providing for his entire family for the much longer duration.

> *Hurry and go up to my father and say to him, 'Thus says your son Joseph, God has made me lord of all Egypt. Come down to me; do not tarry. You shall dwell in the land of Goshen, and you shall be near me, you and your children and your children's children, and your flocks, your herds, and all that you have. There I will provide for you, for there are yet five years of famine to come, so that you and your household, and all that you have, do not come to poverty.' (Genesis 45:9-11)*

Joseph clearly demonstrated to his family that they were more important than his pride; helping them was of far greater value than punishing them for wrongs they had committed years earlier; seeing the will of God being presented before their very eyes was of far greater joy than attacking them to "get even."

Also noteworthy, Joseph did not threaten his brothers to tell their father the truth of his vanishing; he did not force them to admit their guilt. This was not an issue for him. Joseph had forgiven his brothers, had accepted the sovereign design of God, had seen God's gracious working in his life, and now in his family. The past sins held little significance in comparison to the present blessing.

We are not told what the discussions were like among the sons and their father regarding the "how" of Joseph's disappearance or his arrival in Egypt and newfound prominence. We do not know if the brothers confessed their sin or continued speculative lies. It does not matter to us; we do not need to know. The important lesson: Joseph chose to live above the fray, to live above the sins of others, above past offenses, and give God glory in His magnificent design and present blessings.

Jesus said to His disciples:

> *"But I say to you who hear, Love your enemies, do good to those who hate you, bless those who curse you, pray for those who abuse you. (Luke 6:27-28)*

And Paul reiterated this same thought to the church at Rome:

> *Bless those who persecute you; bless and do not curse them. (Romans 12:14)*

The Lord's intention is for us to never pronounce judgment through revenge. Rather, He calls His children to live above the fray, to demonstrate mercy and grace, to proclaim to others that life is more than justifying ourselves in the presence of having been wronged. We should not focus on "getting even," for life is not about "getting even." It is about having the attitude of Christ, demonstrating the work of His Spirit, and realizing the things of eternity have far greater value than my reputation.

Again, Jesus, in talking with His disciples, instructed them to "live above the fray," to not be distracted by the sins of others:

> "You have heard that it was said, 'An eye for an eye and a tooth for a tooth.' But I say to you, Do not resist the one who is evil. But if anyone slaps you on the right cheek, turn to him the other also. And if anyone would sue you and take your tunic, let him have your cloak as well. And if anyone forces you to go one mile, go with him two miles. Give to the one who begs from you, and do not refuse the one who would borrow from you. "You have heard that it was said, 'You shall love your neighbor and hate your enemy.' But I say to you, Love your enemies and pray for those who persecute you, (Matthew 5:38–44)

Answering the following five questions will help determine if our attitude is one that pleases God:

Question #1: Am I desiring to give God glory?

Our desire for vengeance never brings glory to God. In choosing to live above the fray we can unquestionably give glory to God, knowing that He is in control and that He is working together in His sovereign plan those things which seem to be happening contrary to my desires and wishes. Participating in giving the Lord His Glory is by far the greater goal than seeking my own earthly glory.

So, whether you eat or drink, or whatever you do, do all to the glory of God. (1 Corinthians 10:31)

Question #2: Am I demonstrating the attitude of Christ?

In choosing to live above the fray, we demonstrate the attitude of Christ. Though it has become popularized and commercialized, the phrase, "What would Jesus do?" is worthy of consideration. We are told to follow in the footsteps of Christ (1 Peter 2.21), and we will only be able to do this as we are intent on knowing Christ. We want to know the attitude of Jesus Christ. He did not look at situations with His best interest in mind; He did not consider others for how He could be benefited. Rather, He always lived to bring glory to God first and then humbly considered us; He always thought about what would be best for us. Had He not, there would not have been motivation to go to the cross, to suffer the agony of crucifixion, to bear the penalty of our sin. In humility He gave Himself totally for our benefit.

Have this mind among yourselves, which is yours in Christ Jesus, who, though he was in the form of God, did not count equality with God a thing to be grasped, but emptied himself, by taking the form of a servant, being born in the likeness of men. And being found in human form, he humbled himself by becoming obedient to the point of death, even death on a cross. (Philippians 2:5–8)

Looking to Jesus, the founder and perfecter of our faith, who for the joy that was set before him endured the cross, despising the shame, and is seated at the right hand of the throne of God. (Hebrews 12:2)

In humility, Christ is our example. In living to accomplish a purpose, Christ is our example. We are to give; we are to think of others. We are to recognize that regardless of the actions of others, our responsibility is be usable to the Lord, to have our heart in right relationship with Him whereby He is able to work through us for His glory.

Question #3: Am I rejoicing in God's work?

In choosing to live above the fray we openly rejoice in God's work. It is a delight to see good things happening. We can easily rejoice in "our team" winning the game, in someone getting the awaited promotion or raise, or in our child reaching a much strived for accomplishment. But, a far greater delight is seeing the working of God in people's lives, in seeing His sovereign plan developing for a good we could not have foreseen. Our desire should be to have the perspective that regardless of what others have done, regardless of the personal offenses incurred, God is at work. This was the attitude of the prodigal's father – seeing his son come home (Luke 15:11-31). This was the attitude of the crowds seeing the lame man walking (Luke 5:17-26). This was the attitude of Naomi in seeing blessing come to Ruth (Ruth 2:20). This was the attitude of John in seeing believers growing in Christ.

> *I have no greater joy than to hear that my children are walking in the truth. (3 John 4)*

Question #4: Am I demonstrating a desire for revenge?

In choosing to live about the fray, we give assurance to others that revenge is not on our agenda. When others are confident our goal is not to "get even," then reconciliation is possible and probable; the potential of working together, living together, or serving together moves to a whole different arena. Whether the rift is in a marriage, a family, a church, or any other relationship, the intention of the "body" working together can then be realized.

> *For by the grace given to me I say to everyone among you not to think of himself more highly than he ought to think, but to think with sober judgment, each according to the measure of faith that God has assigned... So we, though many, are one body in Christ, and individually members one of another. Having gifts that differ according to the grace given to us... Love one another with brotherly affection. Outdo one another in showing honor... Bless those who persecute you; bless and do not curse them... Live in harmony with one another... Repay no one evil for evil, but give thought to do what is honorable in the sight of all. If possible, so far as it depends on you, live peaceably with all. Beloved, never avenge yourselves... Do not be overcome by evil, but overcome evil with good. (Romans 12:3-21)*

Our desire is not to harm God-given relationships and the ministry of Christ, but rather to do all possible to build His Church, to demonstrate the unity of the body, and in so doing to bring glory to God.

Question #5: Am I desiring good for others?

Fourthly, in choosing to live about the fray, we seek to bless, not curse; to encourage, not discourage; to build up, not tear down; to find the good, and not be focused on the bad. Joseph provided for his family through provisions in Canaan, provisions in transition, provisions in Goshen. He used what the Lord had given to him to bless others. He did not look only after his own wellbeing, but rather saw how God was using him for the benefit of others. Knowing he was in a position of power by the gracious act of God, he accepted that God wanted to use his ability and authority for helping others, for displaying before others the mighty works of the Lord, for proclaiming to others the glory of God.

> *Do nothing from selfish ambition or conceit, but in humility count others more significant than yourselves. Let each of you look not only to his own interests, but also to the interests of others. (Philippians 2:3-4)*

When all was "said and done" Joseph didn't change his position. He was consistent to the end. His actions of kindness and generosity were not for the benefit of his father Jacob, or his brother Benjamin. All he did was rooted in his firm belief of God's working through the events of life, whether seemingly good or bad, to accomplish His plan.

> *When Joseph's brothers saw that their father was dead, they said, "It may be that Joseph will hate us and pay us back for all the evil that we did to him." So they sent a message to Joseph, saying, "Your father gave this command before he died: 'Say to Joseph, "Please forgive the transgression of your brothers and their sin, because they did evil to you."' And now, please forgive the transgression of the servants of the God of your father." Joseph wept when they spoke to him. His brothers also came and fell down before him and said, "Behold, we are your servants." But Joseph said to them, "Do not fear, for am I in the place of God? As for you, you meant evil against me, but God meant it for good, to bring it about that many people should be kept alive, as they are today. So do not fear; I will provide for you and your little ones." Thus he comforted them and spoke kindly to them. (Genesis 50:15-21)*

Critical in our relationship with others is to be reminded of the entirety of God's redemptive plan. We don't know how the situations of our lives fit into the larger picture of history, but we do know that God knows, and that all He does is absolutely perfect. We must look at the "fray" as an evil component to our sinful nature that is seeking to bring about a digression in our attention from God's glory to our glory. Seeking revenge will only provide a momentary satisfaction at best. Living above the fray allows us to follow the exhortation given by Paul:

> *If then you have been raised with Christ, seek the things that are above, where Christ is, seated at the right hand of God. Set your minds on things that are above, not on things that are on earth. (Colossians 3:1-2)*

God delights in using His people in His ministry for His glory. When our eyes are focused on the sins of the world, the offenses of others, the wrongs committed against us, we are no longer focused on God's glory or His working, nor are we willingly giving Him all our praise.

Consider:

1. Have I struggled with revenge, with wanting to "get even" with a particular person who has offended me in the past? If so, what have I done?
2. What does God want me to do when another offends me?
3. What do I consider to be most unusual regarding Joseph's actions with his brothers?
   What was the reason Joseph was able to have this response?
4. How does Philippians 2:5 relate to 2:3-4?
   What do I need to do to change my attitude

DECISION TEN

to make it more like Christ?

5. Romans 12:3 states: Do not think of yourself more highly than you ought. Are there particular areas of my life I struggle with this, where I do think of myself better than others?
6. Is there a certain individual I know the Lord would have me to bless?
   What will I do about it?
7. What sin do I need to confess; what thinking needs to be transformed; what practice needs to change?

DECISION ELEVEN

I Choose to Forgive Others

Forgiveness is not easy. It means I have to let something go; I will not be able to hold it against another person any longer. In regards to forgiving another, the following comments are often heard.

"I have forgiven them," and then with a vengeful tone continue saying, "but I haven't forgotten."

"I will forgive them in time, but not now; I will have to wait to see if they change."

"I forgave them, but the consequences with what happened won't let me go forward."

"I forgave them, but if I never see them again, that will be fine with me."

The Christian wants to forgive, because they know God calls us to be forgivers. But, at the same time, we don't always want to let go of the offense. There is something within us, something lurking within our sinful nature, where we don't want to heal a broken relationship caused by another's sinful act. We are prone to want someone else to "pay" for their crime against us. It is difficult for us to accept that others have so wrongfully sinned against us, while at the same time we excuse our sin against another; we will hold the banner of our imperfectness, while expecting others to act perfectly in relationship with us.

However, a relationship cannot be healed without forgiveness. A husband and wife will never be able to restore their marriage unless they are willing to seek and grant forgiveness. Children will not be able to grow into a sibling relationship that provides support and help without a willingness to seek and grant forgiveness. A local church body will never be the vital organism God intended unless the members learn to seek and grant forgiveness. This is God's design. Jesus is the author and leader of forgiveness; He is the initiator and motivator of forgiveness; He is the example and standard of forgiveness.

Difficult situations will occur in our lives. We have already clearly seen where those unplanned turns in the course of our lives can totally change our direction, cancel our plans, and put us on a new and unknown path. From the first decision needing to be made, we know that God is in control and there is nothing that happens which is not measured in His sovereign design. We know that He is at work through the most awful of times, as well as in the times of great blessing, and everything in between, to bring about His glory and our good as He shapes us to be more like Jesus. When faced with the need to forgive another due to a personal violation or offense, truth must not be forgotten. Refusing to forgive reverts back to our discussion in Decision Ten, where we choose to seek revenge.

Not forgiving and "living above the fray" are not compatible. To live above the fray I must forgive; to refuse to forgive is intentionally continuing to judge another, wanting them to compensate us for their deed – having to do something to gain forgiveness, to be acceptable before God, or in this case, before others. There is the desire for another to "work" their way to forgiveness, to pay back what they owe. In refusing to forgive, we seek to hold power over another and resist the work of the Spirit in healing.

As Jesus spoke to his disciples about our treatment of and relationship with others, the disciples asked a question, and Jesus initially gave a short and concise answer.

> *Then Peter came up and said to him, "Lord, how often will my brother sin against me, and I forgive him? As many as seven times?" Jesus said to him, "I do not say to you seven times, but seventy-seven times. (Matthew 18:21–22)*

Forgiveness should have no limits. We are not to say, "I forgave him yesterday, and that's it; once is enough." In our Lord's forgiving His people, He never says, "I forgave you yesterday, or last week, or for that same sin once before; you had your opportunity; now you have to pay for it." nor should this passage be taken in an unnatural literal sense, intending for someone to keep tabs of his "forgiveness moments" and quit when he reaches seventy seven (or as some translations state, seventy times seven; or 490 times). In following the example of Christ, our forgiving others should also be unlimited; as His mercy is unending, so should be ours.

Jesus continued to further explain forgiveness with the following parable.

> *"Therefore the kingdom of heaven may be compared to a king who wished to settle accounts with his servants.*

> *When he began to settle, one was brought to him who owed him ten thousand talents. And since he could not pay, his master ordered him to be sold, with his wife and children and all that he had, and payment to be made. So the servant fell on his knees, imploring him, 'Have patience with me, and I will pay you everything.' And out of pity for him, the master of that servant released him and forgave him the debt. But when that same servant went out, he found one of his fellow servants who owed him a hundred denarii, and seizing him, he began to choke him, saying, 'Pay what you owe.' So his fellow servant fell down and pleaded with him, 'Have patience with me, and I will pay you.' He refused and went and put him in prison until he should pay the debt. (Matthew 18:23-30)*

At the servant's pleading, his master had graciously cancelled the debt and did not hold it against him. He had forgiven it; the debt was gone from the page. However, the forgiven man did not follow his master's example. Finding a fellow servant who owed him money, he took the man before the authorities and had him imprisoned until the debt could be repaid. Though he wanted mercy for himself, he knew nothing of demonstrating mercy to others. His calloused action only demonstrated his lack of appreciation for what his master had done for him.

The believer who understands the gracious forgiveness of God, who realizes the enormity of his sinful debt Jesus took upon Himself on the cross, who knows what it means to be set free from the bondage of guilt, sin, and sin's punishment will be eager to demonstrate the same mercy to another. We must realize that only by the grace of God are we forgiven; only by the blood of Christ are we forgiven; only by the delight of God's mercy are we forgiven. Knowing He has been merciful to us, sinners, unworthy of any grace, how can we boldly say that another's sin is greater than mine, that another's sin should not be forgiven, that another should remain accountable for the penalty of his sinful actions? Are we better than the other person? Are we more deserving of God's mercy? Are we more worthy to be redeemed? Are we more valuable and should be forgiven when we have sinned? Absolutely not! In seeing ourselves before the Holy God, we should all say with Paul: Wretched man that I am! Who will deliver me from this body of death? (Romans 7:24). Every believer should see himself in this wretched condition only deserving the fullest punishment of hell under the wrath of the Almighty God. Yet God, in His mercy grants us full freedom from any bondage of sin, so that now the believer can say, There is therefore now no condemnation for those who are in Christ Jesus (Romans 8:1).

Another argument often used to justify our unforgiving hearts can be heard in the words, "but, I'm not God; God is perfect; He can forgive; I can't." Wrong. Has God ever asked us to do anything we cannot do; has He ever placed a command before us which cannot be kept?" Absolutely not! Forgiveness is a decision: a decision not to hold on to past actions, not to have past offenses dictate our negative actions towards another, not to allow another's sin grow into bitterness that is deeply rooted within our hearts.

Is this truth not reinforced with the words of Christ in instructing us how to pray, when He said, forgive us our debts, as we also have forgiven our debtors (Matthew 6:12)? The point is this: we seek forgiveness as we forgive; we forgive as we know we have been forgiven.

The situation should not determine forgiveness. The magnitude of sin should not determine forgiveness. The hurt and pain experienced should not determine forgiveness. The forgiveness of God should determine our willingness to forgive and give us the enablement, the heart's desire, to forgive.

Decision Eleven: I choose to forgive others, and not accept bitterness.

Although the word "forgive" is not specifically used in these fourteen chapters of the Joseph account, the principle is clearly demonstrated; his actions indicated forgiveness. From the following passages, there is unquestionable evidence that Joseph did not let the sins of the past separate him from what God was presently doing. All his interactions expressed heart-rooted forgiveness.

When forgotten by the restored cupbearer, we can only imagine how Joseph felt. The hopes he had of being out of prison and into a better place slowly faded away into oblivion. The cupbearer had other things to do, other responsibilities, other motivations. Remembering Joseph was not his priority. In our way of thinking, we could understand Joseph becoming angry and bitter. Once Joseph was out of prison, we would not have faulted him if he would have chosen to look up the cupbearer and bluntly remind him of his failure and punish him for his forgetfulness. However, we see nothing of this activity. The indication is that Joseph forgave; that he moved forward; that he did not allow the failure of another to hinder what he could do. There appears to be nothing of bitterness toward him. When offended, in the absence of bitterness we can know there has been forgiveness.

From the moment Joseph saw his brothers, there is no suggestion of anger and bitterness. Rather, the opposite is evident.

> *Then he turned away from them and wept. And he returned to them and spoke to them… (Genesis 42:24)*

Every indication points to these being tears of joy. Joseph was seeing his brothers for the first time in 13 years. There was no bitterness; there was no animosity; there was no desire for retaliation. He had already chosen, whether this happened on the road to Egypt or at some other time, to forgive his brothers and not to hold their actions against them.

Initially Joseph placed his brothers in prison: And he put them all in custody for three days (Genesis 42.17). He could have kept all ten of his brothers in prison. He could have made them pay through hard labor for their sin against him. But, he did not. Rather than hold the past against them, he knew the grace and design of God held far greater importance.

> He replied, "Peace to you, do not be afraid. Your God and the God of your father has put treasure in your sacks for you. I received your money." Then he brought Simeon out to them. (Genesis 43:23)

Well knowing how the money was restored, Joseph's steward assured the brothers that the returned money in their sacks was an act of God. Joseph chose to bless his family. He had no need to gain from them, no need to add to his wealth or that of the nation because of their misfortune. Having a willingness to bless those who have acted offensively indicated a forgiving heart.

> Then Joseph hurried out, for his compassion grew warm for his brother, and he sought a place to weep. And he entered his chamber and wept there. (Genesis 43:30)

Seeing his brother Benjamin, along with the others, brought tears to Joseph's eyes. His overwhelming joy in seeing Benjamin was a far greater joy than any bitterness against his brothers who sold him into slavery could ever have been. The act of unkindness was long past; the joy of the present was consuming; knowing God was at work was reason for rejoicing. True rejoicing is evidence of a forgiving heart.

> *So Joseph said to his brothers, "Come near to me, please." And they came near. And he said, "I am your brother, Joseph, whom you sold into Egypt. And now do not be distressed or angry with yourselves because you sold me here, for God sent me before you to preserve life. For the famine has been in the land these two years, and there are yet five years in which there will be neither plowing nor harvest. And God sent me before you to preserve for you a remnant on earth, and to keep alive for you many survivors. So it was not you who sent me here, but God. He has made me a father to Pharaoh, and lord of all his house and ruler over all the land of Egypt. (Genesis 45:4–8)*

Again, there is no anger in Joseph's voice; there is no hostility; there is only delight. There was a wonderful sense of relief in revealing himself to his brothers. Having known it himself, but now being able to convey to them the design of God in bringing him to Egypt is absolute joy. There is no need for their fear; there is no need for their concern. All regret of sin is past. Joseph knew of their guilt they felt deep within, as they had previously conversed with themselves in his presence without knowledge of his full understanding. Giving God credit in accomplishing His purpose is further evidence of a forgiving heart.

> *Then they said to one another, "In truth we are guilty concerning our brother, in that we saw the distress of his soul, when he begged us and we did not listen. That is why this distress has come upon us." And Reuben answered them, "Did I not tell you not to sin against the boy? But you did not listen. So now there comes a reckoning for*

his blood." They did not know that Joseph understood them, for there was an interpreter between them. (Genesis 42:21-23)

In being able to convey to his brothers his identity, he was able then to relieve them of all fears. This was not God punishing them; Joseph was not to punish them. Rather, they could now rejoice in the wonderful work of God's design.

There is one further indication that forgiveness had happened in Joseph's heart. He had freedom to be with his brothers, and certainly assured them of their freedom in his presence.

> 'Say to Joseph, "Please forgive the transgression of your brothers and their sin, because they did evil to you." ' And now, please forgive the transgression of the servants of the God of your father." Joseph wept when they spoke to him. His brothers also came and fell down before him and said, "Behold, we are your servants." But Joseph said to them, "Do not fear, for am I in the place of God? As for you, you meant evil against me, but God meant it for good, to bring it about that many people should be kept alive, as they are today. So do not fear; I will provide for you and your little ones." Thus he comforted them and spoke kindly to them. (Genesis 50:17-21)

It is only mentioned once that Joseph's brothers asked for forgiveness, and then it is under the guise of their dad making the request on their behalf. It is interesting to note, that in this final chapter of Joseph's life and relationship with his brothers, they are deceitful. There is no indication Jacob had ever made this request; there is no indication that Jacob thought Joseph might hold their earlier sin against them; there is no indication Jacob even knew of their sin. Yet, it their lack of faith in God's working and in their doubt of Joseph's words of assurance, they used the authority of their dead father for their own benefit. They had not learned.

However, Joseph's response clearly indicated his forgiving them was complete. Forgiveness had happened a long time prior to this meeting. Joseph had accepted the providential plan of God. He knew his brothers had sinned. But, he chose to not hold this sin against "their account." He let the sin go; he put it behind him, as he realized the design of God to accomplish His plan in the redemption of His people. Not holding on to past sins is evidence of forgiveness.

Yes, there are consequences to sin. Joseph faced severe consequences. However, those consequences do not have to be looked at as a negative mark in our lives. Rather, we must remember the full truth of Scripture, and claim what Paul wrote,

> *And we know that for those who love God all things work together for good, for those who are called according to his purpose. (Romans 8:28)*

If we believe this, then we cannot choose to hold grudges, bitterness, anger, or any other negative emotion or action against another person. We look for healing and restoration. Though we cannot change the past, we can learn from it, and choose to move forward as the forgiven children of God, better equipped and more conformed to the image of Christ in the doing of His will.

Unrequested forgiveness

One question should be answered: How do I grant forgiveness when it has not been requested? The answer is simple: the same way as when it is requested. When the brothers asked Joseph, supposedly on behalf of their father to grant them forgiveness, Joseph did not specifically respond to this. Why not? First, they did not ask. Secondly, as previously discussed, this had been a matter settled in his mind and heart a long time previously. Whether or not someone asks us to forgive them, we can still grant it. We can still seek to have the relationship healed; we can still determine to never bring it up again or go hold it against them; we can still resist any desire to hold bitterness or anger against them. Our forgiving is not dependent on the other person. It is dependent on our decision in response to God's grace.

Christ's forgiveness of us is not based on anything we do; there is absolutely nothing I can do to gain His favor. True, in conviction of sin, I seek His forgiveness; but His forgiving is not dependent on my request. Likewise, my forgiving another should not be dependent on their request.

Bearing with one another and, if one has a complaint against another, forgiving each other; as the Lord has forgiven you, so you also must forgive. (Colossians 3:13)

If there has been offense, I should choose to forgive. When one comes under conviction of the Spirit and chooses to request forgiveness, then they have the joy of knowing the application of forgiveness in their lives. Then relationships can be reconciled because they have been obedient to the Spirit of God working within them.

Forgive others, regardless[38]

---

38 There is a strong opposing view which I resist. It says that forgiveness can only happen when one requests to be forgiven; I cannot forgive without another seeking to be forgiven. I believe there are sufficient examples in Scripture to dispel this. For instance: In the account of the forgiving father and returning son, the son never asks for forgiveness; the father has obviously forgiven the son before ever seeing him in the distance (Luke 15:20). Paul exhorts believers to be forgivers (Ephesians 4:32). And, does not Christ forgive us of all sin, and not just when I specifically ask Him to forgive me? Are there any sins that are not forgiven by Christ? Therefore, when Paul exhorts us to forgive as Christ forgives, does he expect we will hold on to sin until another comes

DECISION ELEVEN

Having gone through difficult times, having been the victim of another's offense, having repeatedly faced unexplainable trouble at the hands of another, the following principles in choosing to forgive others should be remembered.

In requesting forgiveness, the one being spoken to has to do something; there is a question that must be answered. When we seek God's forgiveness, He forgives – fully and completely.

> *If we confess our sins, he is faithful and just to forgive us our sins and to cleanse us from all unrighteousness. (1 John 1:9)*

When we forgive another, we are making a decision which involves a commitment to them.

First, we agree to not repeatedly bring it up, to not hold the sin against the other person.[39] Holding it against them means we choose to continue punishing the person because of past deeds. Forgiveness means "gone."

Second, we are agreeing to not let it, by any means or in any way, asking.

The missing element when forgiveness is not requested is the restoration of broken relationships. This is true in regards to our relationship with the Lord as well as others. When we have sinned and do not seek forgiveness, there is a break in fellowship with the Lord and we cannot expect His blessings. When a husband sins against his wife, he cannot expect the Lord to answer his prayers, until forgiveness takes place. Similarly, in relationship with others, the broken relationship cannot be restored until there is a willingness to seek forgiveness and to forgive. Then two individuals who have been severed by sin are able to rejoice in the restorative work of God.

39 Not continuing to talk about a previous sin is critical in forgiveness. This recognizes that the sin, though it may result in lasting consequences, has no value in discussion. Similarly, it is important to never talk about the offender's sin to others, to rehearse what they had done, or to speak in slanderous tones.

Only when mutually agreed upon and for the purpose of bringing help and encouragement to another, should the previous sin be brought into a conversation. In this, it is never discussed in an insulting or condemning manner, but as an example to help others overcome sin and demonstrate the difference made because of the mercy of God and of a forgiving believer.

separate future relationships. Therefore, saying "I forgive you but I never want to see you again," is not an option.

Third, we want any torn relationship to be healed. When Christ forgives us, there is no more separation in our relationship, and in forgiveness there should be no separation in our relationship with others.

Fourth, knowing that we do not have a perfect "forgetfulness" as does God, we agree to not dwell on the past sin, to put it out of our mind, to not repeatedly entertain negative thoughts as to the sin or the one having offended, to not hold it against the other person, and to not let it have any bearing on our future relationship.

As we are called to not harbor anger or bitterness toward another, but rather to be willing to forgive others of any offense against us – we must follow through and do it!

> *Let all bitterness and wrath and anger and clamor and slander be put away from you, along with all malice. Be kind to one another, tenderhearted, forgiving one another, as God in Christ forgave you. (Ephesians 4:31–32)*

Our forgiving is not to be limited. The Lord calls us to be a forgiver of others, regardless of the incident, the impact, or the reoccurrence.

Forgiveness guidelines:
- Forgiveness should never be optional for the believer, regardless of the circumstances.
- Forgiveness frees the believer to love and to serve both God and others.
- Forgiveness is not solely dependent on another person asking for forgiveness.

- Forgiveness encourages the healing of broken relationships.
- Forgiveness is always motivated by our being forgiven by God.
- Forgiveness is a command.

Be kind to one another, tenderhearted, forgiving one another, as God in Christ forgave you. Therefore be imitators of God, as beloved children. And walk in love, as Christ loved us and gave himself up for us, a fragrant offering and sacrifice to God. (Ephesians 4:32–5:2)

The Joy of Forgiveness

In forgiveness, there is great blessing; in forgiveness restoration is possible. Apart from forgiveness there is no restoration; without forgiveness bitterness develops a strong root in one's life. God chose to forgives us and bring us into relationship with Himself. He delights in forgiveness. Our response should be no different but to delight in forgiving others in order to have and enjoy restored relationships which can bring glory to God.

Consider:

1. How do I respond to being forgiven by God; to being cleansed of all sin?
2. How does being forgiven impact my daily living?
3. Are there certain people I do not want to forgive; that I have a difficult time forgiving?
   What is my response to these individuals when I think about them or see them?
   What response does God desire I have toward them?
4. Have I seen a relationship restored in direct response to forgiveness?

Do I think some relationships are beyond restoration?

5. Am I more prone to say "I'm sorry" than "Would you please forgive me?"

   What is the difference between the two?

6. What is the commitment I make when I tell someone I forgive them?

7. What sin do I need to confess; what thinking needs to be transformed; what practice needs to change?

DECISION TWELVE

I Choose to Serve Others

Blessing and serving are closely related. Blessing is using what we have to encourage, support, or to build up another individual in their current situation. Serving is blessing with an added dimension. It is doing something; it is going out of our way, using our abilities and resources to help another person in their needs. It is doing for another something they cannot necessarily do for themselves, or taking what they can do and doing it for them. Serving is using the gifts God has given us to bring glory to His Name.

Moms are servants. My wife, Barbara, has certainly demonstrated this character quality over the years in a commendable manner. She served our two children when they were infants. They did not realize it, but all those diaper changes, clean-ups, spoon-fed meals, clothes changes, coats on and off, laundry done are certainly clear expressions of serving at its height. She served, expecting nothing in return; she served, knowing they depended on her; she served with a heart filled with love and grace.

As our children grew, and two had grown to three, she never quit. There was still laundry to be done, school lunches to prepare, meals to prepare, homework to help with, schoolwork to motivate to do, housework to complete; plus being a taxi driver to multiple events and requirements, and an encourager and disciplinarian. All the time serving; sometimes appreciated, and sometimes not. Again, her motivation stemmed from a heart-rooted love for our children and the joy received from her God-given privilege of being a mom.

Regarding our son Jonathan, serving has taken various twists through the years. From taking him to an early-childhood program at age eighteen months, to sitting in numerous meetings with "professionals" trying to determine the best course of action to take in helping him develop his abilities, to working with him in varying programs and therapies, to driving him to various appointments, to labeling his clothing—she has served him. And in return? Generally unaware of her sacrifice in serving, there are those rare but special times Jonathan will give a winning smile that says "Thank you, Mom."

Though years have passed since our children were small, and now that all of them live in their own homes, serving takes on a different form. Sometimes it comes through watching grandchildren or helping from a distance. But, she still serves, keeping the focus on others, not on herself.

This is service. It is not about us, about what we gain, or how we might benefit. It is about others. And, it is about seeing others through the eyes of the Lord.

In seeing the difficult situations of our lives, it is easy to become self-focused. We can easily spend our days thinking about what we don't have, have missed, or have lost; or in the serving venue, thinking about how unappreciated we have been. This only brings us to a downward spiral of discouragement and depression. We only want to do what is going to be of benefit to us that will help us through the next hour, the next day, or the next week. It takes work to think about others; it takes effort to be in a place where others are. However, we must remember, the Lord does not suggest we should "hold up" in a shelter until everything is going the way we want it to go. Rather, it may be that in the midst of the difficult situation the Lord wants us to serve; in His sovereign design He may have placed us there for the benefit of someone else. We must look beyond ourselves to see what God is doing, and wants to do in and through us, for His glory.

Paul gave this encouragement:

> *Do nothing from selfish ambition or conceit, but in humility count others more significant than yourselves. Let each of you look not only to his own interests, but also to the interests of others. Have this mind among yourselves, which is yours in Christ Jesus, (Philippians 2:3–5)*

Decision Twelve: I choose to serve others, seeking a right focus.

Contrary to what may have been called, "popular opinion," Joseph was right where God wanted him, doing what God wanted him to do. The unusual set of circumstances put him in positions he would not have initially chosen. However, he chose not to focus on himself, but rather willfully chose to serve others. He saw needs, and knew that God had gifted him to meet those needs.

His service likely began back in Canaan. From what we can discern, he served his father without hesitation. He watched sheep when he was told to watch sheep; he went to his brothers when he was told to go. He understood honoring and obeying parents.

Taken to Egypt, he was a model servant. In Potiphar's house, he excelled in all he did. When removed from the position of honor with Potiphar, he served the prison warden commendably, and then ultimately he served in Pharaoh's court. Was there benefit in this for him? No doubt. Perhaps he saw the potential of promotion, of better living quarters, of better meals, or more responsibility and prominence in the future. But, perhaps there was also an inner drive the Lord had given him to do the very best he could in whatever he did. Regardless of the full motivation, he didn't rebel when put in places of service. He served, and He served well.

In regards to selfless service, a clear example is seen in relationship with his brothers. He could have been kind to them; he could have blessed them; he could have provided for them, all without fully serving them. But he went beyond this to give of himself he served. He had them brought to his home, and they realized that to have virtually "unknown travelers" brought into the home of a national leader was indeed an unusual gesture.

> *When Joseph saw Benjamin with them, he said to the steward of his house, "Bring the men into the house, and slaughter an animal and make ready, for the men are to dine with me at noon." (Genesis 43:16)*

A meal was prepared of fine quality, and the brothers were carefully seated according to their age. In doing this, he honored them by clearly giving the place of prominence to the eldest. Each was given a goodly portion, but Benjamin's was five times as much. Now, whether he ate that much more than his brothers, or if it was just an emphasis of privilege, we don't know. The point: Joseph went well beyond what would have been expected, in order to do what God expected. He served.

> *And they sat before him, the firstborn according to his birthright and the youngest according to his youth. And the men looked at one another in amazement. Portions were taken to them from Joseph's table, but Benjamin's portion was five times as much as any of theirs. And they drank and were merry with him. (Genesis 43:33–34)*

After having revealed himself to his brothers, again Joseph's desire to serve his brothers, their families, and his father is seen in his making provisions for them. Though having ruling authority in the nation, in order to bring his entire family to live in Egypt demanded Pharaoh's permission; and this was granted. He could have decided just to provide for them; to continue giving them grain along with the assurance that as long as the famine existed, their needs would be met. However, he didn't stop with the minimum; he went further to bring them to Goshen.

> *Joseph said to his brothers and to his father's household, "I will go up and tell Pharaoh and will say to him, 'My brothers and my father's household, who were in the land of Canaan, have come to me. And the men are shepherds, for they have been keepers of livestock, and they have brought their flocks and their herds and all that they have.' When Pharaoh calls you and says, 'What is your occupation?' you shall say, 'Your servants have been keepers of livestock from our youth even until now, both we and our fathers,' in order that you may dwell in the land of Goshen, for every shepherd is an abomination to the Egyptians." (Genesis 46:31–34)*

Joseph never quit serving. Evidence of this is seen following the death of his father, as Joseph continued to provide for his brothers and their families. He wanted to help them, provide for them, and gave of himself to make it happen. He assured his brothers:

> *So do not fear; I will provide for you and your little ones." Thus he comforted them and spoke kindly to them. (Genesis 50:21)*

God placed Joseph in Egypt to serve; to serve Him and to serve others. He wasn't there to bemoan his plight, but rather to open his eyes to what he could do. Throughout Joseph's life, the significance of his service is clearly seen in the development of God's redemptive plan. Though the people would be provided for during the days of Joseph, they would eventually fall into severe bondage. Then, after years of oppression they would eventually be released in a remarkable exodus orchestrated by the hand of God. This would then begin their trek to the Promised Land. What is seen through this? This is God's wonderful picture of our redemption, of our deliverance from the bondage of sin, from the hopelessness of despair to deliverance and freedom. God used Joseph, his life and service, along with his attitude to accomplish His purpose and fulfill His design, determined before the earth was ever formed.

In serving, the following six principles should be kept in focus:

Principle #1: *God made us to serve*

Having designed us with purpose, we were made to serve; to serve God and to serve others. We were not made to satisfy ourselves and our desires, to fulfill our goals and have fun in the days of life we have been given on the earth. This isn't to say, we can't have goals and fun; I am saying that we must recognize our primary purpose is being an instrument of God, for use in His hands for His glory.

> *...Present yourselves to God as those who have been brought from death to life, and your members to God as instruments for righteousness. (Romans 6:13)*

Christ is our example. He came as a servant.

> *...even as the Son of Man came not to be served but to serve, and to give his life as a ransom for many." (Matthew 20:28)*

> *For to this you have been called, because Christ also suffered for you, leaving you an example, so that you might follow in his steps. (1 Peter 2:21)*

We have been made to serve, to accomplish God's purpose. When we fail to serve, we fail to please God.

> *For we are his workmanship, created in Christ Jesus for good works, which God prepared beforehand, that we should walk in them. (Ephesians 2:10)*

Principle #2: God has made us to serve, where we are

Joseph served where he was: at home under his father's authority, as a servant, as a prisoner, as a brother, and as a leader. God called him to serve others, and he did. Paul followed the same principle. Whether in churches, homes, on the street, or in prison he recognized God had called him to be a servant. Our desire should be no less. We don't have to wait until _____ in order to be effective as a servant. We can begin serving now. How do we do this? We resign ourselves under His authority to do His will in every way in this day.

> *It is my eager expectation and hope that I will not be at all*

> *ashamed, but that with full courage now as always Christ will be honored in my body, whether by life or by death. (Philippians 1:20)*

> *Therefore do not be ashamed of the testimony about our Lord... But I am not ashamed, for I know whom I have believed, and I am convinced that he is able to guard until that Day what has been entrusted to me. (2 Timothy 1:8, 12)*

Though the circumstances may be difficult, and we end up in what would be called "odd" situations, those not according to our liking or design, this is where we are, and this is where we should be serving.

Principle #3: God is teaching us to serve, where we are

Every situation of our lives is used by God, and equipping us for the next. We could not successfully face the situations of today had He not already brought us through others. Each has purpose, each is in order. Joseph was not equipped to be ruler under Pharaoh when he was taken out of the cistern. There was first preparation time. All events were groundwork for the next. The slavery, the imprisonment, and the disappointments, were all used in training Joseph to lead.

We can expect God working within us and through us in similar ways. Every situation is being used to develop us to serve our Lord and to serve others.

> *Blessed be the God and Father of our Lord Jesus Christ, the Father of mercies and God of all comfort, who comforts us in all our affliction, so that we may be able to comfort those who are in any affliction, with the comfort with which we ourselves are comforted by God. For as we share abundantly in Christ's sufferings, so through Christ we*

> share abundantly in comfort too. If we are afflicted, it is for your comfort and salvation; and if we are comforted, it is for your comfort, which you experience when you patiently endure the same sufferings that we suffer. (2 Corinthians 1:3-6)

Principle #4: God has opened our eyes to serve, to see other people where they are

In the new birth, God has given us new eyes that we might see other people as He sees them. In being made new, we have a new vision toward others. This allows us to see people as those who are yet condemned, and facing an eternity in hell, or to see them as participating with us in the church as the redeemed.

> Therefore, if anyone is in Christ, he is a new creation. The old has passed away; behold, the new has come. (2 Corinthians 5:17)

> "For who has understood the mind of the Lord so as to instruct him?" But we have the mind of Christ. (1 Corinthians 2:16)

In regards to sinners, yet lost, God calls us to go to them with the Gospel, to proclaim to them His wonderful grace. He wants us to see their need and to do all possible to bring them to the Savior.

> Then he said to his disciples, "The harvest is plentiful, but the laborers are few; therefore pray earnestly to the Lord of the harvest to send out laborers into his harvest." (Matthew 9:37-38)

In regards to believers, He desires we see them as those who have been redeemed just like ourselves; to see them as sinners rescued by

God and cleansed by the blood of Christ; to see them as those not yet perfected, but being perfected through the continual work of His Spirit in our lives. We are no better than they; we are together members of the body of Christ.

> *For you were called to freedom, brothers. Only do not use your freedom as an opportunity for the flesh, but through love serve one another. For the whole law is fulfilled in one word: "You shall love your neighbor as yourself."* (Galatians 5:13-14)

Principle #5: God has designed us to serve others, not to be self-serving

Joseph was intent on serving others. Jesus was intent on serving others. We should be so intent on serving others. As members of the body of Christ, He has called us to serve together in His body. We are not isolationists, alone doing what we are comfortable in doing. Rather, we are part of a body the Church of Jesus Christ.

> *So then you are no longer strangers and aliens, but you are fellow citizens with the saints and members of the household of God, built on the foundation of the apostles and prophets, Christ Jesus himself being the cornerstone, in whom the whole structure, being joined together, grows into a holy temple in the Lord. In him you also are being built together into a dwelling place for God by the Spirit.* (Ephesians 2:19-22)

Principle #6: God has gifted us to serve

God does not make us useless; He does not place us on this earth to be ineffective; He does not want us to do nothing. He has made us to serve; He has gifted us to serve; He has commanded us to serve in

DECISION TWELVE

love.

Joseph was uniquely gifted by God. From the account of his life we can discern one of his gifts was in administration; he had a heart of compassion and he desired to serve. He used these gifts in accomplishing the purpose God intended. Having been transported to Egypt, he didn't sit back and say, "OK, my life is done; there is nothing I can do; I will just do the minimal to get by and call this one wasted life." No, he took every opportunity and he became a servant before others, using what God had given to him.

Every believer has been uniquely gifted by God and called to use those gifts in the body of Christ.[40]

> *For as in one body we have many members, and the members do not all have the same function, so we, though many, are one body in Christ, and individually members one of another. Having gifts that differ according to the grace given to us, let us use them: if prophecy, in proportion to our faith; (Romans 12:4-6)*

Gifts are not for us to keep to ourselves, but rather to be used. He has enabled us in the fulfilling of His purpose, to serve Him and others. When we limit God's ability to use us in the less than desirable situations of our lives, we sin; we doubt God; we neglect to trust that we are usable to God.[41]

---

[40] Many volumes have been written regarding the gifting of believers. The "gift lists" in Scriptures have been evaluated, dissected, and scrutinized with the goal of identifying how God gifts people. Evaluation tools have been developed to help individuals determine how they have been gifted. My response to these things: 1) It is true that all believers are gifted; 2) God desires every believer to use his gifts as He has intended; 3) The "gift lists" are a guide to help believers understand giftedness. However, I believe we can identify our gifts by asking three questions: 1) What am I good at? 2) What do I enjoy doing? and; 3) What have others affirmed as gifts in me? Then, our response: use our gifts, doing that which pleases the Lord, effectively serving others.

[41] Many people struggle with depression and purposelessness in life because they have simply failed to recognize they were made to serve. When individuals fail to do what God has equipped

Service is sacrifice. It is not for my benefit, but for the benefit of others. It is not for my gain, but rather to demonstrate the perfection of God's will.

> *I appeal to you therefore, brothers, by the mercies of God, to present your bodies as a living sacrifice, holy and acceptable to God, which is your spiritual worship. Do not be conformed to this world, but be transformed by the renewal of your mind, that by testing you may discern what is the will of God, what is good and acceptable and perfect. (Romans 12:1-2)*

Serving is contrary to the flesh; the sinful nature calls us to satisfy ourselves first. Therefore, it is important to ask these concluding questions:

- What am I doing for whom?
- Is my life focused on me, or on others?
- How has my current situation given me a unique opportunity to serve?
- What is God teaching me which enables me to better serve others?

When the situations of my life are not going according to my design, I must realize that the Lord has placed me in this unique situation to serve, which is part of His greater plan in bringing glory to His name

Consider:

1. How do I respond when I see others serving?

---

them to do, when they fail to follow through in using their God-given gifts, they can then expect to be miserable. When we are doing what God made us to do, we will know His joy, whatever the circumstances.

2. Do I believe I can serve others?
   In what ways do I believe I can serve?
3. In serving others, do I have the attitude of serving God?
   If not, what is my attitude?
4. Do I enjoy serving others?
   If not, am I trying to serve in a way I have not been gifted?
   If yes, what do I enjoy doing?
5. How do I believe God has gifted me?
   Am I using my gifts in serving others?
6. In what area would I like to serve that I am not currently serving?
   Is it possible for me to serve as I would like?
   What can I do to make it happen?
7. What sin do I need to confess; what thinking needs to be transformed; what practice needs to change?

DECISION THIRTEEN

I Choose to Accept My Emotions

Emotions are always present to some degree. We cannot avoid them. This is the way we are made. How we respond to our emotions can make a great difference in our responses to God and to others.

My emotions can surface at varying times, and sometimes when I would just as soon hide them. For instance, when watching a television commercial my tear ducts can open and flow and I quickly find a reason to leave the room and blow my nose. Why is it I do not want anyone else to know that the silly commercial hit a cord with me? Perhaps I feel vulnerable of what others may be thinking—that I am prompted to cry while watching a staged commercial! Our children just smile, and roll their eyes with that "Oh, Dad!" look.

There are a lot of emotions that swell up within us and can consume us:

- Sadness that comes in identifying with someone who is in great pain or distress

- Hurting for another who is facing a great tragedy and losing all they had
- Observing, from a distance, an entire community devastated by a natural disaster
- Joy in hearing a success story and being excited for the individual
- Anger at a situation where someone has purposefully hurt another
- Gladness at seeing a child's report card
- Hope, joy, or sadness (or all three) in recognizing life will be different as you observe the marriage of a child
- Grieving at the loss of a loved one
- Happiness experienced in being with one you love
- Hurting in being part of a broken relationship
- Despair when we lose perspective in life's journey

All are real; all are a part of who we are. The four following statements should be recognized in regarding our emotions and our response to them:

- Denying our emotions is denying who we are as God has made us.
- Letting our emotions guide us can lead to an unstable life, as they are likely to change with the day or event.
- Recognizing our emotions and keeping perspective can be used to help others in their trouble or growth.
- Accepting our emotions when they surface, resulting from our own difficult circumstances, can help us gain a proper outlook regarding our Lord's continued working.[42]

---

42   I do not propose to develop a theology of emotions or a full discussion of all the emotions of

However, we also realize that our response to emotions can be debilitating, seemingly preventing us from moving another step. They can tend to have absolute control over us and we can relinquish our upcoming path to their directing; or, they can strengthen our appreciation of God's creation and be used to further develop relationships.

Decision Thirteen: *I choose to accept my emotions, honoring both God and others.*

Knowing our emotions are real, and knowing they are going to impact who we are and how we respond in life's circumstances, we should carefully think about how we respond to our emotions, and if we are honoring God and others through them.

In looking at Joseph's life, I note seven particular emotions and Joseph's response to them.

One: the emotion of grief

We can only imagine what Joseph felt as he found his brothers after his long search.

> So when Joseph came to his brothers, they stripped him of his robe, the robe of many colors that he wore. And they took him and threw him into a pit. The pit was empty; there was no water in it. (Genesis 37:23-24)

Overpowered, humiliated, and mercilessly tossed into an empty cistern, Joseph landed with a flood of emotions going through him. Their hatred of him seemed to suddenly spew out like an open geyser. His future was unknown. Years later, when his brothers were standing

---

the Bible. My purpose here is to glean from Joseph and make applications that will be helpful for the believer when going through difficult times.

DECISION THIRTEEN

before Joseph in Egypt, they recounted their disgusting memory of what had happened.

> ...*We saw the distress of his soul, when he begged us and we did not listen. That is why this distress has come upon us."* (Genesis 42:21)

Knowing his life would be forever changed there was likely a deep sense of sadness and grief. He had been rejected by his brothers, separated from his beloved father and brother, and on his way to an unknown place to be involuntarily assigned a new and unknown vocation.

We do not know how Joseph responded to his captors; we do not know his countenance as they traveled to Egypt; we do not know if there were conversations with the Midianites or if he sat in total silence; we do not know if he was mocked by these strangers who had purchased him and brought him under subjection. It does seem apparent, however, that he did not let the vast array of emotions consume him or control him, at least not for long.

People may disappoint us and there may be sadness and grief that grips our hearts. However, we need to consider carefully our responses. Sulking and falling to depression will not change the situation. Thinking that quitting is better than having to endure the misery of a changed life will negatively affect us, those around us, our relationship with others, and our relationship with and witness for the Lord. How do we respond? We accept our situation and claim again the truths from the first decision: situations will happen that are out of our control, but we know that our God is in control. We rest in Him. Then, we accept that there will be pain in the change of relationships or situations, or in Joseph's situation, the severing of relationships with family. We cannot change what has happened; we are not able to turn back the clock and rewrite history. Though some life situations may again change and return to what would be called more "normal," some things will never change, as in the event of a loved one's death or the onslaught of an incurable disease. However, we can make the decision to honor God in it. We can choose to examine our life to see if our actions, thoughts, relationships are being controlled by our emotion, or if we are being controlled by the Spirit of God.

Two: the emotion of fear

The unknown can be fearful. Knowing the course of our life has drastically changed can produce an eerie awareness of walking into unknown and perhaps hostile territory. Fear can be all consuming.

What was Joseph thinking as he cried out to his brothers and they did nothing? Perhaps he heard them laughing, mocking him, telling stories, sarcastically thinking about what life would be like when he was gone. Adding to this, Joseph likely heard them plotting his future, as they devised a plan to sell him to the Midianite slave traders.

> *Then Judah said to his brothers, "What profit is it if we kill our brother and conceal his blood? Come, let us sell him to the Ishmaelites, and let not our hand be upon him, for he is our brother, our own flesh." And his brothers listened to him. Then Midianite traders passed by. And they drew Joseph up and lifted him out of the pit, and sold him to the Ishmaelites for twenty shekels of silver. They took Joseph to Egypt. (Genesis 37:26-28)*

Fear likely riveted through his body as he contemplated the potential of upcoming personal disaster and abuse. What knowledge he had of slavery in Egypt is unknown, but he likely knew enough to know it would not be pleasant. Where would he end up; who would be his master; how would he be treated; what would be the process of being sold; was his life going to be cut short? All these and countless more questions could have flooded his mind, filling him with unwanted fear. However, there is no indication he allowed these thoughts to control him. Rather, there is evidence he moved forward, trusting God's providential care in his life.

Later, when Joseph refused the sexual assaults from Potiphar's wife and ran (Genesis 39:11-12), fear likely pelted through him: fear of his own weakness; fear of his master discovering the incident; fear of Potiphar's wife overpowering him; fear of what would happen. In this situation his emotions helped to reinforce his resolve to purity. He did not want to fall into sin; he did not fall.

Fear can hold us spellbound, immobilizing us, and keeping us from experiencing God's provisions, from knowing His care, from seeing His power, and from seeing His glory. Though there are certainly fearful situations which thwart our expectations, we do not have to allow them to control our future.

> ...for God gave us a spirit not of fear but of power and love and self-control. (2 Timothy 1:6–7)

Fear is not from God; fear is not part of the "Fruit of the Spirit" (Galatians 5:22-23). Fear is of the flesh and used by the enemy to prevent us from trusting God. Our responsibility is to recognize God has sufficiently gifted us to live in His power, love, and control whatever the circumstances of life, and to live in them in such a manner as is pleasing to God and will bring Him glory.

Three: the emotion of anger[43]

Anger is a likely natural response when situations do not please us. We are wronged and we spew out in anger, somehow thinking that our vehemence is going to change the situation. Joseph is not seen as an angry man; there is no indication he was mad at his brothers, angry at Potiphar's wife, angry at Potiphar, or angry at the cupbearer. I mention it here because this emotion is so prevalent among so many. Mistreatment, hurting words, physical attacks, being ignored can all result in an angry response. We respond with, "They had no right to do that to me," or "Do they realize what they just did to me, how my life, my reputation has been changed. You bet I'm angry!"

In anger, it is important to ask two questions:

First, is my anger righteous? Righteous anger is becoming angry at the same things that anger God. Generally, our anger is far from righteous, as it is rooted in our selfish expectations and disappointments when things don't go the way we think they should or people don't respond as we would expect. Somehow our wants and desires are hindered, our pride is impacted, and our fleshly hearts take center stage. We respond in anger.

> *Know this, my beloved brothers: let every person be quick to hear, slow to speak, slow to anger; for the anger of man does not produce the righteousness of God. (James 1:19–20)*

Secondly, what is my anger accomplishing? We somehow erroneously think that by erupting in anger we are going to solicit another's attention and bring them into compliance with what we

---

43   For a greater understanding of anger, I suggest two works: Uprooting Anger, by Robert D. Jones; and "How to be Free from Bitterness" by Jim Wilson (an excellent booklet with valuable articles on anger, bitterness, forgiveness, the tongue, and others).

want to have happen. Wrong! It doesn't happen this way. Our anger generally produces additional anger, from ourselves as well as from others.

A soft answer turns away wrath, but a harsh word stirs up anger. (Proverbs 15:1)

Yelling at a passing car that didn't come to a complete stop at an intersection, humiliating your child for not completing a homework assignment, degrading your wife for not cleaning the house to your liking, or lashing out at an employee for not finishing a task is not going to produce righteousness. It may accomplish a change in behavior, but it is unlikely to do anything to change an attitude or the heart to become more Christ-like; it is more likely to sever a relationship than strengthen one.

What is the better response to those who offend us?

- Pray for those who offend us
- Forgive those who offend us
- Consider any sinful attitudes and responses we may have, and seek forgiveness (Matthew 7:1-5)
- Change what we can change to make the situation better
- Move forward with an expectation of God using our right choices for His glory

Four: the passionate emotion of physical desire

Joseph had been trusted by Potiphar and given full responsibility and authority over his entire household and all he owned. This now common slave had suddenly become a leader among his peers. Any joy he had in this position though was tainted by the presence of and continual sexual assaults by Potiphar's wife. He likely dealt with his own powerful, passionate physical desire. He was a young man. She was willing and tempting. Though he had resolved to not violate his master, we can imagine that his emotions were intense.[44]

Though the consequential results of this incident would be generally termed as less than desirable, Joseph remained faithful. Though his emotions may have been intense, he accepted them for what they were; he kept them in harmony with his convictions, and chose victory over sin. He knew any capitulation would be wrong; he chose not to act on them.

In regards to physical desire and temptation to sin, we must remember that there is never a situation which gives us license to do the wrong thing. No matter the strength of the emotion, we are never justified in saying, "I couldn't help it." This is a lie of the enemy, and must be rejected. We do not have to be controlled by sensually based emotions. God did not create us with the inability to control our feelings; He did not renew us in Christ to fall into sin; He did not indwell us with His Spirit to be controlled by the desires of the flesh.

Five: the emotion of sadness

We have already discussed the sadness Joseph felt when he was rejected by his brothers and thrust into an unwanted path. However, there may have been another time when sadness seemed overwhelming in his life. Though a slave, all was going well for him as he had been placed in charge of Potiphar's house. But then, instantaneously he was taken from a position of responsibility and plunged into prison. He was taken from prominence to confinement without cause; from a probable future of dependability to a dungeon of unknown future.

---

44 I also can accept that Joseph may have been totally repulsed by her, and his physical emotion was not an issue.

DECISION THIRTEEN

Severe loss. Facing the unknown. Subject of unjustifiable judgment. Unable to explain the condemning, misunderstood actions. All these things were a fertile field for great sadness, which could have led to immobility, depression, despair, isolation, and further feelings of not caring and not wanting to do anything. Thoughts can go through the mind of "how can I continue after all this…" For Joseph, he did not allow sadness to override responsibility. No doubt in the midst of confusion and change, sadness was present. However, it did not rule his heart and actions. He kept going. He was in a new place of responsibility, he did his best, and he was given greater responsibility.

When faced with the uncontrolled and overwhelming sadness of events, the believer can look forward. Sad things will happen in our lives. We are not immune from those happening. However, to allow the sadness to control our next step is denying the power and desire of God to use us. Paul wrote:

> *Blessed be the God and Father of our Lord Jesus Christ, the Father of mercies and God of all comfort, who comforts us in all our affliction, so that we may be able to comfort those who are in any affliction, with the comfort with which we ourselves are comforted by God. (2 Corinthians 1:3–4)*

The Lord gives us encouragement. The very thing we have faced, and His gracious working in our lives during those difficult times, may be His specific preparation for using us in the lives of others. The word comfort carries with it the meaning of encouragement. Our Lord encourages us, builds us up with His courage to face the next step in life, and in so doing delights in using us to encourage others to do the same.

WHEN GOD'S WILL AND MY WILL DISCONNECT

Six: the emotion of disappointment

It is that time when suddenly our throat falls into our stomach and we stand with a "deer in the headlights" look. We stop, amazed, that what we were certain was going to happen doesn't. Probably this is what Joseph dealt with when the cupbearer "forgot" the one who had perfectly interpreted his dream, as well as that of the executed chief baker.

Disappointments will happen. We need to accept them, but we don't have to let them rule our future. Our disappointments are based on our expectations that are rooted in our desires. The problem? It is all about us. Our responsibility is to be faithful; to be responsible before the Lord, anticipating His continued working for His glory.

> *For those who live according to the flesh set their minds on the things of the flesh, but those who live according to the Spirit set their minds on the things of the Spirit. (Romans 8:5)*

Is our mind set on the Spirit of God and His working, or is our mind set on us?

Job understood disappointing disaster. Having lost his entire family, except his wife, and all his earthly possessions we would not be overly critical of him had he sulked in disappointing grief. However, he did not sin; he did not curse God; he did not allow his emotions to control his responses.

> *And he said, "Naked I came from my mother's womb, and naked shall I return. The Lord gave, and the Lord has taken away; blessed be the name of the Lord." (Job 1:21)*

> *But he said to her… "Shall we receive good from God, and shall we not receive evil?" In all this Job did not sin with*

DECISION THIRTEEN

his lips. (Job 2:10)

When we remember the first decision, "that I am not in control" and trust that God's control is perfect, we don't need to be disappointed. Rather, we can be thankful, knowing our Lord has interrupted our designs to accomplish His perfect purpose.

> *I have said these things to you, that in me you may have peace. In the world you will have tribulation. But take heart; I have overcome the world." (John 16:33)*

> *Peace I leave with you; my peace I give to you. Not as the world gives do I give to you. Let not your hearts be troubled, neither let them be afraid. (John 14:27)*

Seven: the emotion of joy

Joseph's situation had taken him down new and never imagined roads. Likely he had come to accept that he did not know what was next, or would not begin to predict what roads his future may take. He had lost much, suffered much, struggled much, and been given much. At the time of seeing his brothers, according to the world's standards, he was at the height of success. We could presume that he was happy. He had a great position and was well respected, had a wife and two sons. Everything seemed to be going well for him.

However, none of this seems comparable to the joy he experienced in seeing his brothers and father. Repeatedly the joy of Joseph's heart swells up within him as he realizes God's working in the past and now his reunion with his family, which he possibly thought would never happen.

Then he turned away from them and wept. And he

> *returned to them and spoke to them. And he took Simeon from them and bound him before their eyes. (Genesis 42:24)*

> *Then Joseph hurried out, for his compassion grew warm for his brother, and he sought a place to weep. And he entered his chamber and wept there. (Genesis 43:30)*

> *And Joseph said to his brothers, "I am Joseph! Is my father still alive?" But his brothers could not answer him, for they were dismayed at his presence. (Genesis 45:3)*

> *Hurry and go up to my father and say to him, 'Thus says your son Joseph, God has made me lord of all Egypt. Come down to me; do not tarry. (Genesis 45:9)*

> *Then he fell upon his brother Benjamin's neck and wept, and Benjamin wept upon his neck. And he kissed all his brothers and wept upon them. After that his brothers talked with him. (Genesis 45:14–15)*

> *Then Joseph prepared his chariot and went up to meet Israel his father in Goshen. He presented himself to him and fell on his neck and wept on his neck a good while. (Genesis 46:29)*

Joy expressed in weeping. Joy expressed in revealing himself to his brothers. Joy expressed as he anticipated their quick return to Canaan and then to return with their father. Joy in reunion with those he loved.

Additionally, joy was evident in Joseph's life when his brothers came to him after the death of their father and he could reiterate to them once again God's providential design; when he assured them that he held nothing against them, that he was not about to judge the providential working of God, that they had nothing to fear. These are moments of joy, knowing and delighting in the eternal design of God being worked out in our lives and before our own eyes.

Joy—a wonderful emotion given by our Lord. As believers we have every reason for our joy to abound and be made known. When those unexpected and unwanted situations happen, may we have joy in the perspective of our Lord who is in control. Regardless of events, there can be a deep and satisfying permeating joy in our lives as we are reminded and focus on who our Lord is, what He has done, is doing, and promises to do in the future.

Our Lord's joy was not focused on His trials or on the pain of the Cross, but rather on the redeemed. His joy is our example, as we rejoice in His work, knowing we are, by design, a part of His gracious working.

> *Looking to Jesus, the founder and perfecter of our faith, who for the joy that was set before him endured the cross, despising the shame, and is seated at the right hand of the throne of God. (Hebrews 12:2)*

Though not joyful about our trials, we can have joy in our trials, because we know our Lord is at work. They are not empty, painful moments that purposelessly plague our existence, but rather are being used by a gracious and loving Lord who is masterfully using them for His glory and our perfection.

> *Count it all joy, my brothers, when you meet trials of various kinds, for you know that the testing of your faith produces steadfastness. And let steadfastness have its full effect, that you may be perfect and complete, lacking in nothing. (James 1:2-4)*

Our joy is not determined by the present difficulty, but focuses on that which is yet before us. We know our Lord to be the victor, and we know that there is coming a day where our faith will be sight.

> *Though you have not seen him, you love him. Though you do not now see him, you believe in him and rejoice with joy that is inexpressible and filled with glory, obtaining the outcome of your faith, the salvation of your souls. (1 Peter 1:8–9)*

I have a plaque hanging in my office that places this truth succinctly:

"Joy is not the absence of suffering, but the presence of God."

Joy is not in what we do, have, or experience—joy is in knowing the Lord and the Truth of His Word.

Consider:
1. Do I allow my emotions to control my responses?
   In what situations is this most prevalent?
2. Of the emotions mentioned, which one/ones seem to be prominent in my life?
3. What emotions do I seek most often to deny?
4. How have I observed God's "encouragements" in my life?
   How do I see the Father of mercies and the God of all comfort [encouragement] (2 Corinthians 1:3-4) active in my life?
5. How would I perhaps have responded as one of Joseph's brothers upon realizing I was in his presence?
   Can I be encouraged in the encouragements of others?
6. How does Hebrews 12:1-2 help me keep a right focus in regards to my emotions?
7. What sin do I need to confess; what thinking needs to be transformed; what practice needs to change?

DECISION FOURTEEN

I Choose to Celebrate with Others

When attending a wedding ceremony, we celebrate with others what God has done in the life of a man and woman as they are brought together in marriage. Seeing how God has individually worked in their lives through their years, and then bringing them together in chosen love is exciting. The newly married couple celebrates, families celebrate, and friends celebrate. This is a time to share the celebration; the couple wants others to know and share their joy. It has often been a great privilege of mine to stand with the groom at the front of the church, watching him watching his bride, and watching her watching him as she slowing makes her way down the aisle. This is a precious, unique moment, and we celebrate these two; a man and a woman, as they become one in God's providential design.

I can become glued to political commentaries and closely watch debates preceding an election day, listening to a plethora of "promises." In the evening I watch the returns come in, and become excited when "my candidate" is in the lead. I enjoy doing this, but there is something great about being with others who share my views and "celebrating" a victory.

When our son, Barry, was in school we attended many soccer games. Watching him in the goal box was unnerving at times, as he seemed to fly across the goal box to stop the opposing teams point. Every time there was a victory, we celebrated together. Parents and students gathered in the stands took great joy in seeing their child, and the entire team, do well and gain another victory.

Awhile back we sat in church and heard the testimony given by a middle aged woman dying from cancer. It was just within the last two years she had committed her life to Christ. After living a life of wrong choices and battling varying sinful habits, she came to the Cross, and there accepted Christ as her Savior. Finally she knew the power of His cleansing blood. As she lived through the final stages of cancer, she had a new hope and joy. Her sister stood with her as she spoke, and wiped tears of joy from her cheeks. As she finished, the church rejoiced. Believers together celebrated in what God had done in her life.

Yes, rejoicing can happen in isolation; rejoicing can happen when no one is around to share the good news. However, God has designed for people to live together in community, to share together in life's experiences. Having faced the difficult, the seemingly impassable troubles, and getting through them, there is great reason for rejoicing, and for others sharing in what God has done. He does not want us to keep silent, but rather to tell and to celebrate His sovereign working.

DECISION FOURTEEN

Decision Fourteen: I choose to celebrate with others regarding God's gracious working.

Joseph did not celebrate alone when he realized what God had been doing, and that He was using him in the development of His sovereign plan. He talked about it; he shared it with joy; he wanted his family to be aware of God's work. They celebrated together. Although these passages have been quoted previously, they once again remind us of this truth: share with others God's gracious working!

> *And God sent me before you to preserve for you a remnant on earth, and to keep alive for you many survivors. So it was not you who sent me here, but God. He has made me a father to Pharaoh, and lord of all his house and ruler over all the land of Egypt. Hurry and go up to my father and say to him, 'Thus says your son Joseph, God has made me lord of all Egypt. Come down to me; do not tarry. (Genesis 45:7-9)*

> *You must tell my father of all my honor in Egypt, and of all that you have seen. Hurry and bring my father down here." Then he fell upon his brother Benjamin's neck and wept, and Benjamin wept upon his neck. And he kissed all his brothers and wept upon them. After that his brothers talked with him. (Genesis 45:13-15)*

- Celebrate what God has done—God sent me before you
- Celebrate what God has done—He made me… ruler of all the land of Egypt
- Celebrate what God has done—tell my father
- Celebrate what God has done—he kissed all his brothers

There was nothing here that Joseph wanted to keep to himself. He shared God's working and rejoiced in what had happened. Though the times had been difficult and filled with trials, he was able to share with his brothers and rejoice. I wonder what the conversations entailed as these twelve brothers talked with each other. From the eleven, it could well have been about things "back home:" how people were doing, who had died, who had been born, progress in the shepherding business. From Joseph, he could well have shared with them some events of his time in Potiphar's house and his time in prison, as well as what it was like to rule in Egypt. They likely laughed, and perhaps they cried; the conversations could have gone from the most serious to the hilarious. But in all of it, there appears to be a constant thread of rejoicing together as they realized the sovereign work of the Almighty God.

Times of difficulty can often set the stage for future times of great rejoicing and celebrations. It is in these times we realize God had been working, accomplishing His purpose, and fitting together the varied pieces of our lives. It is after the struggles we are able to see the foundational joy, after the dark and tumultuous storms we appreciate the freshness of the new day.

The following four accounts from Scripture are given as examples of this principle: celebrating with others following the times when God's will seemed so very contrary to what we thought would be best.

Crossing the Red Sea

God called Moses to lead the people of Israel. After the unsuccessful attempts before Pharaoh to "let my people go," God changed Pharaoh's heart. It was Passover night. The people of Israel had been given specific instructions as this holy memorial was instituted. They were to kill a lamb, place some of its blood on the doorposts of their homes, and stay inside and eat the meat (Exodus

12:1-11). That night the death angel swept through all of Egypt and the firstborn of every household was killed, except where the blood was on the doorposts; there, the death angel passed over. Pharaoh in his uncontrollable grieving released the Israelites to go. With the protection of God they came to the edge of the Red Sea, where God then miraculously parted the waters. Israel crossed on dry ground. They had been in Egypt as a people for 400 years, much of that time in slavery. Their bondage was great, and there was no human hope for freedom. But God worked, and there was no doubt in the people's minds that God alone was setting them free.

After having crossed the Red Sea and seeing the waters powerfully coming back together and destroying Pharaoh's army, Moses led the people in celebration.

> *Then Moses and the people of Israel sang this song to the Lord, saying, "I will sing to the Lord, for he has triumphed gloriously; the horse and his rider he has thrown into the sea. The Lord is my strength and my song, and he has become my salvation; this is my God, and I will praise him, my father's God, and I will exalt him. The Lord is a man of war; the Lord is his name... "Who is like you, O Lord, among the gods? Who is like you, majestic in holiness, awesome in glorious deeds, doing wonders? You stretched out your right hand; the earth swallowed them. "You have led in your steadfast love the people whom you have redeemed; you have guided them by your strength to your holy abode... The Lord will reign forever and ever." (Exodus 15:1-3, 11-13, 18)*

Then Miriam, Moses' sister led the women in repetitious chorus, proclaiming the work of God, rejoicing together. They had seen God at work, and they could not keep silent.

> *Then Miriam the prophetess, the sister of Aaron, took a tambourine in her hand, and all the women went out after her with tambourines and dancing. And Miriam sang to them: "Sing to the Lord, for he has triumphed gloriously; the horse and his rider he has thrown into the sea." (Exodus 15:20-21)*

Following the time of difficulty, walking an unknown path and crossing a dried sea bed, the people realized the work of God and together they lifted their voices in praise.

Though we may endure great trials and difficulties, though our life may be very different from what we had at one time planned, though our trouble may have been exhausting, we can know this is not where God leaves us. Our joy is in recognizing the presence of the Lord and the work of the Lord through our journey, recognizing His victories given along our way—all which then leads us to times of great celebration.

Rebuilding the temple

Seventy years had passed since the first people of Judah had been taken captive into Babylon. They were forced to leave their homeland and all that was familiar. The city of Jerusalem was in ruins, the surrounding walls had been torn down, and the temple destroyed. Though Jeremiah had prophesied their return, for many the reality of this coming to pass was hard to believe.

Then God worked in King Cyrus, and the proclamation was made allowing Jews to return to Jerusalem to build the temple.

> *In the first year of Cyrus king of Persia, that the word of the Lord by the mouth of Jeremiah might be fulfilled, the Lord stirred up the spirit of Cyrus king of Persia, so that*

DECISION FOURTEEN

> *he made a proclamation throughout all his kingdom and also put it in writing: "Thus says Cyrus king of Persia: The Lord, the God of heaven, has given me all the kingdoms of the earth, and he has charged me to build him a house at Jerusalem, which is in Judah. Whoever is among you of all his people, may his God be with him, and let him go up to Jerusalem, which is in Judah, and rebuild the house of the Lord, the God of Israel—he is the God who is in Jerusalem. (Ezra 1:1-3)*

Not only did he allow them to go back, he clearly stated that God had appointed him to send people back to build the temple. The long trek of rebuilding had begun.

However, there was opposition. Cyrus had died, and Artaxerxes was in power. He was convinced the work should be stopped. After a ten year break and following the Persian takeover in 521 BC and under the reign of Darius, the rebuilding restarted in 520 BC. Fourteen years later it is completed in 506 BC. Nearly 100 years since the first people had been taken captive the temple once again stood and sacrifices were being offered. The people celebrated. They saw God at work and their hope was restored.

> *And this house was finished on the third day of the month of Adar, in the sixth year of the reign of Darius the king. And the people of Israel, the priests and the Levites, and the rest of the returned exiles, celebrated the dedication of this house of God with joy. (Ezra 6:15-16)*

Together they celebrated—and they celebrated with joy! They could not keep silent as they realized God had worked among them.

In their celebration they worshiped God. There is a close link between these two, for celebration directed to the Lord is worship, and true worship is a celebration of our Lord.

> *They offered at the dedication of this house of God 100 bulls, 200 rams, 400 lambs, and as a sin offering for all Israel 12 male goats, according to the number of the tribes of Israel. And they set the priests in their divisions and the Levites in their divisions, for the service of God at Jerusalem, as it is written in the Book of Moses. On the fourteenth day of the first month, the returned exiles kept the Passover... It was eaten by the people of Israel who had returned from exile, and also by every one who had joined them and separated himself from the uncleanness of the peoples of the land to worship the Lord, the God of Israel. And they kept the Feast of Unleavened Bread seven days with joy, for the Lord had made them joyful and had turned the heart of the king of Assyria to them, so that he aided them in the work of the house of God, the God of Israel. (Ezra 6:17–22)*

Following the difficult days of captivity, and then the difficulty and trouble ensued during the time of rebuilding, the people could celebrate. When a troubling time is past, we must be very careful not to forget Who worked, Who led through the trouble, and Who provided in the midst of trouble. Our celebration is of the Lord's working, and together with believers we can rejoice in what our Lord has done.

The Resurrection

Our Lord's life on earth was far from easy and problem free. Some followed and hung onto His every word while others connived on how to put a stop to His teaching. He was praised and insulted, loved and hated. Some thought He had come to establish His kingdom and free them from the bondage of Rome, while others looked at Him as a threat to the establishment. There were those who listened to His

DECISION FOURTEEN

words and heard a message of peace and hope, while others listened and only heard scorn and division.

His disciples walked with Him for three years. They heard it all, and at times they had their own questions about what He did, who He was, and what was going to happen. They, too, had great hopes; their lives had been changed; and they could not imagine life without Him.

But then came the celebration of the Passover Meal together in the Upper Room. There He talked with them about His body being broken and His blood being given for them. He gave thanks to His Father in heaven and passed the bread to them, telling them that as they ate to remember Him; He did the same thing with the cup of wine. Then they went to Gethsemane and prayed. The disciples fell asleep; they had not begun to understand the depth of this moment, of what was happening, of what Jesus was praying.

The soldiers came, arrested Jesus and took Him to trial. The disciples, in fear, scattered. Peter and John followed. They likely thought their hopes and future were soon to be crushed. The following day He was condemned and crucified. Some watched; some grieved; others went into hiding. Joseph of Arimathea, along with Nicodemus, was granted permission to place His body in the tomb. It seemed as if this "chapter of life" was over, their hopes gone, and life would soon return to some sort of "normal" as they had known it before Christ—though it would never be the same. Likely despair and confusion struck them. The passing events were not supposed to happen, in their thinking; this was not what they had planned; this was not what they had expected.

They did not know; they did not understand the purpose of God, His amazing redemptive plan unfolding before their very eyes. But then Sunday came. Certain women went to the tomb to anoint His body. There had not been time to do this properly when He was buried, and it was prohibitive for them to do it on the Sabbath. They took their first opportunity. However, in coming to the tomb they unexpectedly were faced with an unimaginable "shock." The grave had been opened, and an angel addressed them.

> *But the angel said to the women, "Do not be afraid, for I know that you seek Jesus who was crucified. He is not here, for he has risen, as he said. Come, see the place where he lay. Then go quickly and tell his disciples that he has risen from the dead, and behold, he is going before you to Galilee; there you will see him. See, I have told you." So they departed quickly from the tomb with fear and great joy, and ran to tell his disciples. (Matthew 28:5–8)*

With fear and great joy they were told to tell his disciples. Don't keep this news to yourself! Rejoice—and share your rejoicing! What they had thought had ended, had not; what they thought was over, was not; what they thought was done, suddenly had a very different beginning. They could not keep silent.

And then, on the way to share the good news, they met Jesus.

> *And behold, Jesus met them and said, "Greetings!" And they came up and took hold of his feet and worshiped him. Then Jesus said to them, "Do not be afraid; go and tell my brothers to go to Galilee, and there they will see me." (Matthew 28:9–10)*

The message is the same: tell others; rejoice together; celebrate!

Later we are told of two disciples who were walking on the road to Emmaus. Though not immediately recognizing Him, they soon learned they were walking with Jesus. Having stopped to eat, Jesus broke break with them, and suddenly their eyes were opened, and they quickly knew this stranger to be their friend; this one who they thought to have been dead was alive. When Jesus left them, they did not just sit and talk about what happened; they did not travel to their own homes and wait for something else to take place; they did not look at this as another "ho-hum" event. No. They hurried back to Jerusalem to verify with the disciples what they had already heard. Jesus was alive. Together they rejoiced.

> *And they rose that same hour and returned to Jerusalem. And they found the eleven and those who were with them gathered together, saying, "The Lord has risen indeed, and has appeared to Simon!" Then they told what had happened on the road, and how he was known to them in the breaking of the bread. (Luke 24:33–35)*

From the depths of despair and disappointment can come rejoicing, as is evidenced in this psalm of David:

> *I will extol you, O Lord, for you have drawn me up and have not let my foes rejoice over me. O Lord my God, I cried to you for help, and you have healed me. O Lord, you have brought up my soul from Sheol; you restored me to life from among those who go down to the pit. Sing praises to the Lord, O you his saints, and give thanks to his holy name. For his anger is but for a moment, and his favor is for a lifetime. Weeping may tarry for the night, but joy comes with the morning. (Psalm 30:1–5)*

Note his words: Sing praises to the LORD, O ye his saints and give thanks to his holy name. Together, rejoice in the work of God; together, give Him praise.

Though events may seem as thick, non-dispersing, dark clouds hanging over our lives, we don't have to stay under their shadow. By the grace of God we are able to look beyond them and rejoice in His gracious working and His ultimate victory; we are able to rest in hope and rejoice with others regarding God's great work. He does not call us to be silent, but rather to openly confess His name, to clearly proclaim His truth, to joyfully share with others what great things He has done for you (1 Samuel 12:24), and in all this to celebrate the resurrection of Jesus Christ.

Building the Church

The people celebrated in the first century as the church began, and we certainly have reason to celebrate today.[45] Whenever the Lord is worshipped, when people are saved and lives are changed, and when believers are growing in the faith and knowledge of Jesus Christ, we have reason to celebrate.

> *Some indeed preach Christ from envy and rivalry, but others from good will. The latter do it out of love, knowing that I am put here for the defense of the gospel. The former proclaim Christ out of selfish ambition, not sincerely but thinking to afflict me in my imprisonment. What then? Only that in every way, whether in pretense or in truth, Christ is proclaimed, and in that I rejoice. Yes, and I will rejoice, for I know that through your prayers and the help of the Spirit of Jesus Christ this will turn out for my deliverance, (Philippians 1:15-19)*

To build the church, truth must be taught and the Scriptures must

---

45 We cannot celebrate the many factions among churches, the many factions within churches; the bickering, fighting, and unholy attitudes and actions which can be so very prevalent. We cannot celebrate the commercialization which has happened within the church nor the worldliness which has crept into the church or at times leapt into the church, all under the guise of reaching the lost and worshipping God. We must be careful to celebrate what God celebrates: true worship by His people, the exaltation of His Name, the testimony before the world, and unity of the body.

be upheld; the Word of God must be our authority; and we must be bold standard bearers for truth.

The early church was under the power of the Holy Spirit of God, led by its Head, the Lord Jesus Christ. The believers were committed to doing the right thing, to standing firm on the Word and the person of Jesus Christ, and reaching out to others.

> *And they devoted themselves to the apostles' teaching and the fellowship, to the breaking of bread and the prayers. And awe came upon every soul, and many wonders and signs were being done through the apostles. And all who believed were together and had all things in common. And they were selling their possessions and belongings and distributing the proceeds to all, as any had need. And day by day, attending the temple together and breaking bread in their homes, they received their food with glad and generous hearts, praising God and having favor with all the people. And the Lord added to their number day by day those who were being saved. (Acts 2:42–47)*

Note the key aspects of the early church.

Together they celebrated what God was doing. Together they praised God, not because of their great accomplishments and evangelistic efforts, but rather they celebrated God's work among the people, and they gave Him the glory.

They celebrated in their times together—remembering His working, teaching and learning, praying together, and enjoying true fellowship.[46]

- They celebrated seeing lives changed as people came to trust

---

[46] True fellowship in the church is not eating meals together and playing games. Rather, true fellowship is the Body of Believers intentionally celebrating God's working. This is not to say that food cannot be a part of fellowship; but that it is much more than food. It should be focused around God and what He is doing in the lives of believers and in His Church.

Christ as Savior.
- They celebrated in their mutual exaltation of Jesus Christ.
- They celebrated in their ministry to each other, as they shared together from the blessings God had given to them.
- They celebrated together as they saw the blessings of God among His people.
- They celebrated praising God for His great work.

In celebrating, we must:
- Believe God has been at work.
- Believe God's work is good.
- Believe God's work has a sovereign purpose.
- Believe God wants us to celebrate.

In celebrating:
- We do not have to understand the design of God.
- We do need to understand God has a perfect design.
- We do not have to enjoy the trials of life.
- We do need to recognize God is at work through our trials.
- We do not have to see victory over our trials.
- We do need to know that the Lord is the ultimate victor.

May it be our desire, our goal, our delight to be involved in celebration of our Lord and what He is doing among His people and in His Church. May our hearts and voices ring with the familiar Doxology and words of Scripture:

> *Praise God from whom all blessings flow; Praise Him all creatures here below; Praise Him above ye Heavenly Host; Praise Father, Son, and Holy Ghost.*

DECISION FOURTEEN

To the only God, our Savior, through Jesus Christ our Lord, be glory, majesty, dominion, and authority, before all time and now and forever. Amen. (Jude 25)

… "Worthy is the Lamb who was slain, to receive power and wealth and wisdom and might and honor and glory and blessing!"… "To him who sits on the throne and to the Lamb be blessing and honor and glory and might forever and ever!" (Revelation 5:12-13)

Consider:
1. Do I enjoy celebrating, or do I tend to just look at life circumstances with little response?
2. How do I respond when seeing others celebrating God's working?
3. Celebrating is a choice. How can I celebrate when it appears there is nothing to celebrate?
4. What are ten things I can celebrate that God has done in my life? *What are ten things I can celebrate that God has done in the lives of others?*
5. What have I learned about celebrating from the four Biblical illustrations given?
    The Crossing of the Red Sea:
    Rebuilding of the Temple:
    The Resurrection:
    The Building of the Church:
6. What additional Scriptures point me to celebration?
7. What sin do I need to confess; what thinking needs to be transformed; what practice needs to change?

WHEN GOD'S WILL AND MY WILL DISCONNECT

DECISION FIFTEEN

I Choose to Glorify God

Knowing our son Jonathan is indeed "Jehovah's gift" and that our Lord has been at work in and through his life, we are able to give glory to God. Though some days are definitely more difficult than others, we know the Lord has been and is working. At times this evidence isn't readily seen, and at other times, there is greater clarity in God's design. One situation during a military transition time demonstrates both of these thoughts. In recapturing the event, Barbara wrote:[47]

> As our time in New Jersey was coming to a conclusion we faced our next duty with mixed emotions. Hawaii seemed like a faraway place but we were finding a perspective— counting our Sovereign Lord to be working it all together for good and His Glory. We'd been, since early spring, faced with a set of brand new concerns, as Jonathan was presenting some

---

47 In her book (not yet published), *Even this Lord?... For Good and for Glory!* Barbara has consistently demonstrated God's working and glory as she recounted the story of her life, of Jonathan's life, and of our lives as a family.

DECISION FIFTEEN

new and severe symptoms. They manifested quite suddenly as we noticed swelling in his knee joints that had him down and crawling in order to be mobile. We, of course, got him in to see his doctor, whose initial assessment communicated concern for the possible onset of Juvenile Rheumatoid Arthritis. He gave us a referral to a specialist and we awaited our appointment. We managed to take a short, little family vacation to explore the wonders of Washington, D.C. and Mount Vernon. This was on our "want to do" list before we were off to our next duty in Hawaii. We pushed Jon in a wheelchair which he submitted to very well.

The outcome of our appointment with the Rheumatoid Specialist was another confirmation of our loving Heavenly Father's care for His children. This doctor had upon examining Jon ordered blood work to check Jon's Lyme titer levels. He, to our ongoing amazement, had been involved in the research that led to the discovery of Lyme Disease and was suspect that this was the case for Jon. His suspicions were confirmed with the return of the lab work. Jonathan's levels were extremely high. Perhaps on our family walk in a New Jersey park on Easter Sunday afternoon Jon had hosted an infected tick? We praised God that the truth of this matter was revealed. Jon was treated aggressively with Tetracyclamine which resulted in improvement and eventual total recovery. We were celebrating God's faithful timing in this as had we not had these providential connections and treatments prior to heading off to Hawaii, Jon's prognosis would likely have had a far different outcome.

Why Jon encountered Lyme Disease, we do not know. How and when he encountered it, we think we know. Why we were sent to the specialist, we absolutely know. This was not just the recommendation of Jon's doctor; we know there was sovereign design in protecting and providing. We give God glory. Perhaps someday we will have clearer insight into what we do not know; but now, we don't need to know. Knowing our Lord is working things together for Good and for Glory is enough, and we are compelled to give Him praise.

Decision Fifteen: I choose to glorify God in all things.

When we see the events of life unfolding and know God has orchestrated them specifically, our only response should be to give Him the glory. We can take no credit for whatever we may have done; we must recognize it is not the result of our keen wisdom, careful planning, or ability to influence. God is the One who should receive all credit. He has brought us through; He has provided; He is working His providential plan.

Once again, we clearly see Joseph taking no credit for what has happened in his rise to prominence in Egypt. He never mentions his ability, his giftedness in interpreting dreams, or his boldness in reasoning for an authoritative position. Rather, he sees it as being all of God, and that God definitely should receive the full credit.

> *So it was not you who sent me here, but God. He has made me a father to Pharaoh, and lord of all his house and ruler over all the land of Egypt. Hurry and go up to my father and say to him, 'Thus says your son Joseph, God has made me lord of all Egypt. Come down to me; do not tarry. (Genesis 45:8-9)*

> *As for you, you meant evil against me, but God meant it for good, to bring it about that many people should be kept alive, as they are today. (Genesis 50:20)*

DECISION FIFTEEN

Joseph did not have to reveal himself to his brothers; he did not have to give God credit for what had happened; he did not have to attribute his brother's evil schemes to the providential hand of God; he did not have to relay to his brothers that God was at work in preserving the people. But he did. This desire stems out of the faithful character of Joseph and his deep faith that God was in control. He not only celebrated truth with his brothers, but he glorified God before them.

When we fail to give God glory

In our life situations, no matter how difficult or unplanned they may be, we rob God, ourselves, and others when we harbor resentment and bitterness, when we choose sinful responses rather than accepting the truth that God has been at work. We rob God, ourselves, and others when we do not acknowledge God's providential design and that His will is better than ours, that He knows what He is doing, and that all He does is good.

We are not the ones to receive glory—but God alone as He completes His sovereign plan.

> *Not to us, O Lord, not to us, but to your name give glory, for the sake of your steadfast love and your faithfulness! Why should the nations say, "Where is their God?" Our God is in the heavens; he does all that he pleases. (Psalm 115:1–3)*

When we choose to not give Him glory in all things, we choose to bring glory to ourselves or to others. In doing this, we rob God. We rob Him of His glory; we rob Him of the credit that is rightly due His name. We rob Him of crediting Him with truth when we brood in despair because things have not worked out the way we think they should have. We rob God of His reputation before others, claiming what He has done to be the results of our working or of someone else.

We rob ourselves of His joy permeating our life. When we harbor sinful responses because we have not favored the situations in our life, we know nothing of the joy and peace He alone can give. We rob ourselves of the privilege of submission before His Throne, resting in Him, knowing that His will and His care are absolutely perfect.

We rob others of celebrating in the joy of the Lord's working, of allowing them to share in the realization that God's divine plan has meaning and purpose. We rob others of the witness that God is God, and there is no other, that God is God and that He is true, that God is God and that all He does is good. We rob others by bringing to them doubt in God's blessings and design, doubt in God's wisdom, doubt in God's care.

We are commanded to give God glory.

Paul said this to the Church at Corinth as he was exhorting them in their relationships with others and in their decisions regarding how to live:

> *So, whether you eat or drink, or whatever you do, do all to the glory of God. (1 Corinthians 10:31)*

God desires to receive "glory" in all things—to be exalted above all, to be seen as worthy over all else.

In worship—we give God glory

In giving God "glory" we worship Him; we join in with all of creation recognizing His supremacy above all.

DECISION FIFTEEN

> *Ascribe to the Lord, O heavenly beings, ascribe to the Lord glory and strength. Ascribe to the Lord the glory due his name; worship the Lord in the splendor of holiness. The voice of the Lord is over the waters; the God of glory thunders, the Lord, over many waters. The voice of the Lord is powerful; the voice of the Lord is full of majesty... The Lord sits enthroned as king forever. May the Lord give strength to his people! May the Lord bless his people with peace! (Psalm 29:1-11)*

In proclamation of His Name—we give God glory.

May the glory of the Lord be known throughout every area where we have ability to proclaim Him. He is like none other; He alone is Holy in His very being.

> *Oh sing to the Lord a new song; sing to the Lord, all the earth! Sing to the Lord, bless his name; tell of his salvation from day to day. Declare his glory among the nations, his marvelous works among all the peoples! For great is the Lord, and greatly to be praised; he is to be feared above all gods.. Splendor and majesty are before him; strength and beauty are in his sanctuary. Ascribe to the Lord, O families of the peoples, ascribe to the Lord glory and strength! Ascribe to the Lord the glory due his name... Worship the Lord in the splendor of holiness; tremble before him, all the earth! Say among the nations, "The Lord reigns!... Let the heavens be glad, and let the earth rejoice; let the sea roar, and all that fills it... Then shall all the trees of the forest sing for joy before the Lord, for he comes, for he comes to judge the earth. He will judge the world in righteousness, and the peoples in his faithfulness. (Psalm 96:1-13)*

In celebration of God's character—we give God glory

In celebrating the work of God in the assurance of God's covenant, His provisions in the building of the temple, and the gifts given by the people, David led the Israelites in a prayer of praise. This is a wonderful portion of Scripture to memorize for a reminder of the greatness and praiseworthiness of our Lord.

> ... *"Blessed are you, O Lord, the God of Israel our father, forever and ever. Yours, O Lord, is the greatness and the power and the glory and the victory and the majesty, for all that is in the heavens and in the earth is yours. Yours is the kingdom, O Lord, and you are exalted as head above all. Both riches and honor come from you, and you rule over all. In your hand are power and might, and in your hand it is to make great and to give strength to all. And now we thank you, our God, and praise your glorious name. (1 Chronicles 29:10–13)*

At the birth of Christ, the angelic hosts gave glory to God. They knew the wonder of His work; they knew the realization of the hope of our salvation; they knew the His redemptive plan was unfolding. They could do nothing less than sing praises to the Lord Most High, giving God all the glory rightfully due Him.

> *And suddenly there was with the angel a multitude of the heavenly host praising God and saying, "Glory to God in the highest, and on earth peace among those with whom he is pleased!" (Luke 2:13–14)*

Having spoken of the wonder of God's redemptive plan, of the depth and extent of His salvation, of His wonderful working throughout history, Paul concluded with this doxology of praise.

> *Oh, the depth of the riches and wisdom and knowledge of God! How unsearchable are his judgments and how*

> *inscrutable his ways! "For who has known the mind of the Lord, or who has been his counselor?" "Or who has given a gift to him that he might be repaid?" For from him and through him and to him are all things. To him be glory forever. Amen. (Romans 11:33-36)*

Because from him and through him and to him are all things, there is none other which can rightfully usurp His glory. Our proclamation should ring loudly, as we see and know His powerful working, learn of His sovereign design, and further realize His Holy character.

In knowing Christ—we are compelled to give God all glory.

In knowing Christ and His great redemptive plan, we are compelled to do nothing less than give God full glory. Here is the concise statement of His sovereign design being fulfilled in the lives of His own. Seeing this, there can be no other response from His children but that of praise—giving Him the glory He so rightly deserves and that which so fully surrounds Him.

> *Blessed be the God and Father of our Lord Jesus Christ! According to his great mercy, he has caused us to be born again to a living hope through the resurrection of Jesus Christ from the dead, to an inheritance that is imperishable, undefiled, and unfading, kept in heaven for you, who by God's power are being guarded through faith for a salvation ready to be revealed in the last time. In this you rejoice, though now for a little while, if necessary, you have been grieved by various trials, so that the tested genuineness of your faith—more precious than gold that perishes though it is tested by fire—may be found to result in praise and glory and honor at the revelation of Jesus Christ. Though you have not seen him, you love him. Though you do not now see him, you believe in him and rejoice with joy that is inexpressible and filled with glory,*

obtaining the outcome of your faith, the salvation of your souls. (1 Peter 1:3–9)

Then, in the culmination of His redemptive plan, in the fullest realization of our salvation, in the presence of our Holy God who has loved us and made us His own, we will take part with the heavenly host in praise before His Throne, giving His glory for all eternity.

And whenever the living creatures give glory and honor and thanks to him who is seated on the throne, who lives forever and ever, the twenty-four elders fall down before him who is seated on the throne and worship him who lives forever and ever. They cast their crowns before the throne, saying, "Worthy are you, our Lord and God, to receive glory and honor and power, for you created all things, and by your will they existed and were created." (Revelation 4:9–11)

Saying with a loud voice, "Worthy is the Lamb who was slain, to receive power and wealth and wisdom and might and honor and glory and blessing!" And I heard every creature in heaven and on earth and under the earth and in the sea, and all that is in them, saying, "To him who sits on the throne and to the Lamb be blessing and honor and glory and might forever and ever!" (Revelation 5:12–13)

After this I heard what seemed to be the loud voice of a great multitude in heaven, crying out, "Hallelujah! Salvation and glory and power belong to our God. (Revelation 19:1)

In making right choices that lead to giving God the glory in all things, the following questions can be helpful to consider:

- Am I delighting in glorifying God?
- Am I motivated to glorify God?

DECISION FIFTEEN

- Am I looking for reasons to glorify God?
- Am I choosing ways to glorify God?

Reminder: glorifying God is not an event, it is a way of life; it is not a single experience, but rather the fullness of living.

Consider:

1. When was the last time I gave glory to God before others?
2. Have I been guilty of robbing God of His glory?
   If yes, how? What will I do differently?
3. Have I been guilty of robbing myself of God's joy permeating my life?
   If yes, how? What will I do differently?
4. Have I been guilty of robbing others of celebrating what God is doing?
   If yes, how? What will I do differently?
5. What are some specific things I can do to give glory to God, and to glorify Him before others?
6. What is the foundational truth that motivates me to glorify God?
7. What sin do I need to confess; what thinking needs to be transformed; what practice needs to change?

CONCLUSION

God is always working. He never quits. He never fails. He is always faithful to all His Word all the time. Regardless of how the events of my life are written, I can be confident God is accomplishing His purpose. In considering who my Lord is and all He is doing, has done, and has promised to do in the future, my responsibility is to make the following choices:

- I choose to accept that I am not in control, that God is in control, and circumstances will happen that are beyond my control.
- I choose to confess my own sin, repent, and claim God's forgiveness.
- I choose to live faithfully before God in imperfect circumstances.
- I choose purity over temptation, recognizing the cost of consequences is of no benefit.
- I choose to trust God to use me even though I do not understand how.
- I choose to accept God's timeframe, knowing His timing is

always perfect.
- I choose to give up my dreams and replace them with God's realities.
- I choose to accept and appreciate God's unusual blessings as His perfect design.
- I choose to remember God's working in the past, knowing He will work in the future.
- I choose to live above the fray and not seek revenge.
- I choose to forgive others, and not accept bitterness.
- I choose to serve others, seeking a right focus.
- I choose to accept my emotions, honoring both God and others.
- I choose to celebrate with others regarding God's gracious working.
- I choose to glorify God in all things.

Making right choices are not always easy, but they will always honor and please God; they will always result in blessing.

Joseph had no concept of what was about to transpire in his life when he was first taken to Egypt by the Ishmaelite traders. God did. Everything was planned.

> *When he summoned a famine on the land and broke all supply of bread,*
>
> *he had sent a man ahead of them, Joseph, who was sold as a slave.*
>
> *His feet were hurt with fetters; his neck was put in a collar of iron;*

> *until what he had said came to pass, the word of the Lord tested him.*
>
> *The king sent and released him; the ruler of the peoples set him free;*
>
> *he made him lord of his house and ruler of all his possessions,*
>
> *to bind his princes at his pleasure and to teach his elders wisdom. (Psalm 105:16-22)*

God knew, and used Joseph in the design and accomplishment of His majestic plan of redemption.

> *"And the patriarchs, jealous of Joseph, sold him into Egypt; but God was with him and rescued him out of all his afflictions and gave him favor and wisdom before Pharaoh, king of Egypt, who made him ruler over Egypt and over all his household. (Acts 7:9-10)*

Joseph was sent ahead by the Lord to deliver His people from the frustration of famine and bring them into a safe place. Through the amazing series of events, God accomplished His purpose without flaw.

But the events do not stop here. For God continued His working and following 400 years of captivity He called for another man to deliver His people out of the bondage of Egypt. Though they were brought to the land with good intent, they were never designed to remain in this place; they were not made to be slaves of Pharaoh for the remainder of their history. God had promised them the land of Canaan, and to Canaan He would take them. This was all part of His perfect design.

CONCLUSION

> *Then the Lord said to Abram, "Know for certain that your offspring will be sojourners in a land that is not theirs and will be servants there, and they will be afflicted for four hundred years. (Genesis 15:13)*

God did not plan for His people to remain in Egypt, and He does not plan for His people today to remain enslaved in sin. Because of the powerful working of the Lord Jesus Christ, we have been taken out of bondage. He did not take us across a body of water, but rather through the shedding of His blood. He took us from the depths of the grave of deadness, having been born under the curse of sin, to the heights of the resurrection through His powerful working. We have the hope that someday we will be removed from the desert wanderings of this earth and brought into the Promised Land, into the eternal heavens and before His Holy presence.

Joseph knew His people would not remain in Egypt. He knew it was but temporary. He gave them hope that a day would come when they would return to the land God had given to their father, Abraham.

> *And Joseph said to his brothers, "I am about to die, but God will visit you and bring you up out of this land to the land that he swore to Abraham, to Isaac, and to Jacob." Then Joseph made the sons of Israel swear, saying, "God will surely visit you, and you shall carry up my bones from here." (Genesis 50:24–25)*

They had hope. We have hope. There is more to come.

Joseph died. He was 110 years old, and placed in a coffin in Egypt (Genesis 50:26). But he didn't stay there. Even though generations had passed, the Israelites remembered their commitment to Joseph and took him out of Egypt.

> *Moses took the bones of Joseph with him, for Joseph had made the sons of Israel solemnly swear, saying, "God will surely visit you, and you shall carry up my bones with you from here." (Exodus 13:19)*

The troubles we face in these days of our pilgrimage on this earth are few in comparison to the joys we will experience for all eternity. When our will, our designs, hopes, and dreams don't coincide with God's will, may we keep our focus on He who has planned it all, knowing He will always do what is best; may we keep our hope on Him who is able to lead us through the desert times of our lives; may we not forget what we know, and hold firmly to the truth of His Word. May we not spend our given days seeking to fit God's will into ours, but rather seeking to connect with His will for our lives.

As Moses was faithful to remember Joseph's bones, so we can be certain our Lord will remember us. Whether we are alive or have died when the Lord returns, He will not forget us; we can expectantly look forward to His return.

> *But we do not want you to be uninformed, brothers, about those who are asleep, that you may not grieve as others do who have no hope. For since we believe that Jesus died and rose again, even so, through Jesus, God will bring with him those who have fallen asleep. For this we declare to you by a word from the Lord, that we who are alive, who are left until the coming of the Lord, will not precede those who have fallen asleep. For the Lord himself will descend from heaven with a cry of command, with the voice of an archangel, and with the sound of the trumpet of God. And the dead in Christ will rise first. Then we who are alive, who are left, will be caught up together with them in the clouds to meet the Lord in the air, and so we will always be with the Lord. Therefore encourage one another with*

CONCLUSION

these words. (1 Thessalonians 4:13–18)

We have much to be thankful for!

May we celebrate joyfully with His people!

Looking forward to that day when we shall celebrate in His presence with praise before His Throne—when we shall be forever perfectly united with our eternal Lord and God.

APPENDIX A

Synopsis

APPENDIX A

Decision One: I choose to accept that I am not in control, that God is in control, and circumstances will happen that are beyond my control.

God has a plan and His design always surpasses ours.

God will always be faithful to Himself and in His working in our lives.

God's Character

- The Lord is Creator
- The Lord is Sovereign
- The Lord is Holy
- The Lord is Powerful
- The Lord is Good
- The Lord is Incomparable
- The Lord is Redeemer
- The Lord is Praise Worthy
- The Lord is Faithful

My Responsibility

In faith we trust God to be God, believing His plan is always perfect.

Therefore:

> We are responsible to believe.
> We are responsible to accept God's design.

Decision Two: I choose to confess my own sin, repent, and claim God's forgiveness.

Sin never happens in isolation; sin is never without consequences.

My Relationship with the Lord.

Rather than harboring a root of bitterness toward another or becoming angry because of what they did, we should follow the clear pattern of Scripture. In confronting sin in our lives, we should follow these steps:

First, we must acknowledge our need for a Savior.

Second, we must desire to be right in my own relationship with the Lord.

Third, we must repent of sin, having the desire for and making the commitment to be free from sin.

Fourth, we must humbly ask for forgiveness from God and claim His forgiveness, and make a commitment to change.

Fifth, we must humbly ask forgiveness from others, committing to being in a right relationship with others.

APPENDIX A

Decision Three: I choose to live faithfully before God in imperfect circumstances.

First, I choose to live faithfully before God in circumstances of horror.

Holding to the truth of 1 Corinthians 10:13 we make these necessary choices:

> We must remember that the temptations we face are not uniquely ours.
>
> We must remember that God knows what we are facing, when we are facing it, and the depth of our struggle.
>
> We must remember that our Lord will always provide a way of victory for us while under temptation; He will always make it possible for us to escape the tempters snare.

Second, I choose to live in faithfulness before God in circumstances of imperfect success.

Third, I choose to live in faithfulness before God in reality circumstances.

Lessons from Paul

- Faithfulness without complaining
- Faithfulness in personal struggles
- Faithfulness in maintaining focus
- Faithfulness in praise
- Faithful in thinking

Choosing to live faithfully, we should then make these choices:

- I will choose to not wallow in unpleasantness.
- I will choose to not murmur or complain—about my circumstances or about others.
- I will choose to not allow my grief to hinder my moving

forward.
- I will choose to not give up when repeated circumstances are against me.
- I will, when all that is familiar is gone, choose to learn my new surroundings and live in them well.
- I will choose to place my heart and mind before the Savior that He might renew them in His truth.
- I will choose to think on these things… (Philippians 4.8)
- I will choose to live faithfully before my faithful Lord and before others, regardless of circumstances.

Decision Four: I choose purity over temptation, recognizing the cost of consequences is of no benefit.
- First, I must choose to say "no" to temptation.
- Second, I must choose to say "no" to repeated temptation.
- Third, I must choose to say "no" when temptation appears to overpower me.

The following principles from Scripture are effective in determining right choices in the face of temptation.
- Principle One: All sin is against God.
- Principle Two: Vulnerability is a reality.
- Principle Three: The Armor of God is effective protection
- Principle Four: the consequences of sin are of no benefit to the believer.
- We must never believe the enemy's lies. Sin always brings consequences; sin's consequences are never good.
- Principle Five: The characteristic behaviors of the unregenerate nature can be eradicated.

In making the following six declarations, the believer is able to

choose freedom and live in purity.
1. One, I declare the holiness of God and His abhorrence of all sin.
2. Two, I declare the desire of God for me to live in complete harmony with Himself.
3. Three, I declare the power of God, through the indwelling Spirit and the resurrection, to free me of all sin.
4. Four, I declare my own sin, confess and repent all known sin, and determine to live pleasing to God.
5. Five, I declare the forgiveness of God, accepting the fullness of His mercy and grace.
6. Six, I declare the joy of God, filling me and allowing me to move forward, free from sin.

Decision Five: I choose to trust God to use me, even though I do not understand how.

In trusting God to use us, four specific decisions must be made.
- First, I choose to be ready for God to use me.
- Being "ready" to be used means I will anticipate God working.
- Being "ready" to be used means I will accept my position before God.
- Second, I choose to do nothing that will detract from my being used by God.
- Third, I choose to have an attitude that is usable and not detrimental to God's purpose.
- Fourth, I choose to be willing to be used by God.

When we are willing to be a sacrifice, then we are willing to be used; when we are willing for our lives to not be conformed to the pattern of our thinking, then we are able to experience the working out of God's will in our lives.

Decision Six: I choose to accept God's timeframe, knowing His timing is always perfect

The following five reminders can help us learn and accept God's timeframe as always best.

One, I will have disappointments.

To redirect our disappointments we must:

Practice truth.

Practice patience.

Practice faith.

Two, God is never surprised.

Three, I live in a perfect timeframe.

When doubting the perfection of God's timeframe, the following questions help us relinquish doubt and live in faith.

When has God's timeframe not been perfect?

When has God failed in the past?

When has God not provided everything I have needed?

When has God forgotten me?

When has God said who I am and where I am is not important?

When has God not been good?

Four, I recognize that time does not stop with the disruption of my timeframe.

Five, I am to practice contentment.

Am I willing to go against God?

Do I realize my decision to be discontented with the way things are doubts God's design?

Do I remember that to doubt God is to sin against God?

APPENDIX A

Decision Seven: I choose to give-up my dreams and replace them with God's realities.

Six areas of examination help us make good future choices and accept a new direction designed by God.

I need to reassess God's call.

I need to review my actions.

I need to rejoice in God's mercy.

I need to reformat my future.

I need to readjust my attitude.

Consider Jesus. His attitude focused on others, on us, as He willingly gave Himself in sacrifice for our redemption.

I need to realize God's answers.

I need to remember God's truth.

Faith in our Lord frees us to release our dreams and replace them with grateful acceptance of His realities.

Decision Eight: I choose to accept and appreciate God's unusual blessings as His perfect design.

When in difficult situations we need to be doing what we should be doing.

When in difficult situations we need to we remember God is working far beyond our purview.

When in difficult situations we need to remember our God does not quit working.

Consider the fullness of the believer's unending blessings.

Decision Nine: I choose to remember God's working in the past, knowing He will work in the future.

This is a decision to remember; a decision to not forget.

Principles for remembering.

Principle #1: Interact with the Word of God.

Principle #2: Meditate on the Word of God.

Principle #3: Memorize the Word of God.

Principle #4: Trust the Word of God.

Principle #5: Walk in the Word of God.

Principle #6: Love the Word of God.

Choosing to remember is a discipline. I remember because I want to remember, because I choose to remember.

Decision Ten: I choose to live above the fray and not seek revenge.

The Lord calls us to be faithful, to make righteous choices, regardless of what others have done. Our choice to sin against another in retaliation to their sin against us is never condoned by God.

Answering the following five questions will help determine if our attitude is one which pleases God.

Question #1: Am I desiring to give God glory?

Question #2: Am I demonstrating the attitude of Christ?

Question #3: Am I rejoicing in God's work?

Question #4: Am I demonstrating a desire for revenge?

Question #5: Am I desiring good for others?

Critical in our relationship with others is to be reminded of the entirety of God's redemptive plan.

Decision Eleven: I choose to forgive others, and not accept bitterness.

Forgiveness is very different from saying "I'm sorry."

When forgiveness is requested of another, a decision must be made. There are only two options: to forgive or to choose not to forgive. If we say, "I forgive you," then we are making a four-fold commitment.

One, we agree to not repeatedly bring up the past, to not hold the sin against the other person.

Two, we are agree to not let it, by any means or in any way, separate future relationships. Therefore, saying "I forgive you but I never want to see you again," is not an option.

Three, we desire to have any torn relationship healed.

Four, knowing that we do not have a perfect "forgetfulness" as does God, we agree to not dwell on past sin and to not let it have any negative bearing on our future relationship.

Forgiveness guidelines:

Forgiveness should never be optional for the believer, regardless of the circumstances.

Forgiveness frees the believer to love and to serve both God and others.

Forgiveness is not solely dependent on another person asking for forgiveness.

Forgiveness encourages the healing of broken relationships.

Forgiveness is always motivated by our being forgiven by God.

Forgiveness is a command.

The Joy of Forgiveness

In forgiveness, there is great blessing; in forgiveness restoration is possible… Our response should be no different but to delight in forgiving others in order to have and enjoy restored relationships.

Decision Twelve: I choose to serve others, seeking a right focus.

In serving, the following six principles should be kept in focus:

Principle #1: God made us to serve

Principle #2: God has made us to serve, where we are

Principle #3: God is teaching us to serve, where we are

Principle #4: God has opened our eyes to serve and to see

other people where they are

Principle #5: God has designed us to serve others, not to be self-serving

Principle #6: God has gifted us to serve

Serving is sacrifice. It is not for our benefit, but for the benefit of others.

Serving is contrary to the flesh; the sinful nature calls us to satisfy ourselves first. Therefore, it is important to ask these concluding questions.

What am I doing for whom?

Is my life focused on me, or on others?

How has my current situation given me a unique opportunity to serve?

What is God teaching me which enables me to better serve others?

Decision Thirteen: I choose to accept my emotions, honoring both God and others.

Joseph demonstrated seven emotions:

One: the emotions of grief and sadness

Two: the emotion of fear

Three: the emotion of anger

In anger, it is important to ask two questions:

- Is my anger righteous?
- What is my anger accomplishing?

A better response than anger:

- Pray for those who have offended us
- Forgive those who have offended us
- Consider any sinful attitudes and responses

APPENDIX A

  we may have, and seek forgiveness
- Change what we can change to make the situation better
- Move forward with an expectation of God using our right choices for His glory

Four: the passionate emotion of physical desire
Five: the emotion of sadness
Six: the emotion of disappointment
Seven: the emotion of joy

Decision Fourteen: I choose to celebrate with others regarding God's gracious working.

We are to celebrate with others following those times when God's will seemed so very contrary to what we thought would be best.

The early church provides a model for our celebrations:

- They celebrated in their times together
- They celebrated seeing lives changed as people came to trust Christ as Savior
- They celebrated in their mutual exaltation of Jesus Christ
- They celebrated in their ministry to each other
- They celebrated as they saw the blessings of God among His people
- They celebrated by praising God for His great work

In celebrating, I must:

- Believe God has been at work
- Believe God's work is good
- Believe God's work has a sovereign purpose
- Believe God wants me to celebrate

In celebrating:

- I do not have to understand the design of God

- I do need to understand God has a perfect design
- I do not have to enjoy the trials of life
- I do need to recognize God is at work through my trials
- I do not have to see the removal of my trials
- I do need to know that the Lord is the ultimate victor

Decision Fifteen: *I choose to glorify God in all things.*
- When we fail to give God glory:
- We rob God of the glory He rightly deserves
- We rob ourselves of His joy permeating our live
- We rob others of celebrating in the joy of God's working

God desires to receive "glory" in all things—to be exalted above all, to be seen as worthy over all else.

- In worship—we give God glory
- In proclamation of His Name—we give God glory
- In celebration of God's character—we give God glory
- In knowing Christ—we are compelled to give God all glory

In making right choices that lead to giving God the glory in all things, the following questions can be helpful to consider:

- Am I delighting in glorifying God?
- Am I motivated to glorify God?
- Am I looking for reasons to glorify God?
- Am I choosing ways to glorify God?

Reminder: glorifying God is not an event, it is a way of life; it is not a single experience, but rather the fullness of living.

APPENDIX B

Scripture Used

Genesis

Reference	Page
1:1	18
3:6-7	308
4:1-14	100
4:5	194
15:13	279
19:17	47
30:21-24	2
30:23	2
35:10	2
37:2	2
37:3	3
37:4	3
37:5	4
37:5-8	4
37:9-10	4
37:11	5
37:12	5
37:13-14	6
37:17-36	100
37:18-20	6
37:20	7
37:21-22	7, 15
37:23-24	238
37:26-28	16, 240
37:31-33	8
37:36	8
39:1	60
39:2-6	64
39:2-4	162
39:5	164
39:6	68
39:7-9	82
39:9	88
39:10	83
39:11-12	241
39:11-15	86
39:20-23	69
40:8	120
40:14, 23	128
41:1	128
41:14-16, 25	121
41:39-43	164
41:55-57	165
42:6-8	176
42:9	177
42:11	197
42:17	214
42:18	177
42:21	239
42:21-24	178
42:21-23	215
42:24	213, 247
42:35	197
43:16	226
43:23	214

43:30	214, 248	**Leviticus**	
43:33-34	227	11:44-45	21, 308
45:2	198		
45:3	198, 248	**Numbers**	
45:4-8	215	32:23	100
45:5-8	198		
45:7-9	253	**Deuteronomy**	
45:8-9	258	6:1-9	187
45:9	248	6:4	24
45:9-11	199		
45:13-15	253	**Joshua**	
45:14-15	198, 248	1:6-9	147
46:29	248	1:8	183
46:31-34	227	3-4	179, 191
50:15-21	205	4:1-7	180
50:17	50	7:1-5	116
50:17-21	216	7:3-5	148
50:20	268	7:1-26	101
50:21	228	7:24-26	116, 148
50:24-25	279	8:1-29	148
50:26	279		
		Ruth	
Exodus		2:20	203
3:2-11	146	**1 Samuel**	
3:11-4:17	146	4:12-22	100
3:14	24	12:24	262
13:19	280	24:4-7	195
15:1-3, 11-13, 18	255	24:6	131
15:20-21	256		

26:9-11	196	29:1-11	271
		30:1-5	261
2 Samuel		34:8	23
11:1-27	101	37:2-8	132
13:2	194	37:25	67
13:15	194	37:31	185
13:32	195	40:1-3	132
		42:5, 11	131
1 Chronicles		43:5	131
29:10-13	272	51:1-3	43
		51:1-10	313
2 Chronicles		51:3-4	88
7:10	161	62:1-2	31
		89:1	28
Ezra		91:1-2	xi
1:1-3	257	92:1-2	x, 154
6:15-16	257	96:1-13	271
6:17-22	258	103:12	168
		105:16-22	277
Job		111:1-10	29
1:21	xii, 246	115:1-3	269
2:10	246	118:6	ix
12:7-10	20	119:1-2	187
		119:9-11	185
Psalm		119:15	184
1:1-3	184	119:16	189
8:1-3	26	119:18	182
19:1, 14	27	119:24	189
19:7-10	189		
27:13	24		

119:26	182	139:23-24	313
119:27	184		
119:30	186	**Proverbs**	
119:33	182	3:5-6	186
119:35	189	15:1	243
119:43	185	16:6	15
119:44-45	187	16:14	30
119:47	190	20:22	196
119:51	186		
119:55-56	187	**Isaiah**	
119:64	182	2:22	99
119:66	182	40:18-20	20
119:68	183	40:21-31	22
119:70	190	40:25-28	25
119:71	183	55:8-9	129
119:72	190	55:11	110, 185
119:74	186		
119:77	190	**Jeremiah**	
119:83	185	31:34	168
119:86	186		
119:88	183, 188	**Lamentations**	
119:105-106	186	3:21-23	71
139	3	3:22-23	28
139:1-12	135		
139:11-12	xi	**Jonah**	
139:13-17	18, 68	1:1-17	100
139:15-16	xi	**Micah**	
139:16	136	6:8	119
		7:19	168

WHEN GOD'S WILL AND MY WILL DISCONNECT

Habakkuk
3:17-19	20, 34

Matthew
5:38-44	201
6:9-13	97
6:12	50, 212
6:26	x
6:30	x
7:1-5	243
7:3-5	42
9:37-38	231
18:15-22	39
18:21-22	210
18:23-30	210
20:28	229
22:37	87
27:1-10	101
28:5-8	260
28:9-10	260

Luke
2:13-14	272
5:17-26	203
5:32	312
6:27-28	200
15:11-32	40
15:24	40
15:20	218
24:33-35	261

John
1:12-13	314
3:1-18	49
3:16	167
3:16-17	310
3:36	310
6:37	44, 65, 306
8:32	xi, 92
8:36	xvii, 93
10:10	xvii
14:1-3	315
14:6	310
14:27	247
16:33	xvii, 136, 247
19:30	313

Acts
2:42-47	263
4:12	310
5:1-11	101
7:9-10	278
12:5-6	155
12:14-16	155
16:31	312
17:30	312

APPENDIX B

Romans

3:10-18, 23	41
3:23	308
3:23-24	58
3:24	41
5:1	58
5:12	309
6:6-18	44
6:13	229
6:23	309
7:15-24	89, 175
7:24	212
7:25	90
8:1	212
8:1-2	58
8:1-39	172
8:5	246
8:17	167
8:17-18	61
8:28	xii, 153, 157, 217
8:37	90
8:39	170
10:9-10	41, 312
10:9-13	48
11:33-36	27, 272
12:1-2	122, 174, 234, 314
12:2	139
12:3	123
12:3-21	204
12:4-5	124
12:4-6	233
12:14	200
12:19	149, 196
12:20-21	149

I Corinthians

1:9	71
2:16	231
6:18	86
10:12	89
10:12-13	87
10:13	62, 85
10:31	69, 202, 270

2 Corinthians

1:3-4	245, 250
1:3-6	230
5:17	231
7:9-10	46, 312
10:4-5	96, 98
10:5	175
11:21-30	72
12:7-10	73

Galatians

1:4-5	26
5:13-14	232
5:22-23	133, 241

Ephesians

1:3-6	156
1:3-14	166, 172
1:4-6	25
2:1-2	309
2:1-10	49
2:10	229
2:19-22	232
4:1	74, 153, 157, 314
4:1-2	119
4:17-19	84
4:31-32	51, 220
4:32	218
4:32-5:2	221
5:1-2	103
5:3	85
5:3-4	101
6:10-13	91
6:10-18	xvi
6:10-20	124
6:14-18	92
6:16	124
6:18	97

Philippians

1:6	67, 156, 157
1:15-19	262
1:20	229
2:3-4	205
2:3-5	225
2:5	118, 315
2:5-8	153, 202
2:10-11	169
2:13	25
2:13-16	73
2:14-16	118
3:12-14	151
4:5-9	75, 77
4:8	78
4:8-9	77
4:11	139
4:19	x, 136

Colossians

1:9	170
1:16-17	18
3:1-2	206
3:1-4	74
3:5-8	101, 152
3:13	218

APPENDIX B

1 Thessalonians
4:13-18	280, 315
5:18	152, 157, 171

2 Timothy
1:6-7	241
1:8, 12	230
2:22	86
3:15-17	96
3:16-17	144, 307
4:7	134

Titus
3:3-7	58

Hebrews
1:1-2	4, 110, 144
4:12	96
9:22	311
10:10	168, 311
10:1-4	311
10:12-14	311
11:1	133
11:6	133
12:1-2	250
12:2	134, 202, 249
13:6	ix
13:8	166

James
1:2-4	249
1:6-8	31
1:17	23, 171
1:19-20	242
2:1-9	3
4:7	63
5:16	50, 50

I Peter
1:3-5	313
1:3-9	273
1:8-9	250
1:15-16	21
1:18-21	25
2:1-3	190
2:21	202, 229, 315
2:24	311
4:19	28
5:7	32
5:8-9	63, 174

2 Peter
1:3	xii, 24, 36
1:20-21	307
2:1-3	190
3:18	139

1 John

1:8-9	48
1:9	xii, 148
	168, 219
3:1-6	102
3:2-3	315
3:3-9	46
3:6-10	49
4:19	87
5:13	314

3 John

1:4	203

Jude

1:25-26	265

Revelation

4:9-11	274
5:12-13	265, 274
19:1	274
20:13-15	30
22:20	316

APPENDIX C

The Certainty of Salvation

"How do I know for certain that I am saved; that I am honestly a Christian?" "How do I know if I really believe the Bible to be true, that it is God's Word?" These are questions many believers have asked. Decisions are made, prayers are prayed, and Scripture is read. But, the question still can be haunting; "Did I really mean it; was it real; am I saved?" The thoughts can come, "I don't feel any different; should there not be some sort of feeling that comes with salvation?"

There may be feelings; perhaps not. The certainty of salvation is not based on what we feel, but rather on what we believe; it is not founded in what we think, but rather on the reality of God's Truth. Salvation comes through a decision of faith; of believing and receiving. This is faith in what we know to be true; faith to believe the Word of God; faith to receive our Lord and His gracious redemptive plan and work.

An underlying reality is found in one's searching, in desiring to know for certain. This is the prompting of the Holy Spirit of God. One who is not a believer, who has no interest in the things of the Lord, who does not hold to the truth of God's Word evidences that they do not know the Lord as Savior. The one who seeks to understand, desires to have absolute certainty, and longs for full confidence in salvation is giving evidence of the Spirit at work in their life. Only through the prompting of the Spirit, only through the life-giving work of the Spirit is one able to come to the Lord, is able to know His saving grace.[47]

Eight truths are critical to believe in coming to salvation and in having the certainty of salvation. When doubts come, we return to

---

47 John 6.37, 44, 65: All that the Father gives me will come to me, and whoever comes to me I will never cast out... No one can come to me unless the Father who sent me draws him. And I will raise him up on the last day... And he said, "This is why I told you that no one can come to me unless it is granted him by the Father."

APPENDIX C

what we know to be true and our confidence in God's Truth.[48]

1. The Truth of the infallibility of God's Word.

There is no other Word of God; there is no other inspired written word which supplements what is written in the 66 books of inspired Scripture. God's Word is Truth. In order to have certainty of salvation we must believe the absolute truth which alone can be found in the Word of God.

> *All Scripture is breathed out by God and profitable for teaching, for reproof, for correction, and for training in righteousness, that the man of God may be complete, equipped for every good work. (2 Timothy 3:16-17)*

We must believe God's Word to be literally true, to understand it as it was intended to be understood. We are not to take our faulty presuppositions to determine what is and is not true, to discern an interpretive style which best fits our desired perspective. Rather, we must accept Scripture as it is—the literal, inspired, and infallible Word of God.

> *Knowing this first of all, that no prophecy of Scripture comes from someone's own interpretation. For no prophecy was ever produced by the will of man, but men spoke from God as they were carried along by the Holy Spirit. (2 Peter 1:20-21)*

2. The Truth of the perfection of God's holiness.

God is holy. All He does is holy; all He does is good; all He does

---

48 This is a synopsis of God's Word and His Truth regarding salvation. The redemptive work of God can be traced from before the foundations of the world. God desires to be in relationship with His people; and for His people to know Him, love Him, and worship Him.

is in perfect harmony with His sovereign plan. God's holiness is descriptive of His absolute perfection in all He is and in all He does. Salvation is not that which is given to us just because we are sinners; rather, salvation is given because God is holy.

> *For I am the Lord your God. Consecrate yourselves therefore, and be holy, for I am holy... For I am the Lord who brought you up out of the land of Egypt to be your God. You shall therefore be holy, for I am holy." (Leviticus 11:44-45)*

God does not make mistakes; He does not change His mind; He does not condone sin. Being holy, He is unchangeable in every aspect of His character; He is constant in and can be trusted in all He says.

3. The Truth of the absolute sinfulness of man.
We are sinners. All are sinners.

> *For all have sinned and fall short of the glory of God. (Romans 3:23)*

Man's sin originated in the Garden of Eden when man chose to go against the commands of God. He thought he knew better than God; he believed the tempter's lies; he chose sin.

> *So when the woman saw that the tree was good for food, and that it was a delight to the eyes, and that the tree was to be desired to make one wise, she took of its fruit and ate, and she also gave some to her husband who was with her, and he ate. Then the eyes of both were opened, and they knew that they were naked. And they sewed fig leaves together and made themselves loincloths. (Genesis 3:6-7)*

Though immediately knowing something had happened, sin

was irreversible. There was nothing man could do then, and there is nothing man can do now, to remove sin or to move backwards to remove the consequences of sin.

Because of Adam's sin, all are sinful. There are no exceptions.

> *Therefore, just as sin came into the world through one man, and death through sin, and so death spread to all men because all sinned—* (Romans 5:12)

Sin is contrary to God; it is contrary to God's holiness. Therefore, it totally separates us from God. In holiness, God cannot and does not look upon sin.

4. The Truth of the total inability of man to do anything to remove his sin.

Because of sin, man is spiritually dead. Dead men can do nothing; one dead in sin can do nothing to gain spiritual life; one dead in sin is fully at the mercy of another to breath into him the gift of life.

> *And you were dead in the trespasses and sins in which you once walked, following the course of this world, following the prince of the power of the air, the spirit that is now at work in the sons of disobedience—* (Ephesians 2:1–2)

> *For the wages of sin is death…* (Romans 6:23)

Dead people are incapable of gaining their own righteousness, of being justified in God's sight. They cannot become acceptable to the holy God.

5. The Truth of the redemptive work of Jesus Christ.

There is only one way of salvation, and this is only through the person of Jesus Christ. There is only one way to be delivered from the bondage of sin, the judgment of sin, and final condemnation, and this is only through the sacrificial work of Jesus Christ.

> *And there is salvation in no one else, for there is no other name under heaven given among men by which we must be saved." (Acts 4:12)*

> *Jesus said to him, "I am the way, and the truth, and the life. No one comes to the Father except through me. (John 14:6)*

None other than Jesus Christ accomplishes salvation. None other can provide forgiveness of sin; none other can cleanse man of the filth of sin; none other can bring man into righteousness; none other can deliver man from deserved condemnation.

> *"For God so loved the world, that he gave his only Son, that whoever believes in him should not perish but have eternal life. For God did not send his Son into the world to condemn the world, but in order that the world might be saved through him. (John 3:16–17)*

> *Whoever believes in the Son has eternal life; whoever does not obey the Son shall not see life, but the wrath of God remains on him. (John 3:36)*

The work of Jesus Christ alone accomplishes man's redemption. On the cross Jesus died; He shed His blood; He took upon Himself the full penalty of man's sin; He suffered death for man. The third day following His death Jesus rose from the grave. He conquered death; He conquered sin; He conquered Satan; He conquered the penalty of sin. Apart from the shedding of His blood, apart from His death and resurrection there is no salvation; there is no hope for sinful man.

APPENDIX C

Christ purchased man's salvation through the cost of His shed blood.

The Law required blood to be shed to bring about forgiveness.

> *Indeed, under the law almost everything is purified with blood, and without the shedding of blood there is no forgiveness of sins. (Hebrews 9:22)*

The Law required animal blood to be shed on a continual basis to maintain forgiveness; sacrifices had to be repeated. There was no assurance of any sacrifice being sufficient to purify one forever before the Throne of God.

> *...It can never, by the same sacrifices that are continually offered every year, make perfect those who draw near... But in these sacrifices there is a reminder of sins every year. For it is impossible for the blood of bulls and goats to take away sins. (Hebrews 10:1-4)*

Only through the shed blood of Jesus Christ is the Law completely satisfied; only through the sacrifice of Christ on the cross was the sacrifice perfect. Jesus Christ was the perfect Lamb sacrificed, once for all; the sacrifice never having to be repeated.

> *But when Christ [being both the priest offering the sacrifice and the perfect sacrifice] had offered for all time a single sacrifice for sins, he sat down at the right hand of God... For by a single offering he has perfected for all time those who are being sanctified. (Hebrews 10:12-14)*

> *And by that will we have been sanctified through the offering of the body of Jesus Christ once for all. (Hebrews 10:10)*

> *He himself bore our sins in his body on the tree, that we*

might die to sin and live to righteousness. By his wounds you have been healed. (1 Peter 2:24)

6. The Truth of repentance and the decision of faith.

We must believe. We are totally responsible for our decision to follow Christ or to remain in sin. We must place our faith in Christ alone, and in nothing else, in no one else.

And they said, "Believe in the Lord Jesus, and you will be saved, you and your household." (Acts 16:31)

...If you confess with your mouth that Jesus is Lord and believe in your heart that God raised him from the dead, you will be saved. For with the heart one believes and is justified, and with the mouth one confesses and is saved. (Romans 10:9-10)

With belief comes repentance. Repentance is the acknowledgement of sin, accepting the responsibility of sin, seeking forgiveness for sin, and making a firm commitment to not follow the same pattern of sin.

...He [God] commands all people everywhere to repent, (Acts 17:30)

I have not come to call the righteous but sinners to repentance." (Luke 5:32)

As it is, I rejoice, not because you were grieved, but because you were grieved into repenting. For you felt a godly grief, so that you suffered no loss through us. For godly grief produces a repentance that leads to salvation without regret, whereas worldly grief produces death. (2 Corinthians 7:9-10)

> *Have mercy on me, O God, according to your steadfast love; according to your abundant mercy blot out my transgressions. Wash me thoroughly from my iniquity, and cleanse me from my sin! For I know my transgressions, and my sin is ever before me. Against you, you only, have I sinned and done what is evil in your sight... Behold, I was brought forth in iniquity, and in sin did my mother conceive me... Hide your face from my sins, and blot out all my iniquities. Create in me a clean heart, O God, and renew a right spirit within me. (Psalm 51:1-10)*

> *Search me, O God, and know my heart! Try me and know my thoughts! And see if there be any grievous way in me, and lead me in the way everlasting! (Psalm 139:23-24)*

7. The Truth of God's completed work.

Our confidence in salvation is complete in Christ; in the truth of the Word of God; in the work of the Holy Spirit to bring us to faith. There is nothing more needing to be done. There is nothing Christ needs to do; there is nothing we can do.

> *...He [Jesus] said, "It is finished," and he bowed his head and gave up his spirit. (John 19:30)*

> *Blessed be the God and Father of our Lord Jesus Christ! According to his great mercy, he has caused us to be born again to a living hope through the resurrection of Jesus Christ from the dead, to an inheritance that is imperishable, undefiled, and unfading, kept in heaven for you, who by God's power are being guarded through faith for a salvation ready to be revealed in the last time. (1 Peter 1:3-5)*

Therefore, in Christ and in His Word we can have complete

assurance that we are saved. Believing His Word, we can believe we are saved because of His work of grace in our lives.

> *I write these things to you who believe in the name of the Son of God that you may know that you have eternal life. (1 John 5:13)*

> *But to all who did receive him, who believed in his name, he gave the right to become children of God, who were born, not of blood nor of the will of the flesh nor of the will of man, but of God. (John 1:12-13)*

Being born again, there will be the commitment to continue growing as a child of God, to be fully committed to being the person God has called us to be.

> *I therefore, a prisoner for the Lord, urge you to walk in a manner worthy of the calling to which you have been called, (Ephesians 4:1)*

> *I appeal to you therefore, brothers, by the mercies of God, to present your bodies as a living sacrifice, holy and acceptable to God, which is your spiritual worship. Do not be conformed to this world, but be transformed by the renewal of your mind, that by testing you may discern what is the will of God, what is good and acceptable and perfect. (Romans 12:1-2)*

Being born again, there will be evidence of this new life in Christ. Having been transformed from one who was dead in sin and bound to condemnation to one who has been given new life in Christ and the hope of eternity; there will be a difference in both heart and actions; there will be a desire to be free from all sin, following the steps of Jesus Christ, and having the attitude of Christ.

APPENDIX C

> *Beloved, we are God's children now, and what we will be has not yet appeared; but we know that when he appears we shall be like him, because we shall see him as he is. And everyone who thus hopes in him purifies himself as he is pure. (1 John 3:2–3)*

> *For to this you have been called, because Christ also suffered for you, leaving you an example, so that you might follow in his steps. (1 Peter 2:21)*

> *Have this mind among yourselves, which is yours in Christ Jesus, (Philippians 2:5)*

If there is no appreciation and thankfulness for the saving work of Jesus Christ, no desire to be free from sin, no desire to have Christ manifested in your life, then there is good evidence you have not honestly repented of sin and believed in Christ as Savior.

8. *The Truth of our eternal hope.*

There is more to come. Life on earth is just the beginning. Those who have placed their faith in the Lord Jesus Christ are able to look forward to eternity in the very presence of God.

> *"Let not your hearts be troubled. Believe in God; believe also in me. In my Father's house are many rooms. If it were not so, would I have told you that I go to prepare a place for you? And if I go and prepare a place for you, I will come again and will take you to myself, that where I am you may be also. (John 14:1–3)*

> *But we do not want you to be uninformed, brothers, about those who are asleep, that you may not grieve as others do who have no hope. For since we believe that Jesus died*

and rose again, even so, through Jesus, God will bring with him those who have fallen asleep. For this we declare to you by a word from the Lord, that we who are alive, who are left until the coming of the Lord, will not precede those who have fallen asleep. For the Lord himself will descend from heaven with a cry of command, with the voice of an archangel, and with the sound of the trumpet of God. And the dead in Christ will rise first. Then we who are alive, who are left, will be caught up together with them in the clouds to meet the Lord in the air, and so we will always be with the Lord. Therefore encourage one another with these words. (1 Thessalonians 4:13–18)

He who testifies to these things says, "Surely I am coming soon." Amen. Come, Lord Jesus! (Revelation 22:20)

We can be certain of our salvation. This is a matter of faith; of repentance; of choosing to believe God and His Word; of relying upon the work of God's Spirit to draw us to Him.

ABOUT THE AUTHOR

Terry Burlingame earned a Doctor of Ministry in Pastoral Counseling from Westminster Theological Seminary and is a member of the Association of Certified Biblical Counselors. After retiring from the U.S. Army Chaplaincy, he served as a senior pastor for ten years. Currently he is a counselor with the Biblical Counseling Center in Jenison, MI, involved in ministries at Jamestown Baptist Church, and is a member of the Board at David's House Ministries. Terry and his wife Barbara have three children and eight grandchildren.